GUNSHIP ACE

GUNSHIP ACE

The Wars of Neall Ellis,
Helicopter Pilot and Mercenary

AL J. VENTER

CASEMATE
Philadelphia & Newbury

Published in the United States of America and Great Britain in 2011 by
CASEMATE PUBLISHERS
908 Darby Road, Havertown, PA 19083
and
17 Cheap Street, Newbury RG14 5DD

ISBN 978-1-61200-070-1
Digital Edition: ISBN 978-1-61200-082-4

Cataloging-in-publication data is available from the Library of Congress
and the British Library.

10 9 8 7 6 5 4 3 2 1

Printed and bound in the United States of America.

For a complete list of Casemate titles please contact:

CASEMATE PUBLISHERS (US)
Telephone (610) 853-9131, Fax (610) 853-9146
E-mail: casemate@casematepublishing.com

CASEMATE PUBLISHERS (UK)
Telephone (01635) 231091, Fax (01635) 41619
E-mail: casemate-uk@casematepublishing.co.uk

INDEX

BOOKS BY THE SAME AUTHOR INCLUDE:

Report on Portugal's War in Guiné-Bissau
Underwater Africa
Under the Indian Ocean
Africa at War
The Zambezi Salient
Underwater Seychelles
Coloured: A Profile of Two Million South Africans
Africa Today
South African Handbook for Divers
Challenge: South Africa in the African Revolutionary Context
Underwater Mauritius
Where to Dive: In Southern Africa and off the Indian Ocean Islands
War in Angola
The Chopper Boys: Helicopter Warfare in Africa
The Iraqi War Debrief: Why Saddam Hussein Was Toppled
Iran's Nuclear Option: Tehran's Quest for the Atom Bomb
War Dog: Fighting Other People's Wars
Allah's Bomb: The Islamic Quest for Nuclear Weapons
Cops: Cheating Death: How One Man Saved the Lives of 3,000 Americans
How South Africa Built Six Atom Bombs
Dive South Africa
Barrel of a Gun: A War Correspondent's Misspent Moments in Combat
War Stories by Al Venter and Friends

To my lovely Caroline

AUTHOR'S NOTE

*G*unship Ace is a book about a combat helicopter pilot who is not only an outstanding pilot but also a very good friend. I have been on operations with him in Angola and while he fought to turn around the rebels in Sierra Leone. In both ventures he was successful, so much so that in a personal letter to me in 2010, General Sir David Richards, then Chief of the General Staff—and today Chief of the Defence Staff in Great Britain—told me: 'He is a great man; I and everyone in Sierra Leone owe him much.'

This is the first time in recent history that the serving head of a Western defence establishment has paid tribute to the role of a mercenary pilot in wartime.

Neall Ellis and I have been friends for a very long time. Indeed, I watched his four children grow up and he observed some of the disturbing antics of mine. In-between we sank a few ales, swopped a few yarns and travelled many different roads together. Writing about old buddies is never easy as you know them far too well to be complimentary about all they do. In a sense, as the saying goes, no general is a hero to his batman.

Nellis is different and, to me, a true hero. An efficient combatant when the occasion demands, had he not beaten the rebels back from the gates of Freetown—both times flying alone in an antiquated Mi-24 and at night—our governments' representatives would today be sharing space with some of Foday Sankoh's barbarians at the United Nations and other world bodies. In Afghanistan, for almost three years he has been flying support missions in Russian Mi-8 helicopters across some of the harshest and most demanding mountain terrain on the planet. This is dangerous work; while preparing this book for the printers in September 2011, these choppers twice came under RPG-7 attack while attempting to land. Nellis wasn't flying at the time, but he was immediately tasked to try to find solutions to what appear to be an insoluble range of problems.

Neall Ellis has led an extraordinarily adventurous life through a dozen wars and more scrapes than he cares to remember. His career has been going on for more than 40 years and in this time he has never been seriously wounded, just scratched a few times.

One aspect of this book that concerned me from the start was that having had *War Dog* published by Casemate in the United States in 2006—much of that action also involving 'Nellis'—there was bound to be a bit of overlap. Most of it has been avoided, but I have once more had to bring to the fore one event that is seminal to the conflict in Sierra Leone. That was the ambush on the road out of Makeni of a convoy of vehicles rushing to meet a turncoat Nigerian general who hoped to do a deal with the rebels. Using all the subterfuge he could muster, Neall Ellis rocketed and machine gunned the column, killing or wounding many rebel commanders. In effect, it was the beginning of the end for Sankoh's Revolutionary United Front as they never recovered from the setback.

Others have helped put this work together and here I must pay tribute to journalist and author James Mitchell, who gave me much of what appears in the two chapters dealing with Neall's time in Sarawak and while he served with a firefighting unit in South Africa. Like Nellis, James and I go way back: he even joined me on a lengthy sojourn across North America in a Hurricane motor home while I was working on the book on Richard David, the man who invented concealable body armour (and who has subsequently saved the lives of more than 3,000 law enforcement officers).

Anita Baker edited this book and because of a plethora of detail, it became an enormous challenge for her to make sense of what was sometimes a jumble of facts, stats and figures. It took an inordinate amount of time and effort, but you can judge for yourself whether or not she succeeded. Thank you Anita—and here's to our next title together.

Libby Braden was the force behind finally bringing this book to fruition, and what a marvellous job she has done. It hasn't been easy because of the enormous volume of material, and trying to fit all of it into what was already a very substantial work.

I also have a special word of thanks for Steven Smith, editor-in-chief of Casemate and another old friend. He is the man who originally decided whether or not Casemate should take on this difficult work. He apparently didn't hesitate, nor did David and Sarah Farnsworth, who own and run the company in Philadelphia.

A final word for my lovely Caroline, the woman who keeps my life, and my love, on track. You have been tolerant, affectionate and understanding during some extremely difficult times darling soul and, indeed, I am a very lucky man.

Al J. Venter
Downe
November, 2011

Neall Ellis at the controls of a former Soviet-Mi-24 helicopter gunship taken during a previous deployment in Sierra Leone. *Author photo*

PROLOGUE

Mike Foster, Neall Ellis' co-pilot, penned the following observations while flying alongside him after take-off from Kabul in summer 2011. The helicopter, a Russian-built Hip registered ZS-RIX, was on its way to Khowst Salerno, a remote military outpost that routinely comes under attack.

He's a tough bugger, this Nellis guy, still flying helicopter support missions in his 61st year and there is no talk of retirement. That's roughly 40 years of action in a dozen or more wars, and he has never been wounded. He says he can't stop now because he's got to put bread on the table . . . too many people depend on him.

A peculiar, likeable fellow, Neall has become something of a legend in his time. He's a father, a military man to his fingertips, a totally unforgiving mercenary fighter when placed in an uncompromising situation and, to his mates, honest to the point of being exploited by those less fortunate than he might be. He is peculiarly sensitive to the problems of others, although he's got a bunch of his own that he rarely talks about, including the recent untimely loss of the woman with whom he shared six good years of his life.

He can also be stubborn, interesting and occasionally infuriating, especially if things involving the machines he flies haven't been done his

1

way. He refers to it as 'survival—straight and simple'. Then he'll add: 'Just do it right and we won't have problems when we least expect them,' which has been his credo throughout his career.

These are all qualities that are typical of the Neall Ellis that I have got to know over the last two or three years. He is physically short, perhaps a bit stocky, but as confident as hell, with a discerning personality and force of character that reflects good leadership. He had probably acquired all that by the time he made colonel in the South African Air Force almost a quarter of century ago.

Neall Ellis has quite a few other accolades, which he won't talk about. He has been acclaimed by quite a few notables, including General Sir David Richards, Britain's Chief of the Defence Staff following victory against the rebels in Sierra Leone. That was the first time in recent history that British armed forces had worked hand-in-glove with an acknowledged mercenary. Before that, he was involved with Sandline's Colonel Tim Spicer, who apparently has a high regard for him. There are others, but he's non-committal about them as well. He just smiles when asked.

Neall also has the gift of being a good listener. There has never been a time when he hasn't made me feel comfortable, even when he has been really busy and I have interrupted him or intruded on valuable time, of which he doesn't have much because he's often still at his desk at 10 o'clock at night working on the next day's flying schedules. He always makes you welcome and gives you his undivided attention. What more can I say?

Neall was in the SAAF with me, but I never had much to do with him then as he was a lot senior to me. I only really got to know him after we'd been deployed to Kabul. Afghanistan is a land of contrast, harsh but pure, arid but green, sweltering heat contrasting with high altitude tables of snow, that's how we pilots all see it. That is also where I really got to understand the man.

Roughly the size of Texas, Afghanistan has very few major roads. The ones that are there are being increasingly monitored and mined by the Taliban. These actions have forced Coalition Forces to rely more on aircraft to move troops and supplies. Indeed, many remote military bases and outposts—particularly in the mountains—can sometimes be reached only by helicopter.

We arrived with the first group of South African Mi-8 helicopter pilots

Above: Bokkie the Mi-17 helicopter that was the real hero of the war in Sierra Leone. Full of holes, battered, but never beaten, this old war bird—with Nellis flying solo— played a major role against the rebels earlier in the war. *Photo: Neall Ellis*

Below: Ambush of a Coalition Forces road convoy in Central Afghanistan. *Photo: Neall Ellis*

in Afghanistan and Neall approached this vast new Central Asian country with discernible eagerness. It was quite a hop, from flying Mi-24 helicopter gunships to being at the controls of slow and meandering Mi-8s. I reckon that it was hard for him to get accustomed to because the Hip is hardly an offensive weapon in this kind of environment. He changed his style of flying as well. These days he takes more of a defensive approach with the Hip—mostly high flying and none of the low-level aggressive stuff he was used to in Africa and elsewhere. You can't help sensing that it is perhaps a little boring for him.

This has come to the fore several times in recent months: an example being the day we were flying along the western fringes of the Hindu Kush when Nellis leaned forward with a curious look on his face. He tugged at the side of his helmet and turned that side of his head towards the window. With an elated grin he happily exclaimed that we were being shot at. Quietly, and without fuss, he pulled his helmet straight again, leaned back in his seat and, with a look of contented nostalgia, continued with whatever he had been doing moments before.

Flying with Neall has its advantages. On long flights he insists that there has to be a break in the middle. That means stopping at a DFAC, usually on the turnabout point. It also means great food and goodies to enjoy. Fantastic! It does a lot for crew camaraderie and is always something to look forward to.

I enjoy going to Kabul with him too. If he wants something he buys it, simple as that. In Afghanistan the art of bargaining is something ingrained in the local psyche from birth. The old story runs along the lines of dividing by two whatever they first ask you to pay but Nellis doesn't have the time for that kind of nonsense. He just hands over the money and doesn't argue. He reckons that 'if you want it, buy it, don't dally around'.

It's basically the way the man runs his life, and has done since his form-ative years growing up in the south of Africa.

CHAPTER ONE

FORMATIVE DAYS IN SOUTHERN AFRICA

Neall Ellis's determination to hew his own path in life can be traced back to his youth and, more precisely, to his experiences as a schoolboy in Bulawayo and, later, in Plumtree, both in the south-west of what is now Zimbabwe. In colonial times it was known as Southern Rhodesia, or simply Rhodesia.

Born of good British stock in South Africa's great mining and financial centre of Johannesburg on 24 November 1949, he didn't live there long. Six weeks later his father moved the whole family to Rhodesia. At the time, Ellis Senior was general manager of Gallo Africa, a major music production and sales company, probably the biggest of its kind in Africa. Originally from Woolwich, near London, he had come out to South Africa with the Royal Navy during World War II. He had served on board the battleship HMS *Royal Sovereign* on Arctic convoy runs, shipping vital supplies to the Soviet port of Murmansk in Russia. His service with the RN also took him to South Africa where, in Simonstown—then a British naval base—Leslie Thomas Ellis met and married Ruby Sophia Hyams. 'My mother's side was very Afrikaans—they were Vissers—while my grandfather's name was Hyams', recalls Neall.

The move to Bulawayo brought many changes, including a number of different homes in the city. As Neall recalls: 'My parents encouraged us to be pretty independent . . . we were strictly disciplined and my mother used to thrash us with a wooden coat hanger, but it would always break, so it wasn't too bad!'

There were two large dams, not far from home, where the kids would fish: 'Mom was petrified whenever we went near either of them, having already lost one son to drowning. However, we were taught to swim at a very young age—something like three or four.'

In one of the family homes, at Hillside, on the side of a *kopje* at the back of the house, the youngsters played their games in the nooks and crannies of the rocks and they would sometimes encounter cobras or other bush creatures that had ventured in from the wild.

> We never thought too much about it—the snakes would give us a wide berth if they sensed our approach and we would duck away if we saw them—got spat at by a Cape cobra a few times, though.
>
> At the time, Dad was very friendly with a man named Alan Boyle, an Australian, and both men were what you'd call 'party animals'. They would go up north into Africa, driving or chartering a light aircraft, the idea being to make recordings of traditional African music which Dad loved. It was all the kind of antiquated reel-to-reel stuff that you never see today, bulky, testy old machines.

Neall believes that his father's interest in this aspect of 'Black Culture' was the start of old man's Eric Gallo's specialisation in traditional African music, for which the company later became known. More important to the Ellis children at the time, their father would return from his trips with lovely ebony masks and other African carvings, curios and a huge variety of native trivia on which tourists today spend good money. Neall recalls: 'One morning I went into the kitchen and opened the fridge. There was a candy box and inside, one great big lump of elephant shit!'

Growing up, young Neall remembers lots of weekends when the family and their friends went up into the Matopos Hills on picnics. Rhodes lies there, watching over the country once named for him, under a brass plate set into granite over his grave on the summit of one of the *gomos*.[1]

Meanwhile, the kids would play games, such as kennietjie. This game would start with a groove being dug in the ground. Then one of the youngsters would take a twig and lay it across the groove, before flicking it with a stick and someone else had to catch it. These were the kind of pastimes that children of the original Pioneer Column must have played of an evening after they had unhaltered—or as we liked to say, *outspanned*—their oxen following a long day's trek. Neall recounts:

> I was fascinated by the historical impact of the area, especially what that tiny band of settlers who had followed in the wake of Cecil John Rhodes' dream had achieved. There were lots of stories of these rugged, tough pioneers, almost all of them frontiersman like Alan Wilson and his Shangani Patrol . . . and their bloody and terrible end under the spears of Lobengula's Ndebele warriors. There was a great lore, a fine historical tradition in all those tales

Early Rhodesian Department of Information photo of troops on deployment in the bush.
Photo: Original Rhodesian government recruiting photo

that were recounted around the fire in the evenings, and I was fascinated. It was the same when my grandmother introduced me to the history of the Zulu people and their tribal cousins, the Ndebele, who moved northwards into Rhodesia long before the white man got there.

It was possibly these interests that helped give Neall the ease with which he later crossed racial and social barriers, some real, some imagined, but strong, for all that. Race, then, was a feature of life in South Africa in the days of apartheid, and, while far less rigid and formalized in the Rhodesia of his youth, he recalls today that you really couldn't miss the innuendos that involved 'them and us'.

Among some of the first of the historic tales that young Neall can recall hearing was one told to him in the late 1950s about what was to become known as the 'First Chimurenga War', or the first liberation struggle of Rhodesia's black population. As with similar rebellions against white settler communities in German-ruled Tanganyika and what later became known as South-West Africa before the start of the First World War, Rhodesia's Chimurenga was an uprising against the white settlers of Rhodes' British South Africa Company.

Most of it, as I recall, was passed on to us young people from the victors' (white) side . . . but then that is how history usually emerges, kind of like 'to the victor the spoils'. They used to have military tattoos at the Bulawayo Showground, with re-enactments of the mounted patrols on their horses, all very well done and actually quite impressive. Then, the African Impis—the black warriors in their proud headdresses, hardened cow-hide shields and assegais—would surround them, and there would be lots of firing and yelling 'and the whiteys would see their *gats*. [An Afrikaans expression, impolitely translated as 'seeing their arses'.]

Those family picnics in the magnificent Matopo Hills also gave Neall what he calls 'the start of my love for the bush'.

We looked for what we called the 'Resurrection Plant'. You found it in Rhodesia on the hills; it never totally dies. It's a growth that survives on top of a rock in the dry winter months, just a blackened twig, but you place that 'dead' twig in a glass of water, and in just a couple of days, its leaves begin to sprout . . . that's the Resurrection Plant.

Neall had one older brother, Peter, whom he never knew: Peter had drowned 'just before I was born—some six months before'. His younger brother Ian today lives in Johannesburg, while his sister Janine (they were born 18 months apart) is married and is in Australia. The family remains in contact and despite distance—he is in Afghanistan most of the time these days—they stay close.

When he was old enough, Neall was sent to Hillside Junior School, which soon enough taught him about the unpleasant consequences of human relationships going awry.

There was a gang of us boys; we used to cycle home together. But it was pretty brutal. If one member of the gang fell out, there would be a fight, either with the leader of the mob, or with someone whom he nominated, in a little 'arena' among the rocks. One might have had absolutely no quarrel with that individual, but one still had to tough it out and it could sometimes be quite vicious.

'From that came my hatred of bullying', he says thoughtfully. Is it too much of a psychological leap to wonder whether this realization would, in future decades, lead Neall Ellis to feel no qualms about meting out swift and terminal justice to those, such as Foday Sankoh's brutal killers in Sierra Leone, whose behaviour had taken them beyond the bounds of normal humanity?

In other ways, growing up in Rhodesia was a marvellous, privileged existence, with a vast hinterland waiting to be discovered and unending promises for the future. There was barely a family who didn't have at least one servant—some of Neall's wealthy friends had four, or even six, one for the garden, perhaps two for the kitchen, a domestic worker for bedrooms and cleaning and perhaps a driver who would take the children to school each morning and fetch them later in the day. It was an idyllic life.

That their country was landlocked didn't keep them from the sea either. Families would sometimes drive, or take the then extremely efficient rail link to South Africa's Indian Ocean coastline and its Natal beaches. So many families would gravitate to Cape Town during the Southern hemisphere summer holidays that there was even a resort near Simonstown which was for many years called Rhodesia by the Sea.

For the young Neall, however, holidays generally meant a much shorter journey. His maternal grandmother, Petronella, had divorced Neall's Hyams grandfather and married Dougal Nelson, a Scot. They lived in Tzaneen, in the Northern Transvaal (now the Limpopo Province of South Africa), and farmed citrus fruits and bananas. They also made a home from home for their visiting grandchildren, a welcome that Neall still recalls with delight. The same applied when the Nelsons sold the farm and moved to Mooketsi, after grandmother Petronella started having health problems from smoking too many of the then-popular Springbok cigarettes.

Life was not always tranquil, however. One day in Tzaneen, he remembers, they were playing and his sister had the role of 'madam' and he was the 'garden boy'.

> I swung the hoe and although it was unintentional, it was a vicious blow and I cut open her head. My granny could be rather a fierce woman and I recall running away and hiding in the bush . . . but grandmother represented overwhelming odds and it was futile to resist and she meted out swift justice, much more efficiently than my mother. . . .

He has many happy memories of his time there as well:

> We would always spend our school holidays there. On the farm we drank fresh milk but not much else but good food and healthy living: there was no electricity, no television, only Springbok Radio to listen to.

He well remembers the British series 'Men from the Ministry'.

Meantime, other interests also took his fancy. 'Grandmother possessed a fine collection of classical music—all old 78 vinyl records—which we played on a battery-operated gramophone'. Neall's eclectic tastes in music remains a feature of his life.

'Those were great times. We used to go into the bush and collect kapok, a form of vegetable down, from the seedpods of the kapok trees to fill our pillows.' He also learned to collect mushrooms—while discarding unsuitable varieties—and today, in his sixties, he can still be seen running around when circumstances allow and inquiring from local residents about spots where edible mushrooms might be found.

'Yes, I am rather interested in mushrooms. If I go into the Knysna Forest, I'll pick them to eat, or to dry for cooking later.'

From Mooketsi, young Neall could look out of the kitchen window towards the Modjadji Hills and marvel at the lightning strikes flickering around the surrounding peaks. They were caused by the incredible electrical storms, which are always a summer feature of the region. 'Perhaps that's why I don't mind loud bangs', Neall comments thoughtfully.

Neall's uncle regularly hunted for guinea fowl and bush pig, all of which supplemented the family's regular diet.

'He took me out into the bush with him. Grandmother had an old Richards and Harrington single-barrel shotgun with a hammer action that could nip you sharply if you weren't too careful. There was also a .22 Savage rifle: I've still got them both,' says Neall, who from the age of ten was allowed by his grandmother to go out alone and hunt.

Wildlife in the area was not always for hunting and eating. 'I'll never forget the snakes, particularly at Mooketsi . . . cobras—lots of them and puff adders. There were also twig snakes and boomslangs . . .' he recalls thoughtfully. 'A black fellow who I got to know quite well taught me about snakes, and also my grandmother, who had a reference library of her own with some quite old books, and I learned a lot about these creatures from them as well.'

As he reminisces, life—and death—could be pretty rough at times, and in those days people simply had to learn from a young age how to accept responsibility and look after themselves . . . and, of course, others.

One time, one of the labourers' wives got bitten by a snake—I was about 14 at the time—and grandmother gave me the snakebite serum and told me to go and find out if the woman had actually been bitten by a poisonous snake and, if so, give her the necessary injection. Not that I'd ever used a syringe before . . . I realise now that had I actually injected her, it would probably have been the worst thing to do. For a start, I had no idea what species of snake it was, or even if there had been a snake to start with. I'm sure she lived, even though I didn't give her the serum, because nobody complained.

Snakes weren't the only danger in this remarkable Garden of Eden south of the Limpopo. 'Grandmother had her own flock of geese and they could be formidable. There was a big gander called Shake and he guarded his flock with a passion . . . he'd nip you on your backside if you were slow and it was amazing how painful the bite could be', Neall recalls.

There was also a large reservoir that was used to store water for the farm, where the young Ellis siblings used to swim. 'But it was full of algae . . . and water scorpions and the little buggers used to bite you.'

Likewise, he says, there were some real scorpions—lots of them—and they were notorious for their ability to inflict one of the most painful of wounds. 'I got stung by a scorpion on my foot, when I was barefoot at night; I heard a dog cry out—he must have been stung first—the next moment it got me. From then on I've hated scorpions.'

Back in Rhodesia, in 1962, Neall was sent to Plumtree High School, on the border with Botswana, which in its day was regarded as one of the best educational institutions of its kind in the region. 'For me,' recalls Neall, 'it proved to be more of a "school for sadists".'

Pupils were forced to undergo two-year periods of what they termed 'initiation'. We call it hazing today and most of it is totally irrelevant to its supposed purposes of teaching new entrants how to live in harmony among themselves and with their supposedly more responsible elders. In his first pupils' residence as a boarder—Hammond House, he recalls:

We weren't allowed to have any hot water for those first two years . . . even though it got so cold during winter months that the bird bath outside froze solid and the outside water pipes would ice up.

The seniors were allowed to beat us as well … or at least, it was kind of accepted that they had the freedom to do that.

In his view, it was no better that what was referred to as the 'fagging system' which had become institutionalised in many English Public Schools. In truth, he felt it could be both demeaning and painful at times . . .

Those bastards were absolutely dominant, a kind of law unto themselves. Although the masters were aware of what was going on, they did nothing because it had always been part of the "traditional system". When I tried to protect some of the others, particularly a few of the younger boys, I reckon that was possibly the worst thing I could have done, because then the entire cabal descended on me.

On one occasion, when the pressure became too severe, he even ran away from school. 'It just became too much for me to handle. Remember, I was still basically an immature youngster and, to this day, I react strongly to anybody who is a bully. Perhaps that is why I am invariably with the underdog, and have been so throughout my life.'

Nellis' philosophy is basic. People who browbeat or intimidate those who are weaker than themselves, he maintains, are at the bottom of his chain of ethics and deserve harsh retaliation. 'The unfortunate thing is that I tend to get emotionally involved in such fights, which has often placed me in a bad situation.'

Academically at Plumtree—which was what his schooling there was all about—Neall Ellis was regarded as being fairly 'average', and he admits that only some of the sports caught his fancy. 'I tried cricket and rugby … and even some hockey, but none of that was for me. However I did well in swimming and water polo.' Perhaps his sessions in his grandmother's farm reservoir did end up paying a few dividends, because Neall ended up belonging to the school swimming team and getting his colours for water polo.

With his school days almost at an end, there were some serious decisions for the youthful Neall Ellis to make. The short-lived Federation of Rhode-

Typical Rhodesian security force patrol in contested area: normally a 'Stick' was composed of four soldiers or police reservists on active duty. *Author's photo*

sia and Nyasaland had collapsed in disarray, with majority rule being quickly implemented in Northern Rhodesia (which was to become Zambia) while Nyasaland transmuted into Malawi. Everybody could see that Southern Rhodesia wouldn't be far behind. However, with its far larger white 'settler' population (the majority of white residents were born there, rather than having emigrated from abroad), this was not a simple matter, as Ian Smith's Unilateral Declaration of Independence in November 1964 was to show.

With a limited armed guerrilla 'struggle' now underway, Neall was initially faced with the possibility of joining the Rhodesian Army. Had he done so, he would have served with many of the boys from his school. However, his father opposed this course of action and instead he went back to South Africa, this time to try his hand at a law degree course at the University of Natal.

While he should have spent more time than he did on his academic studies, his options rested largely on participation sports, which was why he got involved in canoeing, judo, weightlifting and rowing fours amongst other activities. He also began to show an interest in underwater pursuits, taking up diving and spearfishing as extracurricular activities.

His 'other' extra-mural activity centred on his girlfriend Barbara (or 'Babs', as everybody called her) back in Bulawayo. That meant hitchhiking back to Rhodesia every long weekend, no mean task at a distance of almost 1,000 miles. The good life couldn't last, of course, and the end result of all these pursuits was that the aspirant sportsman didn't even sit his last exam. 'My father was mightily unimpressed', he recalls.

At that point, young Neall was accepted for an officer training course in the Rhodesian Army, which meant he would be based at Gwelo. As the Rhodesian Army was looking for quality rather than quantity it was a particularly tough regimen:

> We had two colour sergeants who, as the saying goes, 'protected our interests'. One, by the name of Simpson, was a particularly hard customer from Yorkshire; the other, Nortje, an Afrikaner, was somebody we all regarded as a terror—he was also our drill ser-geant. Nortje would march us until some of the guys dropped, but curiously, after that initial three-month of basics, he turned out to be quite a pleasant sort of fellow.

> The routine was hard, with daily inspections to keep us on our toes. There would also be a lot of time spent on the range, polishing our so-called shooting skills. Having used firearms in the wild for almost as long as I could remember, I was pretty good at it. Still, we had our hiccups, and Nortje would taunt us with the comment: 'I know what's on your mind . . . you guys all want to shoot me, well go ahead and fire and see how I react'. He would also warn the men: 'but beware if someone makes a mistake!'

> Group punishment was termed 'wildebeest' and was a brutal rough-and-tough, no-option drill. Essentially, it consisted of the entire squad run-ning around like lunatics through a routine that resembled something between a jungle gym and an obstacle course, the only difference being that we'd have to perform all the requisites while hauling each other across our backs.

One day, our mentors decided that we were to be instructed on crowd and riot control. We were teamed up with a Territorial Army cadet officer group and were delegated to perform the basis for controlling a riotous crowd, the Territorials being the crowd. It was all pretty realistic training as the other side was allowed to throw rocks and bricks and a few heads were cracked as a consequence, as might have been expected.

The culmination came when we were herded into a squash court—about 40 of us jammed into a relatively confined space. The doors were jammed shut and two teargas grenades were thrown in. It was the cruel and mindless act of a psychotic, but we were hardly in a position to argue. Obviously, there was immediate panic and some pretty desperate efforts to get clear of the place because we quickly discovered that the gas masks didn't have the requisite filters. We got out eventually, but it was a massive effort because we were all fighting, literally, for survival.

I was as sick as a dog afterwards, but there were others who collapsed, moaning and crying real tears. Still more of the group were vomiting . . . it was horrendous, but then the military in those days was full of the kind of sadistic bastards who would subject us younger guys to mindless trials. Then, if things really did go wrong, they would shrug their shoulders and move on and do the same thing again at a later date. To this day, when I smell tear gas I react badly. The worst part was that it was an unusually hot day and we'd all been sweating from the effort with the rocks and bricks. That meant that whenever we touched our bodies, the chemicals in the gas gave us a severe stinging sensation.

As an officer cadet, Neall Ellis had several personal problems of his own. He was busted for fighting in the corporal's bar, which he had no authority to enter in the first place, and, as a result, he was charged with assault and being drunk. That little episode took place towards the end of the course, after about nine months of training.

Ordered to appear before his commanding officer, he was reminded that officers never drank in the bars of NCOs without being invited in to do so. Even if they were invited, it was just not good form to get involved in a bar brawl.

His reply was curt and totally uncalled for: 'What is the difference, Sir? In 10 years' time, this country will have a black president anyway.'

The next moment I found myself on the floor: I'd been given a short, sharp crack to the side of my head by the Rhodesian Army lightweight boxing champion. He was my escort and had been standing right alongside me.

That one comment effectively terminated Neall's career in the Rhodesian armed forces. However, as he recollects, being thrown off the junior officer's course was probably the best thing that might have happened:

In any event, I was starting to get more interested in flying, and even considered applying for a transfer to the air force for flight training, although whether I would have passed selection there, after the fracas in Gwelo was another matter.

Meantime, he'd also had problems after returning to base from leave, when he'd tried to patch up things with Babs, his girlfriend—their relationship had become rocky due to his extended periods away.

We were doing a survival course in the bush which, as usual, turned into something gory. The thrust of it centred on teaching us the basics of survival under the most arduous bush conditions imaginable . . . and in Africa it can sometimes be *really* difficult!

As he recalls, the instructors had their own ways of doing things, like forcing the men to carry boxes of sand over long distances in difficult terrain. They were required to go in search of food because everything was taken from them, including sleeping bags and any warm clothing they might have brought. As Neall remembers, being winter it was a really hard call because after dark, in the Rhodesian countryside, temperatures tend to plummet.

After some days of that bullshit, we were given some bricks which we had to put into our packs. We were then split into groups, or 'sticks' of three. They said that they would give us food to start with, and, indeed, they did—all of a couple of tins of bully beef for an unspecified period and no water.

We were then ordered onto an antiquated Rhodesian Air Force DC-3 Dakota and flown to Buffalo Range in the south-east of the country, where our first operation was to reconnoitre an old gold mine. Map coordinates were provided, together with a specific destination where we were to be debriefed after our so-called recce.

Meanwhile, we had every Territorial Force unit in creation chasing after us, and for those who were caught, it was really fierce: some men were stripped down naked for interrogation—not pleasant in the middle of winter—while others were made to stand on rocks in a flooded quarry. I was lucky because I seemed to be quite good at escape and evasion. In the end we were all captured, but I missed the interrogation part because by the time I was hauled in, the allocated period for that phase of the exercise was up and so I was spared the 'torture'.

Thankfully, says Neall, the time on that leg of the course went quickly. On the fourth day, something happened that was to change his life forever.

I was waiting there, on the edge of the airstrip when out of the sun came this bright, shiny little aircraft, a South African Army Cessna 185. It landed, taxied towards where we were waiting, and from it emerged a pair of shiny polished brown shoes and an immaculately dressed guy in neatly pressed khaki clothes, wearing a tie and Ray Ban sun glasses with a great big watch on his wrist. His blond hair was perfectly combed and somewhat longish by military standards. When he got close up you couldn't miss the after-shower deodorants, which I suppose wasn't difficult, because we hadn't washed for more than a week. Under other circumstances he would have been quite nondescript, but there, way out in the bush, he was unique. The man was an army pilot serving with the South African police and he looked like he was having the time of his life.

It's funny how small things become etched in your mind, which was how it was with me. At that precise moment I decided that I would become like him: I would become a pilot, I told myself. I met him afterwards—Captain Piet van der Merwe—and his daughter later became quite famous as a Miss South Africa. That same young lieutenant—as he then was—ended up flying some of us northwards, straight over the magnificent Chimanimani Mountains, and I already knew where my future lay. It certainly would not be with the 'Brown Jobs', a term which aviators sometimes disparagingly use when they refer to soldiers.

Meanwhile, on the orders of my father, I was required to give the academic world another bash. I enrolled at Witwatersrand University in Johannesburg for a legal degree, or what is known locally as Bachelor of Arts, Law. My deal was that he paid my fees while I was required to earn enough to keep my head above water.

My first job was pretty mundane: tending tables at the Spur Steakhouse in Rosebank. The other waiters couldn't believe that I was actually working for a weekly wage and that I refused the tips clients gave me. In the end, I put all that extra money into their pool as they only earned what they were tipped.

Meanwhile, there had been some other changes as well. My folks moved back to South Africa from Rhodesia while I was in the army and Babs, my girlfriend, wasn't talking to me. So at the end of it, there was nothing left for me in Rhodesia and I left the country for good. One of the first things I told Dad was that I wanted to join the South African Air Force, but being ex-military himself, he saw no future for his son in uniform and gave me a pretty explicit thumbs down.

Then, when my second stint at university also turned sour, mainly due to boredom, I simply upped sticks and signed on the dotted line at the headquarters of the South African Air Force in Pretoria.

CHAPTER TWO

EARLY DAYS IN THE
SOUTH AFRICAN AIR FORCE

S ince an early age, Neall Ellis had been interested in all aspects of flying, including reading about aircraft and World War II combat heroes and, of course, talking to the occasional pilot he would encounter while serving in the Rhodesian forces. Had he not queered his own pitch by a series of untimely comments, he might even have tried for the Rhodesian Air Force (RhAF).

Having moved to South Africa which, because of historical ties, regarded Rhodesians (as well as other whites from neighbouring territories) as de-facto Southern Africans, it was a lot easier to enlist in the various arms that made up the South African Defence Force (SADF). That included the South African Air Force (SAAF).

I joined the South African Air Force in 1971. Because of my military service in Rhodesia, I was exempted from the usual three months basic course at Swartkops, the air base on the southern outskirts of Pretoria. It was a good thing, as I dreaded being thrust in at the deep end with a bunch of rookies, not that I was much older than most of them.

Instead, since I had volunteered for pilot training, I was

shipped off to the Cape to undergo a formative course at the Saldanha Military Academy, a South African version of Sandhurst and West Point. The idea was that I, and a bunch of like-minded recruits, would be prepared for the necessary at the nearby air force base at Langebaan Road.

It wasn't the happiest of situations to begin with, in part because Afrikaans was the lingua franca throughout and my appreciation of the language was somewhere close to zero. Not that I had anything against Afrikaans, I'd just never had much need to use it before then.

It was an interesting experience nonetheless, but the academics soon bored me, which was why I started playing hockey and made the academy team. The move wasn't without the usual ulterior motive. Basically, if you played sport you usually got to go to Cape Town on a weekend pass, which made a change from Saldanha which lay 150 dusty kilometres north of the Mother City. During that period I also met my wife Zelda, and we were married two years later in 1973.

My time at the academy was little more than transitional, which was probably just as well. Saldanha was basically a fishing village with few features worth mentioning. The only restaurant in town was beyond the limited resources of us new recruits and when the wind blew in from the fish factories that lined the coast, the entire area stank, sometimes for days at a time. Also, the surrounding ocean, which should have offered some kind of diversion to those of us who might have been off duty, was not only uninviting but could also be dangerous.

Although Saldanha stood on a great natural lagoon—where, through two world wars, Allied ships would gather to form convoys before proceeding north—the ocean was freezing cold almost all year round, in large part because of the icy and sometimes treacherous Agulhas current that sweeps in from the Antarctic.

Most of my colleagues didn't complain. Our accommodation on 'The Kop', a windswept, barren hill, was reasonably comfortable and, anyway, this was the year that the movie MASH appeared on the circuit and, one and all, we were addicted. Like the rebel doctors in the movie, we named our bungalow 'The Swamp' and we tried to emulate some of our limited excesses according to what we'd viewed, although the only 'war' we had at Saldanha was with our instructors.

Not long after I passed through the military academy at Saldanha, I was ordered to grab my things and head a few miles down the road to Langebaan Road, one of the country's largest air force bases, where most young pilots were put through their paces. Like a handful of others, I was actually being taught to fly by a host of experienced aviators, some with combat experience in Korea, and a few old timers from World War II.

Almost overnight, I was in my own special kind of heaven. Moreover, it wasn't just any old plane I was climbing into each time I went aloft. My friends and I were put through our paces in South Africa's newly acquired Impala jet trainer/fighter, a solid sophisticated machine well suited to the African environment in which it operated.

The Impala was my first aircraft, and I spent so much time in these delightful little jets that I got to appreciate their quirks and foibles very well indeed. They are certainly among the most reliable planes I have ever flown.

Not many people are aware that outside the United States, the 'Imp'—or more correctly the Italian-designed and built Aermacchi MB-326—remains one of the most successful jet trainers ever built. There were more than 600 of them wheeled out of factories in half a dozen countries including Australia, Brazil and South Africa. Pretoria ordered 165 of them and, except for the first 40, they were all built locally by Atlas Aircraft Corporation, which had its facilities adjacent to the old Jan Smuts Airport in Johannesburg. It is called Denel Aviation today.

The plane's performance specs—with a lifespan of about 5,000 hours—were awesome. An Imp would take off at maximum load in 800 metres and, in doing so, could clear a 15-metre obstacle at the end of the runway. At light weight, it needed only about half that much runway. Its maximum speed was upwards of 500mph and it could achieve a rate-of-climb rate of 3,000 feet-per-minute. The plane set many category records including one of the very first for a small, single-engine jet fighter/trainer: an altitude record of 56,807ft (17,315m) set in March 1966.

I achieved a great sense of satisfaction in getting on to the training programme and was only made aware much later that I was a member of a pretty exclusive little band of trainee pilots. There had originally been more than 5,000 applicants. Of them, only 250 were chosen for the second selection phase, of whom only half went to the academy and half again—or 60 pupils in total—were accepted for actual pilot training. By the time it was all over, only 27 of our original group got their wings.

Learning to fly jets at Saldanha was never an easy option. Langebaan was exposed to the sea and the winters could sometimes make things a little hairy. With north-west storms constantly roaring in—the region lies in a winter rainfall area—cross winds and down drafts were routine. When the quirks of some of our mentors were added into the equation, things got more complicated still.

My first instructor was Budgie Burgess, an experienced pilot who preferred to shout his orders at you instead of telling you what was required. I just couldn't take his bellowing and ended up doing the unthinkable for a new recruit: I asked for somebody else to teach me. It says a lot that I wasn't kicked off the course, which suggested that someone higher up must have spotted a little promise from this Ellis boy.

Burgess was clearly upset, but the order came down that I was to be handed over to another flying instructor and after that, there were no problems. In later years, Budgie and I ended up being good friends. In fact, he was of immense help when I landed in a spot of serious bother in the Congo (Brazzaville) many years later.

Langebaan Air Force Base always promised to be a tough regime for us youngsters, enthusiastic as we no doubt were. But then, as aviators of all generations will tell you, flying is also a great leveller. There was an inordinate amount of pressure on each of us to succeed and our instructors during the 13-month course—from

ground school to getting our wings—were demanding as well as
tough. They were all professional aviators and totally non-judge-
mental. Apart from flying, everyday rigmarole at the air base was
coupled to a measure of military discipline that would sometimes
make newcomers blanche.

Add to this a series of lecture sessions, regular exams, fatigues
and being completely base-bound with no weekend passes to get
away to Cape Town, all of which made my time there more than
challenging. Having said that, always being head of the pack when
it came to getting things done, if I did not get a pass to leave the
base, I simply went AWOL every weekend and headed for Cape
Town and Zelda. Interestingly, I never got caught, although I had
my share of close calls. I would almost certainly have been bumped
from the course had I been, because others were.

Fortunately, towards the end of the year the instructors relaxed
somewhat, which was more than a good thing. I was sneaking
down the back stairs of our quarters one evening when Buck
Buchanan, my instructor, was heading up them.

He asked: 'You going to visit Zelda?'

I said: 'Yes.'

'Have you got a pass?'

'No,' I replied quite brazenly.

'Well, then I don't think I've seen you, have I? Have a good
time!'

For all that, I wasn't the best student in our class. In terms of
reference (I discovered much later) my overall performance was
rated as mediocre. However, my instructors were aware that while
I might have occasionally struggled with maths and physics, I
appeared to adapt almost naturally once I was strapped into a jet
trainer and prepared for take-off.

Then, as I was to learn rather dramatically, it wasn't only pupil
pilots who made mistakes. There were times when the instructors
would blunder, and more than once there were lives lost, once
almost my own. This was one of about four occasions in my life
when I've felt this really could be the end. When it happens, as I

know from my own experiences and those of others who have survived a critical moment, you just accept it. Not that you don't keep trying, of course, right on up to the last moment . . .

That incident took place during a routine training exercise one August winter morning. We'd taken off in an Impala from Langebaan Air Force Base and had found ourselves in some fairly heavy cloud. At that point, my instructor came through on the intercom and said he didn't want to do a controlled let down. Moments later he spotted a gap in the huge bank of cloud somewhere over the Hopefield Bombing Range and decided to spiral down. However, the trouble was that when circling down like that, the aircraft's speed increases exponentially. Add to that the fact that the radius of the aircraft's turn also increases and we found ourselves right back into cloud.

The instructor was on visual when suddenly the Impala inverted. Ideally, he should have rolled it level and gone up again, ending with a controlled approach. Instead, he took the plane down almost vertically, his intention, I imagine, being to complete the last part of a giant loop. By the time we'd dropped below 1,000ft, I told myself to eject. However, by then we were pulling so many Gs that I could barely move my arms to get my hands onto either of the two ejection handles. That was when I also realised that had I actually pulled one of those handles, I would have probably been hurled straight into the ground. I had no option but to stick with the aircraft.

We were well clear of cloud when we finally emerged from the loop and all I could do was hold my breath. We must have cleared the ground at around 100ft, or perhaps it was 50 . . . we will never know. It was so close that I remember seeing the low scrub bushes only feet below us. My instructor wasted no time in getting our plane back to base and once we'd landed, he was speechless. He just got out of his cockpit and left it to me to switch off. With that he simply walked away. However, he did come back a while later to apologise. Even today, when I see him, he always jokes: 'Remember that day? I almost got you killed . . .' I usually remind him with a smile that we both almost pretty well caught it on that flight.

During the latter stages of our training we learnt the fundamentals of night flying, something that I've always regarded as a
unique experience. This training was to stand me in good stead
many years later in Sierra Leone when I had to go up on my own
and, literally, drive the rebels from the gates of Freetown. More to
the point, in Sierra Leone, while flying the Air Wing Hind—which
was used to halt the rebel advance—I initially did so without night
vision goggles (NVGs).

I recall the many times I flew over the South Cape, the rolling
South Atlantic Ocean on one side and rows of hills on the other,
often on pitch black, no-moon nights at something like 32,000ft.
I always experienced an incredible loneliness. Most times when we
went up in the dark there was nobody manning the radio back at
base. However, the stars, quite brilliant and incandescent above
our heads, made up for the solitude.

Following the completion of the flying course at Langebaan, in
1972, and the award of our wings, we went on leave. On return,
I was posted 'to the tower' for air traffic control training, but
halfway through was ordered back to Langebaan as a 'station pilot'
which, in the lingo, is half-a-step ahead of a gofer aviator and a
ferry pilot. Basically, my job was to be on round-the-clock standby.

This work wasn't without its share of experiences, not all of
them pleasant. Captain John Wesley and I once had to fly an
Impala 1,000 miles from the Cape to Atlas Aviation in Kempton
Park. There we picked up another Impala, which had just been
serviced, and headed back south. We'd re-fuelled at Bloemfontein,
and then suddenly found ourselves caught in a massive storm
between Kimberley and Upington, which lies on the Orange River.

We were flying at about 37 000ft and we picked up comms
from a nearby Learjet at 45,000ft, which reported that it was only
just above the weather. Meanwhile, we were getting thrown around
at altitude as if we'd landed in a maelstrom: we ended up with bank
angles of up to 60 degrees and severe up and down nose pitching.
At one stage, I felt a kind of twitching in my ears, almost as if they
were being flicked. It was a peculiar sensation and I thought:

'What the fuck is this instructor playing at?' It was as if I was back at school and the science master was flicking my ears with a wax taper when my concentration started to lag. For a few moments I thought he was flicking my ears from the rear seat. Then I thought again. I was wearing a flying helmet so of course he couldn't flick me. Eventually, I realized that the sensation was from static sparks coming through the radio system, my first experience of St Elmo's fire. The hues—muted greens and yellows—and the radiance coming off the nose of the aircraft all added to it. It was really quite eerie.

We got out of the storm eventually and after we'd landed at Langebaan, we noticed that our vertical stabiliser had a two centimetre hole burned right into it. There was also something that looked like blobs of solder scattered all over the wingtip tanks where the static charges had been breaking away. Hail had destroyed some of our navigation lights, and there were dents on the wings from these projectiles which, considering our flying speed, must have hit with considerable impact. There were even dents on our nose cone.

The stress limit for an Impala is 7.5Gs (or seven-and-a-half times the force of gravity), but we'd apparently hit almost double that. The plane wasn't flyable thereafter so they trucked it back to Atlas and basically pulled the aircraft apart for a completely new overhaul. Captain John Wesley, who taught me many of my flying skills in those early days wasn't all that phased by the experience. A real gentleman aviator, he left the air force soon afterwards, enrolled at university and qualified as an aeronautical engineer.

Still a second lieutenant, Neall Ellis was next posted to Bloemfontein with orders to join 8 Squadron, which flew Harvard T-6s, a World War II vintage prop-driven trainer. With the Border War in the north-west gathering a sudden momentum of its own, Air Force Headquarters in Pretoria needed pilots to be trained for conversion to Impala jets, which could be used in cross-border support strikes into Angola.

The T-6 could be a tricky plane to land. However, when I arrived at my new posting, the first Impala jets had been delivered and I was spared the Harvard conversion. So I just continued flying jets.

Life at 8 Squadron under Major Hans Conradie, our officer commanding, was good. Although keen for 'Border Ops'—as the counter-insurgency conflict was referred to—only helicopter pilots were then being sent north on Alouette 111s and I didn't rate. Instead, I trained with a bunch of Citizen Force (CF) pilots, among them a major who'd served in the Korean War.

The unit had a unique set of Standing Orders, one of the most important being that every Thursday night everybody had to be in the pub. Even if you drank only coke, no excuses were accepted. In a peculiar way, that and other quirks under good leadership made for great camaraderie in the squadron. However, with a serious war threatening from Black Africa to the north, the good times couldn't last.

In 1974, the youthful Neall Ellis was posted back to the Cape and Langebaan Road for an operational training course. Almost overnight, he was introduced to air combat manoeuvring, rocket-fire in combat, aerial bombing, air-to-ground attacks and so on. Because of the war, a new dimension had been created for the air force, which had been considered a 'peacetime air force', and the training reflected that.

At heart though, young Ellis was still a schoolboy. During a return visit to the Saldanha Military Academy, he was challenged to climb the ship's mast on the parade square and place a beer can on the top.

Of course, after I had done the dreaded deed we had a crowd of military police on our tail and we ducked out towards the rear of the establishment. The bottom line is that I drove off, had an accident, and while trying to get my gear out of the car, the police arrived and, as it is phrased in the lingo, I 'thumped a cop' for being impertinent.

Not unsurprisingly, Lieutenant Ellis was arrested and, after blood tests to establish his alcohol level, he was taken to the Wynberg Military Hospital in Cape Town to be treated for torn ligaments in his leg which came with the altercation. 'They put me in an empty ward and then just forgot about me. Next morning I had to hobble out and search for food and some attention.' Nothing came of the fisticuffs, though. Taken off the course as medically unfit, he went back to Bloemfontein for a couple of months to recuperate, and then went on to finish the course.

There were four of us doing this advanced training, which included a pilot attack instructor's course, or PAI, as well as operational training. We'd been advised earlier that we had one weekend off a month and for that we'd be given a pair of aircraft. This allowed us to head out Fridays after lunch and report back for duty the following Monday.

But then, towards at the end of the course, they cut the availability of planes to a single machine and, being the junior, the major said that I had to stay in the base. At which point, I suggested that he strongly resembled a part of the female anatomy. That, in brief, terminated my stint in what we had started to refer to as the 'Junior Space Club' and instead of heading on to the next phase, where 'suitable' pilots would fly sophisticated French-built Mirage supersonic fighters, I was 'relegated' to helicopters.

The year was 1975 and Angola was in a state of protracted civil war. Cuban troops had entered Angola in their thousands and Moscow was pushing offensive weapons into the region as if there was no tomorrow. Clearly, I had done myself an enormous favour.

The operational conversion course on helicopters, to which Nellis was assigned, took place at Ysterplaat in Cape Town. The air base had strong World War II link, as many British and Commonwealth airmen had their basic training there. Quite a few of them went on to make names for themselves in the great upheaval then taking place at the far end of the African continent.

The men who were in charge when the still-obstreperous Nellis arrived were among the best aviators in Africa, and included men such as Captain John Church, who ultimately retired from the SAAF with the rank of general. Bloemfontein followed Ysterplaat, where this by-now reasonably experienced helicopter pilot was attached to B Flight, 16 Squadron.

Time spent operating out of the Free State air base involved intensive flight training in the mountains, which meant lengthy spells in the Drakensberg Mountains and advanced training in navigation (of the type that pilots would eventually put into use when they were deployed with their Alouettes in the semi-arid regions of northern South-West Africa), gunnery skills, trooping drills and a lot else besides.

With trooping drills, SAAF choppers followed some of the principles already in operational use in Rhodesia, where that guerrilla war was escalating far too quickly for Ian Smith's government to be able to adequately cope with it, which was one of the reasons SAAF pilots were sent to help out government forces fighting 'terrorists'.

South African Alouette helicopters would usually board four soldiers at a time, five at a pinch, which was just beyond the specified weight limitations of the machine as detailed by Aérospatiale, its French manufacturers. Basically, the 'Enplaning Drill' for an operation—colloquially termed 'Fire Force'—was simple. The troops would approach the chopper in echelon from the pilot's one o'clock position, the 'stick leader' having raised his right arm to show that his group was ready to board and having had a 'thumbs up' from the pilot. To avoid confusion, the 'stick leader' would be the last to board and in the Rhodesian Air Force he would sit facing towards the rear and the rest of his squad, with the MAG gunner to his right. In that war, the troops always had loaded magazines in their weapons and, more often than not, one up the spout. Any additional packs carried by the soldiers would be held in their laps during flight.

In the early days of the war airlifted troops were allowed to retaliate to ground fire while still aloft, but that was soon stopped to prevent their FN-FAL spent cartridges ejecting upwards into the chopper's rotor blades. The MAG, in contrast, ejected downwards, or, in later modifications, the brass was captured in leather pouches attached to the gun.

Neall Ellis was sent to Rhodesia for his first operational bush tour in the winter of 1975. Normally, he would first have spent time in South Africa's then escalating Border War, adjacent to Angola—usually two months at a stretch—but conditions in Rhodesia's guerrilla war had deteriorated alarmingly and he was needed as a stop-gap. Seconded to 7 Squadron Rhodesian Air Force, Nellis and his group went into the neighbouring territory as part of what was termed 'clandestine assistance'.

Prior to departure, the entire flying group was taken to Defence Head-quarters in Pretoria and briefed. They were told they could take no South African identification, money or any other documentation which might disclose their origins if they were shot down. Everything had to be left behind, even their uniforms. Instead, each man was issued with Rhodesian money and told to be at Swartkops air force base in civilian clothes at four o'clock the following morning. There, they were loaded into an unmarked DC-3, flown to the Rhodesian base at New Sarum, again briefed, this time by a Rhodesian officer, given Rhodesian uniforms and identity cards and ordered not to speak Afrikaans. 'But nobody told the poor Afrikaans guys in our group, almost all of whom spoke in broad and unmistakable South African accents . . . it was actually a bit of a farce', Nellis recalls.

Within days, the South African newcomers had relocated into rugged bush country to the north of Salisbury and been told to get on with the war. Neall Ellis was put at the controls of a G-car, which was a trooper. The trooper, unlike the gunship, was armed only with a light machine gun and was used to ferry troops into position. It was in this G-car that Neall experienced his first hostile action against what he soon came to accept was a tough and resilient enemy.

Although described today as a low-key struggle, the Rhodesian War could be extremely hairy at times, especially if the enemy was about, which was often enough. Throughout, it was not nearly as intense or as widespread as similar wars then taking place in South-East Asia. Altogether, about 1,500 members of the security forces died during the course of Rhodesian hostilities. Of the 25,000 people of African origin who were killed, roughly two-thirds were insurgents. The rest were civilians, mostly tribal people, caught in the crossfire of a conflict that many of them did not even begin to comprehend.

Air support—so crucial and so often decisive—was provided by the eight squadrons of the Rhodesian Air Force. There were sufficient Hunter ground-attack fighters, Canberra light bombers and Vampire fighter bombers armed with cannon, rockets and locally manufactured blast, shrapnel and napalm bombs to devastate external camps and other targets. To this tally the RhAF defied international arms sanctions imposed by the

United Nations (UN) and added light aircraft for liaison, reconnaissance and light attack. Most important, though, was a small squadron of French Alouette helicopters. With time, more would be acquired, including some from Spain, and others loaned to the Salisbury government by South Africa.

The 1978 clandestine acquisition of elderly Agusta-Bell 205s from Israel gave the helicopter forces greater range and load-carrying capability and was to play a vital role in enabling the security forces to cut off and surround guerrilla units on larger bush operations.

In a report on the war, appropriately titled *Rhodesia: Tactical Victory, Strategic Defeat*[1], U.S. Marine Corps Majors Charles M. Lohman and Robert I. MacPherson provided an insight into the country's aviation assets. The Rhodesian Air Force, they said, was able to call on 25 ground-attack aircraft (nine Hawker Hunter FGA9s, a dozen antiquated but still-effective Vampires and four OV-10 Broncos) as well as 11 T-55s. There were also 19 trainer reconnaissance aircraft (nine BAC Provosts and 18 Cessna-337s) and 30 counter-insurgency/reconnaissance planes (12 Al-60s and 18 Cessna-337s). Transports included a single Be-55 Baron, six BN-2 Islanders and ten DC-3 (C-47s).

Top of the list were the 77 helicopters fielded by the Rhodesian Air Force. These comprised 66 Sud-Aviation SA 316/-318 Alouettes as well as the Bell 205s bought from Israel. Lohman and MacPherson tell us that the air service was composed of approximately 1,300 personnel, which, considering the paucity of numbers and the extent of the war was remarkable. The two officers reported:

> Pilot training was unique by American standards, but it followed British traditions. The pilots and crewmembers were trained to become individually proficient in the maintenance of particular parts of the aircraft. If the aircraft experienced a malfunction, the entire crew was able to perform fairly sophisticated levels of maintenance. This system included the incorporation of maintenance technicians as members of helicopter and transport carrier crews.
>
> In 1978 the serviceability of the Rhodesian Air Force was 85 per cent. This is exceptional when 60 per cent is generally considered as 'good' throughout the West. This is a greater accomplish-

ment considering the international sanctions levelled against Rhodesia in 1965 and 1970. The majority of its military re-supply was built upon a system of improvisation and invention.

Seminal to the Rhodesian war effort was the Alouette 111, which followed the Mark 11, an early-era combat helicopter that in 1958 set a new world record for rotary craft at more than 36,000ft. The frail look of these choppers was deceptive. Armed with single- or twin-barrelled heavy machine guns poking out the open port door, they could give much more than they got. However, the Alouette did have a chink in its armour, and that was speed. It could maintain a maximum of only 105 knots at sea level and cruise at about 85 knots fully loaded with troops or, in the case of a gunship, loaded to the gunwales with 20mm ammo.

Because of the country's Central African altitude, Rhodesian Alouettes flew at between 65 and 84 knots, with a range of 210 nautical miles. That meant that on distant operations—into Mozambique or the south-eastern or south-western districts of the country—refuelling was vital.

The mainstay of the helicopter Fire Force attack team was what was referred to as the 'K-Car' (Alouette gunship), armed with a 20mm cannon and manned by three crew members. With 600lbs of fuel, it had an endurance of between 75 and 90 minutes. In contrast, the trooper, or 'G-Car', with only 400lbs of fuel and a crew of two packing a 7.72mm MAG machine gun, was able to uplift a 'stick' of four fully equipped troops. The men were usually dropped straight into a contact, the chopper itself often taking hits from the ensuing firefight.

There was no question that the Alouette 111s were always regarded as excellent combat machines for this kind of low-key counter-insurgency war. Both burnt jet fuel, but in emergencies could operate on diesel or gasoline and paraffin for short bursts. They were also able to absorb astonishing amounts of punishment.

Almost overnight, Neall Ellis found himself in an African environment that was like nothing he had experienced before. Although he had grown up in Rhodesia, the region in which the war was being fought was very different from the Bulawayo area, or even the nearby Matopos Hills.

North-eastern Rhodesia, then and now, was a world of undulating

bush and huge granite outcrops, some as tall as skyscrapers. The countryside provided the kind of ground cover that tended to favour insurgents
rather than helicopters. Also, it was a war that came in brief, intense spurts
and firefights that did not always leave bodies behind

> Most of our actions came from sitting perhaps 50ft above ground
> and looking for targets that were elusive and deadly. The AK-47
> was obviously no match for our 20mm cannon, but there were
> sometimes an awful lot of Kalashnikovs, along with the occasional
> blast from an RPG-2 or, in later phases, the more ubiquitous
> RPG-7.
>   I don't like to use the phrase 'adrenaline rush'—I think it's
> overused and more than a little facile—but there is no other way
> to explain the sensation felt when you're in somebody's sights and
> there is green tracer all around you. More to the point, nobody
> had ever used either me or my machine for target practice before.
> In short, I'd never come under fire before.
>   It didn't take us long to get into the war: only hours, in fact.
> We'd gone out, following an urgent call from a Rhodesian African
> Rifles fire force, a mainly black unit with white officers, better
> known as the RAR.
>   Once over the combat area, with the gunner and three or four
> troops in the back, I couldn't have been more than 10 metres off
> the ground when there was a sudden rattling in the cockpit, like
> three or four people banging away at typewriters. I turned my head
> around towards the engineer—which is actually quite difficult
> when you're wearing a flying helmet—to ask him what the hell
> that noise was. However, the spectre that greeted me was one of
> sheer terror. All those sitting behind me had their bodies pressed
> up hard against rear bulkhead as tracer fire came through the door.
> Tracer fire was whizzing through, right between them and the two
> soldiers in front with me.
>   Their eyes weren't exactly the size of saucers, but I got the
> message. Volleys of rounds continued coming at us from the bush
> below. What was astonishing was that the first salvo—probably an
> entire ammo clip—didn't hit any one of us. Talk about luck! For

me, the experience was sudden, unexpected and, frankly, terrifying. But then when you're at the controls, flying low with a chopper-load of people on board and other gunships in the air in the immediate vicinity, you cannot allow yourself to become distracted.

I immediately banked towards some tall trees to my right and ended up doing a complete 360 degree turn, the idea being that the gunner could get in his sights whoever had been doing the shooting. He did exactly that only moments later and the firing momentarily stopped. Early reports indicated that it had been quite a strong force, possibly several dozen enemy troops who had infiltrated Rhodesia from Mozambique several days before. Most were laid out on slabs before nightfall, as a result of the subsequent RAR ground action, when the unit got caught in an effective cross-fire. Clearly, their training hadn't been as good as ours.

Nellis recalls that while that contact went off quite well, it wasn't always easy to work with the Rhodesians. Almost to a man, he recalls, these soldiers were 'very professional, well trained, coordinated and supremely motivated'. It was almost as if they regarded the bush war as an interim diversion from normal life, he reckoned. 'There were unpleasant things taking place out in the bush, but most were mere hiccups before the gooks were run to ground, one of them told me. Moreover, he really believed it.' He added:

> There was no arguing with the Rhodesians, even though operationally, from our perspective, things didn't look too good. We were always reminded that it didn't matter what we thought about the war, we were outsiders who'd been sent in to help the Smith regime stay in power. Even then, we were only grudgingly accepted for offering a hand, although some of our blokes were killed doing it. 'This is our country' they would say, and for the majority who were born there it was all they had.

In part, Nellis suggests, the Rhodesians actually believed they could win their war, if only because their success rate was so extraordinarily high. They were killing insurgents at a rate of something like 20 or 25 to one, but somebody hadn't factored in that a single fatality on their side was likely to count for quite a lot when the entire white population was measured in terms of a few hundred thousand people—men women and children—or roughly speaking, a town the size of Bournemouth in England.

> We couldn't help sensing that the Rhodesians, almost like the Israelis, regarded themselves as superior to everybody else. But then, I suppose, they were, especially when it came to battling the preponderant enemy force against which they had been ranged for several years already.
>
> As far as the Rhodesian Air Force was concerned, we were a bunch of novices, and there were times when that kind of attitude hurt. They certainly rated themselves as superior to the air crews from down south, but then they'd been fighting for a while and knew both the country and the enemy better than anybody. Sometimes we would blunder—it happens in battle—and they'd have to guide us back to base by radio in this vast, bush-covered land with few natural features. Then the word would go around: 'the slopes have got lost again.'
>
> A favourite word for South Africans among Rhodesian fighting men was the word 'slope', which was supposed to refer to the way that the foreheads of some of our people 'sloped' down, almost like a bunch of Neanderthals. I suppose it did with some of our fellows, but they painted most of us with the same disdainful brush, which was a pity because our intentions were honourable.
>
> I was actually quite lucky because I blended in quite well with local crews. I'd been educated in Rhodesia and knew some of their pilots from school so they probably regarded me as one of them.

Towards the end of that Rhodesian tour, Nellis recalls:

The crews operated from a primitive makeshift base near Mtoko— a few hours' drive north-east of Salisbury and at the core of what was then referred to as Operation *Hurricane*. There were no fixed buildings to talk of, and most of the air crews were billeted in tents, with their water coming from a 44-gallon drum suspended over a wood fire. They would bathe in turn in a modest little zinc bath because it was really all there was.

However, the food was always good because the Rhodesian Air Force liked to commandeer all the top restaurant chefs from Salisbury and Bulawayo for their call-ups. The result was that we'd come in after a day's action and cold beers would be waiting at the improvised bar, which, as I recall, was a huge log that had been planed down flat. Then the party would start and often go on until midnight, which was pushing it because first call was usually before dawn.

The air crews would always go over the day's events in some detail once we got back to Mtoko, almost like an informal debrief and quite useful because you could pick up quite a lot from the experiences of others. It was all fascinating combat stuff, of course, and it sometimes made me wonder why there were so few casualties among flying personnel. We were taking enormous risks, yet had astonishingly few casualties when compared to similar conflicts in other parts of the world. I think it must have been down to the inferior training of the enemy and our aggressive approach.

I recall going into a particularly heavy contact, while flying the G-Car, where one of the South Africans on permanent secondment talked me down to land in a maize field, but with my 20mm cannon facing in the wrong direction. Just as I was going through transition, I came under some heavy tracer fire—it was green, so we knew where it came from and it was striking the ground on all sides of us. We were committed to land so I took the chopper in anyway, but then the fire force troops wouldn't get out because of incoming fire.

I turned to the engineer, and told him chuck the fuckers out, which he tried to do. He literally got them by the scruffs of their necks and attempted to force them out of the helicopter's open door, but they resisted. They were staying put, they said and still refused to budge. So in my basic sign language—because of rotor noise—I indicated that we were staying on the ground until they were out of there and they quickly got the message. Moments later they hit the turf running and, curiously, nobody on the Alouette took a hit.

After a spell at Mtoko, Nellis was drafted to the Joint Operations Command (JOC) at Mudzi, but that was short-lived. He was medevaced to Salisbury one evening with what was diagnosed as a gut problem. In fact, it was a bit more serious and later that night he was wheeled into the theatre for an appendectomy and repatriated to South Africa to recuperate. Days later he was rushed back to the military hospital in Bloemfontein with septicaemia. He was out of action for a few weeks and stayed in Salisbury for that time.

While Nellis Ellis spent time after his recuperation as an instructor on Alouettes, conditions in Rhodesia continued to deteriorate. Some South African forces had been pulled out—the South African Police had been forced to withdraw some time earlier because of American pressure on Pretoria—but some of the helicopter assets stayed behind,

Because the Rhodesians were under serious strain again, Nellis was ordered back to Rhodesia. In the nine months between May 1979 and February the following year, he completed six tours of operational duty in the Rhodesian bush, each of which varied between a month and six weeks in duration.

Whereas the Rhodesians previously wouldn't allow the South Africans to fly the K-Car, this time round he was given an Alouette and worked throughout with the RLI fire force. As he says, it was also his first real experiences of controlling troops on the ground during a contact. Much of the tactics were centred on the 20mm cannon mounted at the rear of the cockpit, and although he wasn't to know it then, these sorties formed the basis of his tactical knowledge, which he went on to use in the escalating military struggle in the vast semi-arid region south of Angola, then still known as *Deutsch-Südwestafrika*. All of his experience, he acknowledges, came directly from Rhodesia.

CHAPTER THREE

EARLY DAYS DURING
THE BORDER WAR

S outh Africa's Border War began in earnest for Neall Ellis in December
1975. Posted for an eight-week tour to the Ondangua—the regional
air force base in northern South-West Africa (Namibia today), he was to
work closely with elements of South Africa's Airborne, the Parachute
Battalion or, in the lingo, the 'Parabats'.

As he recalls, just about everything that happened in this regional
conflict filtered through to the operations room, commonly known as the
'Ops Room'. Although it sounded grand, it was little more than a tin shack
with a cement floor that for most of the year was more akin to a sauna
than an important operational planning centre.

The conflict sometimes took hostilities behind enemy lines and
considerable distances beyond internationally recognised frontiers (to the
consternation of Britain, the United States, the Soviet Union and the
United Nations). The South African Army also went into Zambia and
Mozambique several times. There were more clandestine raids further
afield, with South African Navy Daphne Class submarines dropping
Special Forces strike teams off the coasts of some of South Africa's most
outspoken enemies, Tanzania and Angola.

The war lasted a full generation, about 24 years in all, and by the time it all ended, thousands of sons had followed in the footsteps of their fathers and experienced military service. Although casualty figures throughout this conflict were modest, this was largely due to the immense area (by European standards) across which it was fought. There were hostilities in one form or another from the appropriately named Skeleton Coast on the Atlantic Ocean, to a tiny point on the map 1,500km to the east where the frontiers of three nations—South-West Africa, Zambia and Zimbabwe (formerly Rhodesia)—conjoined.

Actual numbers of fatalities and wounded are difficult to assess accurately, in part because the Angolans never opened their archives to the outside world. The South African Army and Air Force (there were few SA Navy casualties because, apart from the briefly resuscitated South African Marines, there were almost no naval personnel directly involved) lost fewer than 800 men during the conflict, roughly three or four a month. The enemy had a casualty rate that was many times that.

In South-West Africa itself, it was the preponderant Ovambo tribal people who initially set the scene for conflict. Always against what they regarded as Pretoria's illegal occupation of their country, they protested at the UN, and when that didn't achieve any results, they asked several African countries for military help to displace what they termed the 'hated racist oppressors'.

Although the Ovambos were regarded by the South Africans as 'primitive and tribal' (this was former apartheid government minister Pik Botha's off-the-cuff phrase, which he used when attending the International Court of Justice at The Hague), they were anything but. Certainly, this African nation followed all the traditional tribal norms, but they were also single-minded in their efforts to dislodge the South African presence from their land. Thus, by the time the war started, they had formed their own political party, the South-West African People's Organisation (SWAPO), and sent batches of troops for military training abroad.

To bring matters properly into perspective, it is essential to look back a little. Pretoria had originally occupied the old German colony of *Deutsch-Südwestafrika* by right of conquest during World War I. That territory was entrusted to Pretoria by a League of Nations mandate. Efforts had already started after the end of World War II to neutralise South African jurisdiction in South-West Africa, but Pretoria hung on resolutely, at one stage even suggesting that the country was already a de facto fifth province of South Africa.

It was then that a group of Ovambo tribal leaders took matters in hand. Having viewed the ongoing 'colonial' war in Angola to the immediate north, and what was then going on in Rhodesia, as precedents, they started a military struggle of their own. Thus a low-key guerrilla struggle was launched in 1965. The consensus was that if Pretoria was not prepared to listen to reason, SWAPO guerrillas, armed and abetted by Moscow and China, would engage Pretoria militarily and force it to relinquish control of South Africa, which was eventually to become Namibia. Obviously, the South Africans viewed all these developments as preposterous.

At the heart of the guerrilla military effort was the People's Liberation Army of Namibia (PLAN), SWAPO's military wing. Although some modern historians tend to denigrate PLAN's efforts, we now know, with the benefit of hindsight, that with dollops of foreign financial and military aid, this moderate-sized group of freedom fighters was finally moulded into an extremely competent and dedicated group of guerrillas. How else could they have kept South Africa—the continent's most advanced industrial country—on a partial war footing for more than two decades?

The war began slowly. A total of six dissident Ovambos, armed with Soviet carbines, infiltrated a remote corner of their tribal homeland in 1965 and established a temporary base. The idea was that more fighters, on their way overland on foot from Zambia through Portuguese Angola (then already in its fifth year of hostilities), would join them. The camp itself, which would become a touchstone of SWAPO leader Sam Nujoma's liberation folklore, was called Ongulumbashe.

The operation launched to tackle these 'infiltrators' mainly consisted of members of the South African Police, with a small army detachment, together with elements from the South African Air Force. The initial operation became known in southern African military lore as Operation *Blouwildebees*. By contemporary standards, the strike was little more than a token effort, launched from what was then still an isolated northern administrative outpost at Ruacana, a small town that straddled the great Kunene River, which had headwaters to the north in Angola. Had it taken place in later years, it would probably have warranted little more than a footnote. South African military historian, Paul Els, wrote a book about it.[2]

The main force comprised four police officers, together with 37 other ranks. There were also four army officers, of whom one was a doctor, and seven NCOs. The South African Air Force contribution was nine, almost all of them pilots. To reduce weight, the eight Alouette helicopters involved in the operation were deployed without their usual complement of flight techs and were able to uplift five men each. It was the first time Alouette helicopters had been used in an offensive role.

By the time the Border War was over, it was estimated that almost half-a-million South Africans had experienced some form of military service, many along a succession of the country's embattled northern frontiers. On the Angolan side, the tally is said to have exceeded a million men in uniform, and cumulatively, over more than a dozen years of fighting, included a couple of hundred thousand Cubans. Their casualties, never confirmed, were rated by unofficial sources in Havana to have totalled into five figures, many more from tropical illnesses such as malaria, typhus, meningitis and typhoid than from actual combat.

There were also scores of Cuban, Soviet, East German and other communist air crews killed during the course of hostilities, a significant number by American Stinger MANPADS[1] introduced into this African theatre of hostilities by the CIA in an effort to counter Moscow's gains. The South Africans did their bit by handing over to anti-government UNITA guerrillas almost all the weapons captured in operations such as Operations *Protea*, *Modular*, *Askari*, *Super* and others.

SAM-7 (Strela-2) man-portable, shoulder-fired missiles captured during these ground operations—and there were dozens of them, similar to the U.S. Army tail-chasing REDEYEs—also went to UNITA and, by all accounts, they did enough damage to cause Cuban and Eastern-Bloc pilots to fly well beyond the estimated 4.2km slant-range of these weapons. That was in sharp contrast to South African military pilots who liked to operate as close to the ground as possible.

Although the Angolans also had low-altitude SAM systems, they hardly ever achieved a lock-on because the South African helicopters were rarely around long enough to become targets, or they hung so low over the forest that heavy foliage interfered with the sighting ability of those handling these weapons. In fact, during the entire war, while there were numerous SAAF aircraft and helicopters brought down by ground fire, not a single

South African (or Rhodesian) helicopter was shot down by SAMs. It wasn't for want of trying. In one major contact during Operational *Super* in March 1982, Neall Ellis in his Alouette gunship dodged three successive SAM-7s fired in about 90 seconds.

As with most wars, much of the day-to-day activity in South Africa's operational area in South-West Africa was routine.

By the time that Nellis arrived at Ondangua, low-key military activity in the region had been on the go for several years. His first deployments came while his helicopter squadron worked with the South African adaptation of the Rhodesian fire force: only Pretoria called it Reaction Force.

The day would start before dawn, with pilots accompanied by their flight engineers and servicing personnel carefully going over their choppers along the flight line. Banter across the hardstand was mostly light-hearted, usually between aircrew and members of the parachute battalion, some of the men taking bets on the possibility of a contact during the day.

The Parabats were active too, checking equipment and filling water bottles. Everything they took into battle had to be secured to prevent loss in the furious activity that usually preceded a contact and afterwards. Once both aircrews and troops were satisfied that everything was in working order, pilots and stick leaders would gather for a preliminary briefing in the operations room.

Typically, the first task of the day would be for crews to remain on standby for an area operation to the immediate north of the base. Other units had been taken in some hours before, cordoned off specific areas and systematically started searching villages—*kraals* in the argot—while looking for insurgents and weapons caches.

Operational experience gained in both the Rhodesian and South-West African Wars was a major factor in the war. Experience had proved that the most efficient method of gathering information on insurgent movements was to either deploy observation posts or send in clandestine patrols (usually disguised as insurgents) to reconnoitre an area where information about an enemy presence might have been received from other sources.

The area was given boundaries and all movement in and out of the place frozen. This meant that no other security force operations could take place while the military remained active there. The same applied to air traffic:

aircraft had either to fly at height over the area, or avoid it altogether.

Patrols sometimes spent days observing local villages from a distance. They would move closer at night and even enter villages to gather information. Obviously, the work was dangerous and only Special Forces troops trained in clandestine operations were employed for the task. Once insurgents were detected, the patrol would make contact with headquarters overnight and the next phase of bringing in ground troops would begin at first light.

Ideally, the composition of a combat ground force team in the Border War was an infantry company, similar to that of a rifle company, with three platoons of three sections of between eight and 14 men each. Each section should have a trained tracker—usually a bushman—and an interpreter for liaison with Ovambo-speaking civilians.

Numbers were essential in the kind of open country in which this war was fought. Because groups of men could be spotted from great distance at even a moderate altitude, most guerrilla movements took place during the dark hours. Should there be a contact during the day, the gunships would be in their element. The bush in South-West Africa is flat and virtually featureless, which made low-level aerial navigation extremely difficult. Nellis commented:

> We dealt with navigation in our own way by initially using 1:250 000 scale maps to an easily recognisable point on the map then, for more accurate navigation to the contact point, we used 1:50 000 scale maps or, quite often, aerial photographs. Because of uniformity and a basic lack of navigation features, we used heading and time and always allowed for wind. Although this might have been regarded as a thumb-suck procedure, the majority of pilots knew the area well enough to be able to navigate quite accurately to the point of destination. In contrast, during the Rhodesian War pilots were thoroughly familiar with their areas of operation and only after they had reached the contact area would they bother to utilize maps for the final run in to target. Of course, that was possible because of the undulating nature of the Rhodesian countryside: on the Angolan frontier we had none of that.

Nellis' Air Force component at Ondangua consisted of an Alouette III command-and-control helicopter (armed with a .303 machine gun) piloted by the mission leader. It would also carry the ground commander, who usually held the rank of major or above. For close air support along Angolan border regions, two Alouette III gunships armed with 20mm MG-151 cannon were preferred.

Along with the Reaction Force gunships there were the troopers, usually two or three Puma helicopters armed with door-mounted 7.62mm light machine guns. For visual reconnaissance and radio relay, a light fixed-wing aircraft such as the Cessna 185 or Bosbok, usually called a 'Telstar', might be sent over the battlefield to keep headquarters primed of developments. If necessary, a larger fixed-wing aircraft, such as a Dakota, would be brought into the mix for dropping a second wave of reserve troops by parachute, usually as a stopper group ahead of the target component. The role of the stopper group was to stop any enemy attempting to escape the attacking force by running in the opposite direction.

Because landmines had already become a feature of all of Southern Africa's regional conflicts, surface movement remained problematical for the four decades that these military struggles lasted. Most of the unpaved roads in the South-West African operational area were mined and could rarely be negotiated at the speeds required to match helicopter assault operations. Also, the road infrastructure in the region was marginal at best. In southern Angola it was almost non-existent, with convoys heading north on cross-border raids making their own tracks through the primitive sand-covered terrain.

During the war, some of the most successful pre-planned attacks on the larger insurgent camps that involved Nellis, resulted from information gathered by aerial photography or by visual reconnaissance by fixed-wing aircraft. These methods became a feature of the conflict in the southern Angolan War. Alternatively, the Reconnaissance Regiment—the Recces—might be tasked to physically confirm that a specific camp was occupied by the enemy.

Operation *Super* in 1982 is still regarded as the single most successful heliborne assault of the war. An attacking force of only 34 troops, all of them members of 32 Battalion, was transported in at dawn by five Puma helicopters. Additional support came from four Alouette gunships, with

Insurgents killed in battle were initially brought back to headquarters in Sector 10 in Ovamboland for fingerprinting and identification. Eventually the volume became so great that those efforts were abandoned, in part because there were many foreign Africans from Tanzania, the Congo, South Africa and elsewhere fighting with the guerrillas. *Author's photo*

Neall Ellis in overall control. The target was a remote SWAPO camp manned by more than 300 enemy troops. By the time the 90-minute firefight was over, 250 insurgents lay dead, for the loss of only four 32 Battalion troops.

It is interesting that, as the war progressed, troops selected for the Reaction Force—in part because of pressure from pilots like Nellis, Arthur Walker and other seasoned veterans—had to be certifiably qualified for helicopter operations. They also had to be thoroughly familiar with all procedures related to emplaning and deplaning. When you are being shot at and some of your mates are wounded or killed, a combination of difficult communication resulting from screaming turbines and rotating blades can cause confusion, especially among unsophisticated African troops from rural backgrounds. There were several instances of soldiers ducking into the tail rotors of helicopters.

Later, while flying against the rebels in Sierra Leone, Nellis commented that they would regularly hear about such incidents. He actually had two of them. One was a Nigerian soldier who ran into the tail rotor of his Mi-

17 while he was airlifting troops out of a dangerous position. Nellis recalled:

> The man killed himself and damaged the blade. My partner, Fred Marafono, a former SAS operator turned mercenary, came forward with big eyes and white face, to report what had happened. We ended up manufacturing a new rotor tip from a steel ammunition box. The chopper vibrated a bit, but was fine otherwise.

It happened again not long afterwards. The blade cut clean through the top of the man's skull. It killed him but, as Nellis recalls, there was luckily no damage to the rotor.

More importantly, says Nellis, helicopters are always vulnerable when they are on the ground during an action and correct procedures must be regularly practised, even in more sophisticated wars like Afghanistan. He reckons that it is worth remembering that more time on the ground tends to decrease survival chances, not only of helicopters but also of crew. Most chopper losses during operations occurred during landing, while on the ground, or on take-off.

Nellis states that the stick leader also has to ensure that each member of his team knows where to sit once on board the helicopter and how to take up a circular defence position immediately after deplaning. Loose straps and articles of clothing have to be properly secured as during flight unsecured objects seem to have a habit of flying out of open doors and fouling tail rotors. Similarly, radio antennae have to be taped down or removed and stored for later use. More importantly, the men must know the exact dimensions of the landing zone (LZ). In the event of a helicopter having to go in and pick up a casualty, or perhaps conduct an urgent uplift under fire, commonly known as a 'hot extraction', such things can have a direct bearing on the survival of everybody in the chopper.

What South African troops were rarely short of during the Border War was the wherewithal to fight. Sections were always heavily armed. In addition to their R5 rifles—the .223 calibre, South African, locally manufactured version of the Israeli Galil—troops carried phosphorous and smoke grenades, mini-pencil flares, 'Day-Glo' stick-on panels for their bush hats (so that they could be identified by circling gunships) and flashlights for searching bunkers and huts. Additional armament per section might be a pair of 40mm grenade launchers, at least one LMG (with the No. 1 and No. 2 carrying 500 rounds of ammunition each) and, in some cases, a light 60mm assault mortar or an RPG-7 rocket launcher.

'With all that equipment on board, chopper pilots had to be aware that the average all-up weight of a Reaction Force soldier was approximately 250lbs or 113k', said Nellis.

Fuel was always a problem for helicopter operations, particularly in the vast Southern African operational region. Because of the largely ruralised infrastructure in Rhodesia, Rhodesian forces were able to place drums of helicopter Avtur at various towns or villages around the country, ensuring that no chopper was more than 10 to 15 minutes from the nearest supplies. The same was true of 20mm ammunition, which could be left in secure storage. Nellis comments:

> The South African forces weren't as fortunate. The only places where fuel could be stored were military or police camps, and these were scattered over a wide area across a region that sometimes extended hundreds of kilometres over the horizon. Distances between these camps could be huge. It was not unusual for a pilot to make a critical decision about whether he should leave the scene of the action in the middle of a firefight because his fuel level said he should—and consequently deprive the Reaction Force of its close air support—or remain over the action and fight. It was either that or land somewhere in the bush afterwards with zero fuel and high hopes that the drums urgently called for over the radio would not be too long in coming. These would usually be ferried in by Puma helicopters.

Routing to the contact area was often a difficult time for aircrew and troops alike. The mission leader and force commander were required to obtain as much information from the forward observation post position as possible and adjust the battle plan 'on the hoof' if necessary. 'In addition,' explained Nellis, 'the mission leader was required to ensure not only that his navigation was correct, but to coordinate the timing for the strike aircraft that were to follow, as well as to ensure that all the helicopters were maintaining their positions in the formation.'

During the latter stages of the bush war in Southern Angola, he recalls, the Angolan Air Force aggressively flew air patrols in the hopes of encountering the South African Air Force in Angolan air space carrying out external missions. In addition, he added, they had a constant ground-to-air threat from SAM-7 missiles, both in South-West Africa and Angola. The fact that they were never able to bring any SAAF aircraft down didn't exactly minimise the threat. Therefore, for mutual support and safety, all helicopters flew in a battle formation, largely to give each other adequate warning of any real or perceived threat. Once a threat was visually acquired, the formation took evasive action. Aircrew in the formation were also required to keep an eye out for evidence of possible enemy activity. According to Nellis, there were numerous giveaways:

> Small things, like the presence of cattle in *kraals* during the middle of the day, told us that there were insurgents in the area. The local population would keep the cattle in the *kraals* so that they could watch over them to prevent the guerrillas from slaughtering them for food. Another indication was the behaviour of local inhabitants when helicopters passed over their *kraals*. Normally, they would just look away when we approached, or completely ignore our presence, even if we flew right over their huts. However, if they tried to hide or run away or perhaps behaved aggressively, maybe by throwing stones at passing aircraft or gesturing with their fists, it was more than likely that there were insurgents about.

Other indications included camouflage clothing near waterholes, women preparing food in the middle of the day, which was unusual because the local population in southern Angola and South-West Africa normally ate only in the early morning and in the evening. The preparation of additional food at midday indicated an alien presence.

Disturbed ground some distance from a village, possibly close to a prominent tree or an anthill—some were metres high—might have told an astute observer that there was an arms cache nearby. All this would be reported to intelligence officers at the post-flight debrief after the choppers returned to base.

CHAPTER FOUR

SOVIET SAMS VERSUS HELICOPTERS IN THE BUSH WAR

The message landed on Neall Ellis' desk at the Ondangua Air Force Base on 8 May 1982. It was succinct: 'your mission: to provide top cover to the Pumas during the recce drop at last light on the 9th and then to be on standby for close air support for the duration of the operation.'

At a subsequent briefing, the intelligence officer told the crews attending that a 'source' had reported an unconfirmed SWAPO presence in the Cambino area, approximately ten kilometres north of Iona, a small, obscure village in a barren wasteland. The area was a remote and desolate semi-desert about 30km north-east of the Marienfluss Valley in north-west Kaokoveld. This barely populated area was extremely difficult to get to overland because there were no proper roads.

Initially, it was explained, the plan was for a reconnaissance patrol to be dropped by chopper into the vicinity to determine whether there was a SWAPO insurgent presence or not. Nellis had been sceptical from the start. He argued that the area was simply too remote and there was no 'local pops' (local population).

> While the ops officer was giving his briefing, I began speculating how big a 'lemon' we were going to have. A 'lemon', roughly de-

fined, is a mission where no contact is made with the enemy, which means no kills. However, as I was aware, not all 'lemons' were unpleasant: the Atlantic Ocean was less than 20 minutes' flying time to the west and I'd never fished off that coast before. The mouth of the Kunene River was supposed to be one of the best locations for some of the big deepwater 'uns' on the west coast. While trying to work out where I could borrow a fishing rod, the ops officer broke my reverie by asking me if I had any questions. We both knew that he had caught me off guard.

After sorting out a few domestic arrangements, my highly experienced wingman, Captain Angelo Maranta, and I were satisfied. We knew what was expected of us and left the briefing room to prepare for a late-morning take-off for the 'Fluss' the following day.

Interestingly, I had been in the Marienfluss a few years earlier and had found it to be one of the most beautiful places I had ever seen. When I visited it again in 1975 it was one vast valley, approximately 120km in length and perhaps 15 clicks wide. The memory that remained with me for many years was suddenly coming upon that expanse of beautiful waist-high, golden grassland with wildlife grazing everywhere. There were gemsbok (oryx), wildebeest, eland, and even elephant, all seemingly unaffected by civilization. However, this time, I was in for a shock. Long before we'd landed I could see that the valley had transmogrified into a barren stretch of desert. There was no grass and no animals of any description.

Our tactical headquarters, or TAC HQ as we would call it, was situated alongside the runway, shielded on both sides by two rows of rusty old 44-gallon drums half buried in the sand. A lifeless windsock flew alongside and by that, surrounded by a ring of whitewashed stones, stood three nondescript army issue tents. This was to be our home for the next couple of days. The trouble was, there wasn't a tree in sight, which meant that there was be no shade to give relief from the stifling desert heat of late summer.

Our commander was an army man, Captain Vissie Verster, and the reconnaissance patrol leader introduced himself as

Sergeant Jose Dennison. He had ten men under him, he said, all of them seasoned fighters. Captain Jan Hougaard headed the modest, 32-strong 32 Battalion attack group. At that stage, the air force helicopter complement consisted of a pair each of Alouettes and Puma transport helicopters. Also mustered was a Bosbok single-engine light aircraft, which would act as 'Telstar' for relaying communications back to HQ while everybody was working in 'Injun Country'. Its role would become crucial once our flight paths took us across the Angolan border.

The morning of the 9th was spent going over planning details with the patrol. Aspects such as radio frequencies were dealt with, including alternative frequencies in the event of jamming by the enemy, battle frequencies, etc. Final briefings were held on escape and evasion for aircrew in the event of any of us being shot down; rendezvous points if crew became separated; and what recognition aids were being carried by the troops and aircrew.

The drop was timed for just before last light, at a point north-west of the suspect area. There, inside Angola, aerial photos showed that a road had been built that followed a river pass through the mountains. Once the patrol had been dropped, they were to mine the road at the entrance to the pass, the idea being that should our chopper drop have been picked up by the enemy, any hostile force entering the pass would detonate the mine and the patrol would be warned.

The drop inserting Dennison and his men was carried out without incident and all aircraft returned to base to wait for the patrol's report. Not long afterwards, shortly after nine, when we'd all settled down around the fire for the evening's usual session of war stories under the stars, we heard a muffled explosion to the north. Somebody had detonated a mine.

'Contact!' shouted one of the officers and there was a crazy rush to the ops tent to find out if Dennison was OK and if he could tell us what was going on. He reported back almost imme-diately: a large Mercedes truck had passed him heading in towards the pass, from which he had just emerged and it appeared to have detonated one of the landmines. At the same time, it became clear that the entire operation had had its priorities enhanced. Early intelligence reports had indicated enemy activity in the area, but there was little substantive proof, which is why it came as such a surprise when a large SWAPO force was suddenly encountered in an area that had been largely passive before. There was obviously some strength to the original intelligence report that there was a suspected SWAPO camp in the Cambino area.

Excitement rippled through our camp and while we were left, beers in hand, speculating about what was going on, the captain spoke to his boss back in Oshakati on the radio. There was an uneasy sense of foreboding about what the morrow would hold for us.

We spent the next day on standby, speculating about whether the team still in the field—and on the wrong side of the border—would run into any enemy patrols sent out to investigate the mine incident. There was nothing to report from the recce team that evening and our enthusiasm started to dampen. A heavy rainstorm followed and went on for much of the night: it was quite an experience hearing the mighty Kunene River—barely two kilometres away—roaring in flood through the mountains.

The following morning saw an early start. Major Paula Kruger, the Puma chief, suggested that we plan a recce along the length of the Kunene River in the area and search for possible insurgent crossing points. Half seriously, he said that the food in the camp lacked the kind of vitamins that could only be found in ocean fish and black mussels. For that reason, he said, the recce would have to go all the way to the sea at the mouth of the river. His choice of 'vehicle' was one of the Pumas and he said he'd also use the opportunity to show some of the cooks and bottle washers what the area looked like from a helicopter.

We took off in good spirits, looking forward to a cool ocean breeze along the beach. However, about 10 minutes into the flight, Kruger passed a headset back towards me and indicated that he wanted to talk. Things had suddenly become serious, he declared. Dennison and his men had a SWAPO patrol of platoon strength in sight and, by all accounts, contact was imminent. It seemed that things were finally happening.

Our immediate problem was to get to Dennison and his patrol before the enemy found them. If that was not possible, their presence could not only be seriously compromised, but they would be heavily outnumbered. If we got to them too late we could end up having to evacuate the entire recce team—or at least those that had survived—to the Sector 10 hospital.

Back at the TAC HQ, we found Verster perplexed. Dennison had just come through by radio and said that they were being attacked. Apparently, the enemy had picked up their tracks and chased them down: there was simply no avoiding a contact.

After a quick briefing about the possible deployment of troops, we took off, the Pumas coming along behind with our 32 Battalion reaction force troops, all 16 of them. Because the Alouettes were much slower than the Pumas, we timed it so that we'd arrive at the destination before the larger helicopters so that we could reconnoitre the area. The sudden arrival of Pumas, we felt, could only compromise the contact as the insurgents knew that troops were likely to be deployed if large choppers started orbiting their position. Also, our Pumas were only lightly armed and were vulnerable to small arms fire. Under the circumstances, it was wise to give the gunships time to check things out and perhaps fine-tune what was still a tentative battle plan, before the Pumas dropped their loads.

Just after take-off, a very unhappy Dennison came through again on the radio. The SWAPO patrol was approximately 18 strong and had begun to fire on his position with light mortars. He was taking evasive measures, he said, but didn't have time to elaborate. After roughly 20 minutes flying time, we arrived over the area and could see evidence of battle below us. The bush had started to burn and that served us well as a homing beacon to where the contact had taken place. The only comment heard from Jose Dennison as we arrived overhead was a sarcastic: 'If you'd have come yesterday, you might have been of some help.'

By then Dennison and his team had taken up a position on a small hill, about 100 metres high. Situated adjacent to a large rocky ridgeline, with steep cliffs overhanging the contact area, the top was flat and easily defensible. He didn't need to indicate any enemy positions: bush cover was sparse and the enemy could easily be spotted, sprawled out flat on their stomachs with their weapons extended in Dennison's direction. For a moment or two I thought they all looked like the little toy soldiers at play, inert and harmless. The insurgents were in a position half way up the hill, the nearest only 40 metres from Dennison's position. They had spread out and were steadily advancing towards the reconnaissance squad, using well-disciplined fire and movement tactics.

We had to decide quickly what we were going to. There was only one section of heliborne troops, so the Puma deployment would be restricted to a single sweep-line with no stopper groups. If SWAPO could be duped into thinking that our small company was a much larger force, our sweep-line might initially act as a stopper group. Once the main punch-up was over, the men on the ground could then go through the contact area and mop up any remaining resistance.

I instructed Sergeant Steve Coetzee, my flight engineer, to target the rear end of the attacking force with his heavy machine gun (HMG). That would create confusion because they would be caught in the crossfire between the gunships and our own forces. Once that became apparent, confusion in the SWAPO ranks was bound to follow and they would try to pull out. The enemy's retreat line could then quickly be ascertained and our troops pushed into position

Both gunships attacking the SWAPO group from the rear, along with the original recce team firing down from their hilltop position, had an immediate effect. The insurgents broke in the direction of open ground, which offered far less cover than before, trapping their entire squad in the open ground. Within a minute they had started to panic and their actions became desperate and totally uncoordinated. Shortly afterwards, the Pumas dropped their troops who were deployed in the direction of the breakout. Meanwhile, Coetzee and Angelo Maranta's gunner were picking off targets at will.

Soviet military hardware, such as this anti-aircraft gun taken inside Angola, were captured in quantity from the enemy. *Photo: Pierre Victor*

It says much for our training, and the ability to be able to think on the hop, that it was over within only a few minutes. Following our hastily devised plan, the attack went splendidly and the men were chuffed. Had we not arrived when we did, it might have been another story. Those guerrillas not killed in the initial onslaught ended up running headlong into the stopper groups. All that remained was for the ground troops to sweep through the area and capture surviving SWAPO cadres; there were only a handful.

By then, both Alouettes were low on fuel. The Puma charged with bringing in the fuel drums had not yet returned, so we had to land and continue managing the sweep-line from the top of the high point that overlooked the contact area where Dennison had initially sought cover. There was no question that the sudden appearance of our gunships had astonished the group and knocked the fight out of them.

We had no casualties on our side, and the final score was 14 SWAPO dead and seven captured. More importantly, the fight had been so fast and furious that the enemy weren't able to alert their own headquarters of the presence of our helicopters in the area. According to the prisoners, there were between 250 and 300 more of their comrades in a camp further into Angola. They confirmed, too, that the unit was equipped with shoulder-launched, anti-aircraft missiles, presumably SAM-7s, but they were unsure about anti-aircraft guns. They also confirmed that their forces were well armed, with the usual Soviet squad weapons including AK-47s and light machine guns which included PKMs, RPDs and RPKs. There were also several RPG-7s. Meanwhile, some of our men returned to the TAC HQ with captured anti-vehicle mines and rifle grenades.

Once we were able to gauge roughly how big the target was, action was quickly taken to fly in extra helicopters and troops along with additional fuel and ammunition. Our main concern was that if the camp were not attacked within the next 24 hours, the remainder of the group would disappear into the bush as they would have become aware, due to the lack of communication, that one of their squads was missing.

Most of that night was spent listening to the interrogation of the prisoners while the senior men threw about ideas for bringing in extra aircraft and men. One of the problems we faced was that we'd never initially planned for anything nearly this big and headquarters back at Oshakati was faced with a critical shortage of fuel and ammunition. To truck it all in from Windhoek might have taken anything up to a week, which meant that a fuel drop by air was requested. This was subsequently carried out by C-130 and C-160 transport aircraft and completed by lunchtime the next day: not a bad feat when one considers that the fuel had to be decanted into drums and flown up from Pretoria, 2,000km away.

Ammunition and the rest of Hougaard's 32 Battalion company were flown in by DC-3s and Pumas from Ondangua and Ruacana, while two more Alouette gunships from Ruacana, headed by Major Charlie Bent and Lieutenant Andre Schoeman, were also attached to the group. By midday, all required forces had gathered.

By now, headquarters elements from Oshakati had become more involved. The general commanding Sector 10, the overall command centre for the entire northern region, decided that we'd have to go in at 16h00 that same afternoon. I countered this, saying that experience had already proved that a camp that large needed an entire day to clear. Moreover, rushed actions usually result in higher casualties. However, nothing would convince the commanding general to delay so we were tasked to take off at 15h40 for a 16h00 strike. Then fate played its hand. We took off after the final briefing, only to have to abort because of a tropical rainstorm that almost turned day into night in the immediate vicinity of the enemy camp. I was mightily pleased as I'd been looking for an excuse to cancel.

In any event, the planning was not at all to my satisfaction. I was almost certain that with only limited intelligence available, the exact location of the camp had not yet been determined. Shortly after we returned to camp, a senior intelligence officer arrived with fresh information that suggested a clearer picture of where the SWAPO camp lay. He had built a sand model of the area and was able to pin-point everything as detailed by the prisoners. That was fortunate indeed as, had the attack taken place as originally planned, we would have put our troops on the ground almost 20 miles from where they should have been.

I awoke at first light feeling quite light-headed. The big day had arrived and finally we were going to go in. Intelligence had already established that the camp was the largest that the South Africans had gone up against for some time. It was also my biggest to date and I was concerned that we were not strong, either on the ground or in the air. Our total forces comprised 45 soldiers from 32 Battalion, led by Captain Jan Hougaard. For backup he had an 81mm mortar group, four Alouette III helicopters and five Puma medium transport helicopters for troop deployment.

Because of the meagre resources available, the plan had to be both simple and thorough: any delay in bringing in troops or lack of fuel at the mini-Helicopter Administrative Group (HAG) would cause us to lose kills. The basic plan was simple. We would initiate the strike at 08h00 that morning. SWAPO units were usually on parade at that time each day, which was also when orders were issued. This suited us because the sun would be high enough to lighten the shadows and to allow us to spot any enemy hiding underneath the bush cover. Maranta and I were to search for the camp and, once identified, we were to order the deployment of both sweep-line and stopper groups. Four Pumas were tasked to transport these men, and another would be detached from the main group to deliver the mortar group to a more distant position overlooking the camp.

Once our forces were in place, the two remaining Alouettes would provide top cover to two small groups deployed towards the far north of the camp and monitor any forces trying to reinforce the enemy. We were also there to prevent any SWAPO forces from escaping while the battle raged.

A mini-HAG was to be established about 12km from the camp, from where the helicopters would refuel and rearm. If a Puma could not get into an LZ in the contact area for a medevac, the casualties would be transported back to that temporary base by one of the gunships. A Puma would then be able to land, uplift the wounded and take them back to the tactical HQ for further treatment. The critically injured would be flown directly to the military hospital at Oshakati.

After a quick breakfast of dog biscuits and plastic coffee, we went over the plan once again. We needed to ensure that the intelligence scenario had not changed overnight, and that everyone understood the communications plan. Someone finished off the briefing with a prayer and we ambled out to the aircraft at about 07h20.

For me, personally, those few moments before take-off are sacrosanct. I actually prefer to be alone and would wander off a short distance to collect my thoughts. It is also a little time for reflection about what all this is about, a time for prayer. Like it or not, I routinely have to deal with what I term the pre-battle butterflies, which I have always felt is necessary in order to create a balance between the feeling of fear and the high that is likely to follow after it is all over and you find yourself not only intact, but alive. Moments later everything is channelled to the task on hand, which usually starts with a final gesture towards the gunner, already strapped in behind his weapon.

The take-off was uneventful and no snags were reported. Captain Maranta and I flew our machines at tree-top height to the target area; visibility was excellent and there were no clouds above us. Once across the Kunene River, it was my job to get down to the serious business of navigation. Generally, the trick is to keep the chopper as low as possible, so that the noise of the rotors doesn't carry too far and give the enemy warning of our approach. However, navigating in rocky or mountainous areas when flying ultra-low can be problematic because of the limited horizon and the many ridges and gullies that can easily cause confusion. Our Alouettes had no navigational aids like those fitted to modern-day helicopters, with the result that I used only my line-of-sight, or what we liked to refer to as 'Eye-Ball Mark 1'. At such times, if the pilot was not up to the situation, it was easy to become disorientated.

At the Two Minute Mark, I called for the climb and confirmed that the Pumas were in the holding area. In theory, according to our earlier planning sessions, that climb should have taken us over a lengthy ridge that overlooked the camp area. For a moment or two I prayed for complete surprise and, like Angelo who was on my wing, was a little disappointed when no enemy base appeared ahead. We were aware that the target area was in a kind of bowl, surrounded by high mountains. Indeed, before us was a large hollow depression in the undulating desert country, completely surrounded by high ground.

There was no option but to continue searching. We set a course close to the nearest flank of a large mountain, hoping that our engine noise, dissipated by all the valleys and canyons in the vicinity, would confuse the enemy. Certainly, they couldn't yet be sure from which direction we were approaching and the muted camouflage paint on our choppers went some way towards preventing visual detection.

At that point I was still apprehensive about anti-aircraft fire, as that capability had not been determined, and I had visions of grinning black faces sitting behind double-barrelled anti-aircraft guns, their sights lined up on my chopper with itchy fingers just waiting for the order to fire.

The trouble just then was that I'd expected to see the camp almost as soon as we got over the crest, but there was still no sign of it. Surely, I told myself, an enemy base that size couldn't be missed. We knew it was expansive—with something like 300 men, it had to be. There would be sleeping quarters, lecture rooms, offices, latrines and the rest. We should have picked it up by now. Still, all we saw was flat scrub.

We went into another orbit over the area, convinced now that even if the camp were deserted, we'd still pick up path patterns and possibly the parade ground. It had to be there somewhere, I knew. Every so often I would check the altimeter as I was subconsciously gaining height which I had to stop doing. All I could see now were large numbers of dew-soaked rocks, dark brown in colour. I sent Angelo Maranta towards the north of the area to have a look. Just then, Coetzee shouted over the intercom that he could see tents below us. I looked down and saw nothing. However, he was adamant. He had tents visual, he shouted into the intercom, describing them as 'squarish and dark brown'.

At that moment another kind of picture unfolded before me. Dark brown rocks became bivouacs and, moments later, a path pattern emerged, almost like a spider's web. Then I spotted uniforms that had been hung out to dry, camp debris and much else that had been concealed. A second later, both Coetzee and I hit the ultimate jackpot: under every bush lay inert soldiers, four or five of them gathered together in some areas where there was more cover. One of the bushes resembled a star fish, legs protruding everywhere.

The enemy had obviously heard us arrive. Almost as if they had been trained to do so, everybody scurried for cover under the nearest bush. However, they couldn't hide their legs, which protruded in every direction. It was a remarkable revelation: I'd never seen so many enemy troops on the ground before; they were all over the place.

Assessing the situation a little closer—at the same time, telling command by radio what we'd found—I could see that the camp was structured around a derelict *kraal*. It must have covered an area of roughly a dozen football pitches and the choice of location was excellent. Everything had been cleverly positioned in a rocky area that offered both natural cover as well as camouflage, much of it small trees and scrub. Ground cover was sparse though, and from the air we could quite easily observe the entire panoply.

By now our excitement had peaked. I was aware that we faced a chance of a lifetime, but our options were curtailed: two tiny gunships ranged against a significant enemy force with who-knew-what firepower. We were on our own until the rest of the group got there and I had to play my game carefully. My first task was to get our troops on the ground. Once the insurgents started to break out, their movements might become a flood, so I had to keep them guessing whether or not they'd been spotted by us. I instructed Maranta to widen his orbit, climb a bit higher and act as nonchalant as possible.

Meanwhile, while we waited for the Pumas to come in, I worked on another idea and decided that we'd change tactics slightly and drop our sweep-line to the immediate west of the camp. The stopper groups could then come in along the river line towards the south-west. There was a rather strategically placed conical hill quite close to the camp, which I thought would be ideal for the mortar team because it overlooked the base. Also, from up high the crew would be able to observe where their bombs were falling and make corrections without us having to give them guidance.

I started another circuit around the base, in part because the enemy had still not made an effort to reveal their positions. From the little I could see, they appeared fairly confident that we hadn't seen anything, which was when some of them started to slowly crawl towards the perimeter. They had made their first move.

Flying in lazy circles above the camp and trying to act as though we were unaware of their presence was disconcerting. I was far too high and very much aware that if they did decide to use their SAMs, it could cause problems for both choppers. Then I spotted the Pumas, approaching fast from the west. Judging from the reaction below, the enemy must have heard the distinctive thumping rotors of these larger machines because some of their troops got up from where they had been lying, which was when I decided to open fire. We needed to slow down their movement; experience had shown that once one person moves in a set direction, the rest usually follow and it would have been difficult to contain large numbers.

The first rounds from our choppers stopped any stampede by the enemy forces encamped below. It also resulted in those already on their feet diving for cover. Then all hell broke loose. I heard a powerful blast towards my rear which rocked the chopper. My stomach muscles tightened when I realised they were using some heavy stuff against us. At the same moment Maranta shouted over the radio: 'SAM launch, six o'clock!'

Out the corner of my eye I saw the distinctive thick whitish-grey smoke trail of a SAM-7 twirling up into the sky towards me. I immediately put on more bank to find the firing position, but as I turned through the half-circle, the missile speeding past harmlessly, I saw a second SAM-7 launch, this time directed at Maranta's machine. It was my turn to shout: 'SAM launch, nine o'clock!'

Fortunately, we were quite low, which meant that by the time I'd called, the missile was already travelling at Mach 1.5; it shot by just in front of his nose. We were now also coming under some fairly heavy weapons fire. The noise was horrific and the curtain of tracer rounds around both choppers seemed almost impenetrable.

The position from which the enemy was firing the SAMs was easy to find. There was no wind so smoke from the launch area rose lazily into the sky, highlighting the command position below. As I arrived over the launch area I saw the missile operators trying to take cover beneath the bushes: Coetzee quickly killed them all with a few well-aimed rounds.

By now our two helicopters were at the receiving end of a huge volume of firepower and RPGs were starting to make life uncomfortable. There were dozens of them, the majority air-bursting over our heads. While I consider them to be fairly ineffective against aircraft, their blasts can be awesome, especially if they explode close by: there is usually an extremely loud bang accompanied by a large puff of black smoke.

Suddenly, another missile—a Strela-2—shot past the nose of my aircraft and, again, after the firing position had been identified, Coetzee did what he had to. Moments later, the Pumas were approaching the newly designated LZ and I moved over to the position to mark it with smoke and to give the troopers a measure of top cover. The LZ was just under two kilometres from the camp and, with the breakout, I'd observed some of the enemy running in that direction. I radioed Kruger in the lead Puma and he passed it on to the others, including the officers who were about to disembark. The sweep-line, led by Jan Hougaard, was already moving forward and things seemed to be developing nicely. The next task was for the remaining Puma to drop off the mortar group and this was done without problems. Having completed their tasks, all five Pumas returned to the 'Fluss' to uplift stopper groups, fuel, ammunition and those personnel needed to form a mini-HAG in the area adjacent to the enemy camp.

Things were not going well for the guerrillas. By now the enemy had realised that they were contained, which was when they started directing heavy fire at me and Maranta, as well as mortar fire onto the troops in the sweep-line. It was quite a concerted effort and although we retaliated, there seemed to be no end to the amount of firepower they were able to bring to the party. Also, their mortar fire worried us. It wasn't very effective, but you didn't need a surfeit of brains to work out that some of their bombs were passing through our circling orbit: It wouldn't have been the first time that an aircraft had been brought down 'by accident'. Fortunately, Maranta found their position and was able to neutralise the emplacement.

Once the troops started moving through the fringes of the camp, they too came under concerted fire and their progress slowed. I radioed to the ground commander that we had the enemy boxed in and that there was no rush. Effectively, we had the rest of the day to achieve our objective and there was no need to take chances. The slower the pace, I said, the less chance of casualties.

At one stage, the fighting on the ground became so intense that Coetzee was killing isolated pockets of enemy within five or six metres of our own troops. The lethal radius of the 20mm cannon shell is five metres and our troops weren't stupid so they kept low each time the cannon barked. In fact, the positions were even more dangerous because some of the troops had to be treated for light shrapnel wounds, picked up from the gunships, after the engagement.

Another time, two of the enemy had climbed the only tree in the area to get a better line of sight on our advancing forces. Coetzee picked them up and killed both with a single salvo. As some of the guys commented afterwards, it was like a scene from the movies.

About 20 minutes after the sweep-line had been dropped, the Pumas were back with the stopper groups. Maranta was detailed to give top cover to the trooper with 'Blackie' as its call sign. As the Puma came into the hover and prepared to make the drop, a fairly large squad of about of 30 enemy soldiers seemed somehow to have managed to move forward to where they reckoned the LZ had to be. Maranta's gunner engaged the enemy and was soon involved in a fairly stiff firefight. After a few minutes, he managed to neutralise the position, but not before his chopper was damaged by small arms fire.

At that stage I was giving top cover to the Puma dropping off call sign 'Nella'. As it came into short finals for the LZ, I picked up another group of enemy troops running along the gully in which the Puma was going to land. The sides of this natural defile were rocky and steep and the enemy soldiers could not climb out of it, although they tried. For Coetzee it was like a turkey shoot. All he had to do was fire above their heads and the ricocheting shrapnel did the rest: the guerrillas dropped, one by one.

After the Puma had taken off, several enemy troops managed

to move forward to within about 50 metres of the LZ. Less than a minute after having put been down, Nella and his group found themselves in a serious firefight with a determined group of guerrillas. Worse, they were in an exposed position and there were a few anxious moments before we were able to neutralise the attackers. Once again, Coetzee's accurate firing saved the day.

By now, both Maranta and I were short on fuel. Also, we were out of ammunition. The two Alouettes, flown by Bent and Schoeman, positioned themselves overhead and took over the dual job of controlling the sweep-line and providing top cover. Jan Hougaard had his first casualty as we were pulling out. One of his sergeants was badly wounded so Maranta landed his Alouette and uplifted the soldier. The rescue took place under heavy fire, with Maranta's chopper landing only metres behind the sweep-line. After refuelling and rearming, both of us headed back to the battle to relieve the other two helicopters.

A lighter side to the battle—which had then been going on for about three hours—occurred when Hougaard's men had moved through the main camp area and were taking a breather. Their instructions were to consolidate and then sweep back through the area in a bid to gather weapons and documents and to clear up any pockets of enemy resistance that had escaped the initial advance. I landed at Hougaard's position to discuss the next move and also to answer a call of nature. While relieving myself next to a tree, there was a loud holler from one of our soldiers, followed by a sharp explosion in the branches above me. All this was accompanied by the whistle of shrapnel flying all over the place. I got such a fright as I dived for cover that I wet myself: there was a lot of banter afterwards about me pissing my pants.

What had happened was that a lone survivor had somehow remained undetected and decided to make a last ditch stand from a nearby hollow in the rocks. I reckon that he thought he would kill the group of people I was talking to before he died. Luckily, Maranta was orbiting the area and was quickly directed over the enemy's position, where his gunner killed the man.

Throughout the battle, we had Impala ground strike jets

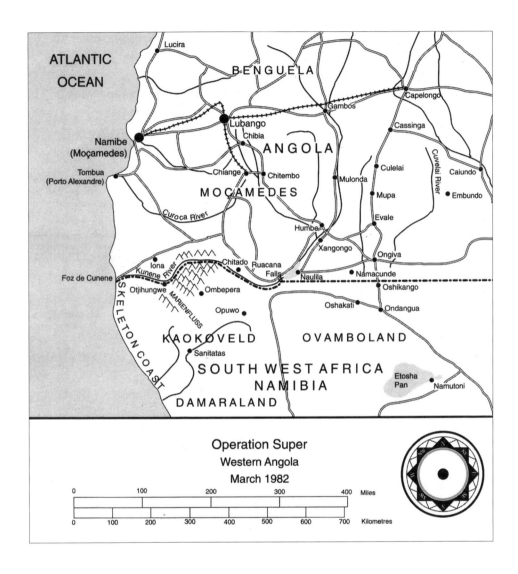

Operation Super
Western Angola
March 1982

orbiting the area for additional close air support. They came in handy when, towards the end of it all, our ground troops encountered a particularly aggressive group of insurgents who had managed to keep our forces at bay. I decided to call in a strike from the Impalas. After passing on the relevant target information and marking it with smoke, I eased away from the area to give the jets a clear run in. I waited and waited some more, but after some minutes there was still no sign of the jets. Still on the radio, I asked them where they were and when they'd be moving in for the strike.

The retort was abrupt: 'We've been orbiting the position you gave us, but can't find any evidence of the battle or see your smoke. Are you sure that you're in the right valley?'

Although most of the enemy force had been neutralised, there were still a few pockets of die-hards. Before we could call it a day and do a final body count, they had to be dealt with. It was then that Hougaard lost two more men, a black soldier and one of his platoon commanders, Lt Nel (Nella), who was posthumously awarded the Honoris Crux (Silver) decoration for bravery. Nella was always regarded as an outstanding soldier, his leadership exemplary. He'd accounted for numerous kills during the action, some of his contacts virtually at point-blank range.

Clearing up took us well into the afternoon and it was only at about four that afternoon—two hours before sunset—that we were satisfied that the guerrillas had either been neutralised or had escaped. The final body count was 187 dead and one captured. The prisoner was the camp cook who, we found out soon enough, was not too interested in making war. Total kills (including the results of the contact two days before) were 201 dead and seven captured.

Troops moving through the area in the days that followed discovered an enormous number of weapons concealed in the rocky slopes of the surrounding mountains. One arms cache alone had 1,000 anti-tank TM-57 mines and anti-personnel rifle grenades. There were also more than 300 mortar bombs in 82mm calibre, ten more SAMs and scores of AK-47s. Not a bad haul when one considers that the operation was supposed to be a 'jolly' and that I'd intended going fishing.

As a direct result of the attack, SWAPO's subsequently disclosed plans for establishing an infiltration route through the Kaokoveld to the west of Sector 10 in Ovamboland took a powerful knock, something from which they were not able to recover for several years.

CHAPTER FIVE

INTO ANGOLA WITH THE GUNSHIPS

Like all things associated with mice and men—conflict included—things don't always pan out as expected and escalating hostilities along the Angolan border were no different. Launching raids into remote and hostile regions, especially in Angola, presented the South Africans with some peculiar sets of imponderables.

Following the abrupt departure of the Portuguese from Angola in the mid-1970s and the entry of Moscow's surrogates, Cuba included, into the political and military void that Lisbon left behind, the South Africans decided that because Angola was on the verge of becoming a Soviet client-state, Moscow's progression needed to be checked.

It was an almost impossible task. Of the three former Portuguese colonies—Angola, Mozambique and Portuguese Guinea (today Guiné-Bissau)—Angola had, by far, the most strategic importance. It straddled a vital region in the South Atlantic and not long after it became independent and communist, it became a major Soviet naval and aviation staging base. It also emerged as one of Moscow's most important surrogates on the African continent. The country contains some of the largest natural resources on the African continent, the most important being oil. There are also diamonds, gold, manganese, iron ore, vast quantities of hardwoods, enormous offshore fishing resources and a host of other commodities. Almost overnight this all landed in Moscow's lap.

Naturally, the Americans were alarmed. With some justification, they feared the same kind of domino scenario that had affected Eastern Europe at the end of World War II. Angola's northern neighbour, Congo-Brazzaville, was lurching towards radical totalitarianism; Zaire had become ungovernable and was beset with secessionist issues and, further east, both Zambia and Tanzania were flirting with Moscow and Beijing. It was not surprising, therefore, that in the winter of 1975 Pretoria, at the behest of American secretary of state Henry Kissinger, launched Operation *Savannah*, the biggest invasion task force seen in Africa since the end of World War II[1]. It was a massive effort and involved several thousand troops, artillery, helicopters, jet fighters and bombers as well as squadrons of Eland armoured cars and a dozen C-130 transport planes. In the end, the South African Army was able to progress northwards, almost to the gates of Luanda.

However, as history has proved, it was too much, too far, too soon with too little preparation. Pretoria simply had no answer for the kind of hardware that Moscow pumped into Angola to stem this advance and it was done on a massive scale. They established the first air bridge across Africa since the Ogaden debacle, some years previously, when Moscow had created an air bridge to supply arms and ammunition to Ethiopia after Somalia had invaded the Addis Ababa's Ogaden Region, claiming it as part of 'Greater Somalia'.

The wherewithal that arrived by sea and air included long-range artillery, BM-21 rocket launchers, a range of heavy 12.7mm and 14.5mm machine guns (some of them two- or four-barrelled weapons) BRDM personnel carriers, T-54/55 tanks and a plethora of fighter jets and helicopters. The materiél passed on by the Soviets wasn't the most advanced in Moscow's armoury, but it was certainly ahead of anything possessed by Pretoria at the time.

Three additional factors militated powerfully against the South African war effort. The first was allies, or rather, an alarming lack of them: UNITA, it will be recalled, was still a fledgling guerrilla body. The second was Holden Roberto's *Frente Nacional de Libertação de Angola* or FNLA, chosen willy-nilly for South Africa by the Americans rather than by Pretoria itself.

Although it was the largest military group in Angola that was still outside the Soviet ambit, it carried no clout. Roberto's ill-trained, badly disciplined army was supposed to have the support of Washington and it got that, but in name only.

Finally, the biggest issue was the number of troops opposing South Africa. By the time Castro had consolidated his forces in this vast West African state, he had at least 50,000 troops on the ground—there are those who maintain that the real figure was closer to 80,000, but we'll never know the truth. More salient, this was no rag-tag bunch of barefoot illiterates. While not an accomplished military force by Western or South African standards, the Cubans at least knew how to handle the hardware passed on to them by the Russians, whereas the African components of the struggle did not. Many of the aviators who flew Soviet jets sent into Angola were Russian, East German or Cuban.

At the end of the day, there were simply not enough South African troops in Angola to stem this flood. After several months of campaigning and demonstrating the kind of initiative and military panache for which the 'Boers'—as Pretoria's detractors would refer to them—became known, they pulled back. They had made the point that it was possible to make gains against a vastly preponderant force, but at heavy cost. Once the South African forces were back behind their own lines, it was a time for the licking of wounds and a comprehensive assessment of the shortcomings of both the army and the air force, taking into account that black nationalist hostilities were creeping inexorably towards the south and the Rhodesians were battling to cope with their own insurrection.

Within months, Pretoria had embarked on the biggest arms modernisation programme yet seen on the continent of Africa. This culminated in the development, in some cases with Israeli expertise, of a range of sophisticated weapons including the introduction of the R4 infantry rifle (a clone of the Galil), an anti-mine troop carrier called the Buffel, a new generation of infantry fighting vehicles like the Ratel and the Casspir (which was actually a South African Police initiative) and the revamping of antiquated British Centurion tanks into sophisticated fighting machines (that included laser sighting devices—also Israeli) called Olifants. This revamped main battle tank eventually proved more than a match for Soviet T-54 and T-62 armour fielded by the Angolan Army.

Also developed were the 155mm G-5 and G-6 artillery series, still among the most advanced weapons of this type. With base-bleed ammunition the G-5 has a range of 42km and over several decades has been marketed in many countries, including Iraq under Saddam Hussein. Many of the mine-proofed vehicles like the Mamba—today deployed in the Middle East, Iraq, several Asian and South American countries and Afghanistan—were originally developed by South African weapons manufacturers.

Not all of it was for foot-sloggers though. Some of the more advanced long-term projects included RSA-2 and RSA-3 medium-range intercontinental ballistic missiles, as well as six atom bombs, ostensibly for arming those projectiles, and concurrently developed.[2] At that stage South Africa was the ninth nation in the world to successfully build nuclear weapons, and it did so without Israeli help and in half the time it took the Pakistanis to achieve the same results.

There were several test firings of RSA-3 missiles, although most of the details remain classified. What we do know is that missiles from the first two launches across the Indian Ocean, from the Overberg Test Base in the southern Cape near Bredasdorp, travelled almost 1,500km and achieved a Circular Error Probable (in relation to missile strike accuracy) of 275 metres when they splashed down in the sea adjacent to the Prince Edward Islands.

South Africa's arms development and procurement programmes were so successful that within two decades the nation had become the eighth biggest weapons exporting country in the world. Well into the New Millennium and decades after Border War hostilities had ended, it was still marketing a variety of arms abroad.[3]

This, then, was the environment into which Neall Ellis and his associates were thrust as the Border War escalated into what finally threatened to become a nuclear showdown between Pretoria and a radical Luanda regime backed by its Eastern Bloc allies. In effect, it was no longer a bush war. With the backing of Havana and Moscow, hostilities escalated to the point where some of the campaigns fringed on conventional warfare, even including tank battles. Warfare in Africa had suddenly become more intense and progressively more sophisticated.

Each year, for more than a dozen years, before the pre-Christmas summer rains set in, hostilities in the southern half of Angola would be moved up a notch or three. Luanda would muster its combined ground and air force assets to try to dislodge the UNITA rebel guerrilla leader Dr Jonas Savimbi from his isolated bush-based headquarters at Jamba in the extreme south-east of the country. Tens of thousands of Angolan soldiers, backed by squadrons of MiG and Sukhoi jets, as well as Mi-24 gunships, would stream out of all major Angolan cities and head south. They would take with them as much heavy artillery as the dismal Angolan road system would allow and, more often than not, scores of sophisticated Soviet SAM systems which were effective enough to stop the South African Air Force from making significant gains.

On the ground, Pretoria would vigorously oppose these efforts and every year the Luanda government and its allies would be beaten back. Year after year, almost like clockwork, FAPLA, the huge Angolan Army, would arrive en masse to occupy huge swathes of territory formerly held by UNITA, fight scores of battles and then, as their losses mounted, would be forced to abandon hundreds of millions of dollars' worth of sophisticated Soviet military equipment as they retreated.

More than once, the Angolans dropped everything (including their rifles and sometimes their uniforms) and ended up leaving behind extremely sensitive hardware. This included a few systems that the West had never before been able to examine, such as the Soviet P-15 'Flatface' early-warning radar and a complete SA-13 missile battery. Codenamed 'Gopher' in NATO parlance, it was the first to be seized by a pro-Western government. Most was passed on to the Americans for 'evaluation'.

By the middle of 1983 Neall Ellis again found himself on the Angolan Border. The war had escalated into the most difficult phase yet as the Soviets had introduced more advanced military aircraft such as the MiG-23.

A UN-imposed arms embargo prevented the South Africans from countering these advances, and they were unable to upgrade their air force, principally because of the government's racially dictated apartheid policies. Apartheid had made the country into a pariah nation and the South Africans had to be circumspect about operating in Angolan air space. They consequently had no answer to Moscow's advanced front-envelope air-to-air missiles.

Already there had been several major cross-border strikes, including

Operation *Protea* (where $500 million worth of Soviet military equipment was captured), Operation *Daisy*, Operation *Askari* and, as we have already seen, Operation *Super*. Then, in July and August 1983, came Operation *Meebos*, which was launched during a period of intensive peace negotiations that ultimately came to nothing.[4]

South African military intelligence sources had indicated that the SWAPO central area headquarters was located in an area known as Evale. This information was fine-tuned and the command centre was eventually pinpointed in the hills just outside Mupa, a few hundred kilometres north of the South-West African border. In order to strike at this base, a South African TAC HQ was established in Ongiva, the biggest town in the region.

While the Portuguese were still around, Ongiva had been a major administrative centre, with moderate-sized office building, banks and shopping centres. The ensuing war had laid waste to it all.

Just then, as Nellis recalls, he was concerned about a new trend that seemed to be developing within the army. This involved the transfer of senior officers, with limited operational experience, from comfortable desk jobs back home to the war front on three-month tours to take command of external operations. As he says, it was an absurd move, like appointing a pilot with only small plane experience to take command of a modern passenger jet. It was also irrational, because the people making these decisions in faraway Pretoria were playing with the lives of many young South African soldiers who were doing their compulsory two-year draft, commonly known as National Service. Nellis comments:

> What worried those of us with good combat experience was that these people tended to be rather conventional in their planning. They had no real understanding of the vagaries of modern warfare and their decisions were predictable, both to us and to the enemy.'

The overall commander of the TAC HQ for Operation *Meebos* was Colonel Pieterse, an officer who had worked his way up through the ranks in anti-aircraft operations. The troops allocated for the operation were two 32 Battalion companies, under the command of Captains Eric Rabie and Tinus van Rensburg, and a company from No. 1 Parachute Battalion, commanded by an old hand in both conventional fighting and counter-insurgency operations, Major Jab Swart.

To ensure that the Luanda government would not intervene after we crossed the border—it was known that there were Angolan FAPLA elements nearby—a Combat Group of 61 Mechanised Brigade, under the command of Commandant Roeland de Vries, was put on standby. Air support took the form of seven Alouettes: six gunships armed with 20mm cannon and a single command-and-control trooper.

For airborne troop transport, there were nine Pumas and a clutch of French-built C-160 and American-supplied C-130 transport aircraft. These could be tasked for airdrops, while the older Dakotas were used solely for resupply. To give the onslaught a bit of muscle, should that be deemed necessary, two squadrons equipped with Mirage fighter aircraft arrived at the Ondangua air base and stayed there for the duration of the campaign.

Operation *Meebos'* first attacks were launched in the last week of July, 1983 and continued sporadically for a week. The object was to hunt for isolated groups of SWAPO insurgents and uncover arms caches. A number of minor contacts occurred with the enemy, but their elusive headquarters was never found. Several times 32 Battalion reconnaissance teams would discover enemy camps but, once the main body of South African troops arrived, they would either find a hastily deserted base area, or hear the last of the guerrillas leaving the camp by truck.

Captain Harry Anderson and Major Pete Harvey, both flying gunships, made contact with a small element of SWAPO's eastern area headquarters and, after a short sharp action, 15 insurgents were killed and two captured, with the majority of fatalities being caused by gunships. The captives said afterwards that they were the last elements in the camp, with orders to clean up and destroy anything that might give the South Africans a lead to their new position.

The period was fraught with numerous frustrations, both for the chopper crews and the men on the ground. The intelligence picture was confused and there was a clear lack of experience with both army and air force staff officers at the TAC HQ. Matters were not helped by the air force restricting the use of helicopters in combat.

As Nellis wryly commented afterwards, orders came through that prior to any attack, each target had to be clandestinely surveyed by furtive squads on the ground for AAA potential. All reconnaissance work was carried out at night and the order proved impossible to implement. It was a rather stupid tactic for a fundamental reason: the moment enemy troops found evidence of reconnaissance teams during their early morning security patrols, the camp would be vacated within an hour. As a result, numerous opportunities were lost because senior commanders would not allow the men on the ground to make the kind of decisions that had always produced good results in the past. Under the new system, attacks came too late to be of any use.

To aggravate issues, the TAC HQ was situated too far from the area of operations. Flying time by gunship from Ongiva to the nearest troops was almost an hour and necessitated a refuelling stop at a mini-HAG before contact could be made. Nellis explains:

> If you allowed 15 minutes for a fuel stop, the soonest that any call sign would be likely to get effective fire support would be at least 75 minutes. As a rule of thumb, an insurgent on the run, very much aware that his life was at stake, could easily maintain a rate of 10 or 12kph because those buggers were both fit and strong. By the time helicopter support was overhead the original designated area, they would be miles away.

Finally, a day or two before the campaign was due to end, Captain Willem Rutter, the 32 Battalion reconnaissance commander located the missing SWAPO command post. He'd earlier been deployed in the forward area to establish whether a suspect camp was 'alive' or not and first reports were optimistic: enemy manpower was approximately 150 strong, with several anti-aircraft positions that included 23mm and 14.5mm AAAs. Also, the entire base was well dug in, with an elaborate system of trenches and underground bunkers, typical North Vietnamese style.

The basic plan was to drop a full company of airborne troops to the north of the camp from a C-160 Transall, and parachute hour was designated at 05h00 the following morning. While the Parabats moved into position, more soldiers from 32 Battalion would be taken in by Puma helicopters and dropped at first light on three of four sides of the enemy camp. Nellis' gunships would already be in place for close air support, but only after the AAA threat had been eliminated. Neall Ellis takes up the story:

I was wakened at 04h45 by a C-130 Hercules aircraft flying low overhead on its way to the drop zone. Unable to sleep, I went through to the operations room to monitor the position. Captain Rutter was on the radio requesting that the air drop be held off as his men were experiencing problems in marking the DZ. Apparently, while crossing a river—which was deeper than anticipated— the homing beacon for marking the target area had fallen into the water and had not been recovered. As fate would have it, time doesn't stand still and when TAC HQ realised what was going on, the transports were circling over the SWAPO camp in search of the DZ. It was already too late to order the plane to move to another position.

The result was that without the homing beacon, the aircraft were unable to find the DZ and the planes were told to return to Ondangua. This was a critical setback to the plan, with the attack obviously compromised. Shortly afterwards, Rutter confirmed a sudden intensity of activity within the camp: SWAPO was pulling out.

At that point, time became the most critical issue. The loss of the parachute battalion stopper group to the north of the camp meant that the escape route was open to the insurgents. Meanwhile, the Pumas had arrived at Ongiva and were tasked to return to Ondangua to uplift and ferry the original group of Parabats to the target. This meant that the whole operation would have to be further delayed by hours and would no longer be a first light attack as originally planned. It was mayhem.

The Alouette gunships, led by me in the command-and-control trooper, took off from Ongiva for the mini-HAG not long afterwards. We put down just before eight o'clock and headed for the command Ratel. The atmosphere was fairly relaxed because

nobody seemed to have a clue what was going on, so we decided
to brew some coffee.

We hadn't quite settled down, and were still swapping stories
with the 'Browns', when we heard a peculiar whistling noise followed immediately afterwards by a loud explosion about 800
metres west of us. It was now our turn for a little intense activity.
In their wisdom, some bright sparks in the army had established
their headquarters and our mini-HAG within comfortable range
of the Angolan Army D-70 artillery guns at Cuvelai. Our entire
camp was packed-up and deserted within ten minutes.

The new HAG was moved a few kilometres to the east, towards the edge of the Cuvelai River and it wasn't long before it
was operational again. Meanwhile, the Puma helicopters had
returned with their Parabat component and the deployment
started once more; we were going to hit the artillery base that had
lambasted us earlier.

Captain Harry Anderson and his wingman, Lieutenant Mike
Kohler, were tasked to give top cover to the Puma drops around
the enemy camp. During this deployment, Anderson detected a
Soviet-built Gaz truck secreted under some trees and moved his
gunship closer. As he did so, the driver decided to scurry off and
try to outrun the pursuing helicopter. His flight engineer, Jock van
der Westhuizen, killed both the driver and passenger with a single
salvo.

What could have been a significant setback to PLAN forces,
turned out to be a missed opportunity for the South African Army.
The destruction of a major insurgent command post would have
successfully put a stop to any joint SWAPO and FAPLA plans to
retake either Ongiva or the riverside city of Xangongo, both then
under South African control. For the loss of one 32 Battalion
soldier, from Lt van Staden's Company, SWAPO lost two vehicles
and five men. The rest of the SWAPO fighters disappeared into
the bush. At the end of it, South African forces pulled back behind
their own lines and started preparations for another cross-border
onslaught, of which there were scores during the course of the
conflict.

The Soviets issued the Angolans and the guerrillas with scores of SAM-7 (Strela) hand-held, supersonic anti-aircraft missiles. Also known as MANPADS, these weapons were extensively deployed against the SAAF, but they were never instrumental in bringing down a single helicopter, essentially because the South Africans tended to hug the ground when operating against what was accepted as a resilient and aggressive enemy. *Author's photo*

Thereafter, a lot of effort was spent preparing for an assault on SWAPO's 'A' Battalion, one of the most active enemy units in the region. Air reconnaissance had confirmed the site of their camp and the decision was made to carry out an attack without deploying the usual reconnaissance teams.

The base was situated on the edge of what locals called a *chana*, a huge open area that resembled a dry swamp, alongside the Jamba River which seemed ideal for a heliborne assault operation. It was estimated that there were about 200 enemy soldiers and, going by aerial photos, there was at least one clearly visible anti-aircraft position to the north of the camp. Intelligence specialists said the anti-aircraft gun was a Soviet ZSU-23 twin-barrelled, optically guided weapon, which concerned us. These guns had already been used to good effect in other wars, Beirut included, and a single hit could knock one of our Alouettes out of the sky.

From a close examination of the aerial photos of the camp, I felt that there was more than one gun and that they were not ZSUs. I suggested that they were actually single-barrelled ZPU-14.5s. However, either could be deadly against all types of aircraft, helicopters especially, and if they were not neutralised in the earlier stages of the battle, the weapons could prove to be decisive in the outcome of any battle that might develop. The secondary role of the guns would obviously be to fire on our advancing infantry, and experience had shown often enough that the effect could be deadly.

The region was sandy and few of the trees were mature enough to provide much protection, especially against our advancing ground forces coming across open areas to the north and east of the camp. The most obvious enemy escape routes were to the west and south of the camp.

The initial plan, drawn up by Pieterse and his staff, was to kick off with a bombing strike by Mirage F1s. Half the squadron would be tasked to attack the anti-aircraft sites, with the rest focussing their bombs on the camp area. There would also be two F1s on standby for close air support, should that be necessary. Immediately after the bombing run, the main assault group, consisting of Eric Rabie's company, would be choppered in by Pumas and move into a position on the far side of the open *chana*, directly opposite the camp. Additionally, stopper groups would be deployed to the west and south of the camp, also using the Pumas. Our gunships would play a critical role as stopper groups, at least until all anti-aircraft firepower had been neutralised. We would then move across the camp to give support to the men working the sweep-lines and stopper groups.

My initial gut reaction was to disagree with the overall concept of the plan. For a start, I reasoned, Rabie would have some serious problems on his hands if the Mirages didn't knock out all the anti-aircraft guns. If they failed, the guns would almost certainly be redirected either at us or at our ground forces. My view was that we should place the assault group to the west of the camp, where ground cover was thicker, so that advancing troops would not then be threatened by the anti-aircraft guns while moving ahead.

CHAPTER SIX

DEATH OF A GOOD MAN

The following day was perfect for making war. There were no clouds in the sky and no wind. This was a good omen as the strike aircraft should have no difficulty in finding the target, and without any other distractions, our Alouettes could maintain a perfect orbit. The bush fire hazard to those on the ground would also be reduced: Africa always burns furiously during and after a battle because of the tracers used in modern wars.

In the pre-strike briefing, we discovered an amendment to the original plan. A pair of Impala jets loaded with napalm would drop their ordinance approximately four kilometres to the west of the camp at the same time as the main bombing strike. The rationale was that the camp inhabitants would see and hear the napalm tanks explode and this, together with the subsequent firestorm, would send them all off in the opposite direction.

At first I thought this was a joke and I said so. Whoever had come up with the idea obviously knew very little about who we were up against. However, the napalm drop stood and, I felt, it reflected not only inexperience on the part of some of our commanders but a misunderstanding of the nature of the war. I pointed out that anybody on the ground in that kind of bush country would be able to see very little beyond a few hundred

metres. Also, all they would hear from the napalm drop would be
a faraway explosion which could just as easily be a landmine, yet
someone believed the enemy would observe the strikes from four
kilometres away!

The commander of Sector 10, Brigadier '*Witkop*' (white head)
Badenhorst ended up agreeing with me and said that he was going
in with us. He would fly in my command-and-control helicopter
because he felt he needed first-hand information about the battle.
He talked of 'future reference'. Commandant Pieterse would normally have accompanied me in the Alouette and monitor his
ground forces from there. He was obviously unhappy with the
decision, especially when I told him that the fuel on board would
allow for only one passenger. With his immediate commander on
the chopper, he would have been superfluous anyway.

At 10h30, we strolled out to the flight-line for our pre-flight
inspections. All six gunships and my command-and-control chopper fired up satisfactorily for the lift-off 20 minutes later. Flying
time to the target was 16 minutes: we were coordinated to arrive
five minutes after the bombing strike. Just before the jets went in,
I made contact with the crew of the Mirages and they said the
strike time would be delayed by three minutes. This suited me as
we would arrive over target while there was still a lot of confusion
in the enemy camp following the bombing raid.

Colonel Dick Lord was in the lead Mirage and on the radio I
heard him calling the roll-in—soon afterwards the first bombs
exploded. From where the brigadier and I were flying, it was an
awesome spectacle. Also, listening to the running commentary, I
gathered there had been no anti-aircraft fire. Moments later I heard
another voice over the radio shouting, 'Going underneath!' The
next moment an Impala fighter passed right below me, almost like
a flash, followed by the distinctive roar of a jet engine which rocked
our helicopter. It was close. I'd been hovering about 150ft above
the trees and there couldn't have been much room between me
and the Imps, then heading home after dropping their napalm
tanks.

Our contribution started in earnest as I approached the camp from the south-west. We were abeam of the target when the familiar typing pool noise began and tracers began to flash past our nose. As leader of the formation, and with Brigadier Badenhorst sitting next to me, I fought the temptation to remain and, instead, climbed in order to determine what types of weapons were being used against us. It was then I realised that 'incoming' was not just small arms fire but also coming from some big stuff—12.7mms and 14.5mms. I banked hard and searched desperately for the anti-aircraft site. Moments later I picked up one of the guns. It was quite easy to see as, out of a small cloud of dust kicked up by back-blast, there protruded a series of pink flames about two-metres long, the distinctive ZPU 14.5mm auto-cannon signature.

By this time our formation had split to fly to our pre-planned orbits, with Pete Welman and his wingman west of the target and Mike Hill and his wingman to the east. Anderson was supposed to cover the south, but I told him to stay with me as I didn't fancy attacking a 14.5mm gun-site with just my .303 machine gun. I also felt that with the huge volume of fire heading in our direction, it would be nice to even the odds a little. That was when I called Mission 262, our Mirage close air support pair, to do another strike on the gun position.

This time, the Mirages used their rockets against the enemy position and Anderson and I tightened our orbit to put us in a more favourable firing position. We were greeted by an amazing sight. As the jets moved away and we started moving towards the anti-aircraft position, the enemy gunners, almost like ants, swarmed out of their bunkers and again took up their positions on the guns. I understood perfectly what they were up to. The gunners would have seen the Mirages put their noses down, ready to attack with rockets, and ducked into nearby bunkers for cover. Once the rockets had detonated, they emerged from underground to man their guns again.

By then, we were one of a handful of targets over the camp and it seemed as if everybody on the ground was shooting at us: the volume of small arms fire, including dozens of RPGs, suddenly became very intense. For identification by our own forces, I had

the usual illuminated panel stuck on my tail boom and, because
of the volume of fire, I thought they might all be aiming at that.
However, Anderson came on just then and said that he was also
picking up a lot of flak.

Within moments, the battle had developed into a duel between helicopters and anti-aircraft guns, with the two Mirages
returning several times in strike after strike until all ammunition
was expended. The two jets actually broke all the rules in trying
to silence the guns. At one stage, in a bid to improve their accuracy,
their approach was so low that I was a little concerned they might
collide with us in our orbit. Fortunately, they managed to destroy
one of the larger gun installations before they were done

I was aware then that it would take another hour or more for
the Mirages to refuel, rearm and return, so it was now up to us to
knock out the two or three other installations. Also, until were we
successful, Rabie and his men on the ground could not be deployed effectively, which was essential for the operation to succeed.

Anderson and his wingman did a magnificent job. They hung
in above one of the gun positions and gave just about all they had
back to the enemy, killing many of them in the process. It was intimidating to watch it all take place from so close. Elongated
tongues of flame would reach into the air when the enemy fired at
us and dozens of RPG-7s exploded all around. At that point I
became concerned that we might lose a chopper and crew, which
was when I ordered two of the other gunships to lend a hand.
Anderson came on the radio moments later: 'They're gapping it
now', he shouted. 'They're running, ah fuck . . . taking the gap!'
There was relief in his voice when he shouted that the enemy was
on the run. Anderson was decorated for bravery after the action.

As soon as all anti-aircraft guns had been silenced, I called in the
Pumas that were transporting Rabie's company, and they were
deployed. It wasn't all that simple. Rabie's right and centre flanks
ended up in some heavy firefights with enemy troops who had
taken shelter in surrounding bunkers with entrances that were
often concealed in the undergrowth. However, his unit did manage

to cross open ground with only one casualty; an African soldier who took a light gunshot wound.

The Pumas returned soon enough with their airborne detachments, which were deployed into pre-planned positions towards the west. Meanwhile, a number of the guerrillas had begun to break out in that direction, and for a while I was concerned for the safety of the Pumas as the enemy, still potent in their desperate flight, had progressed almost to within sight of the LZ. In fact, once Swart and his paratroopers had deployed and formed up in a sweep-line, they immediately made contact with escaping SWAPO, and still more battles developed.

Once the enemy realised there was a stopper group in position towards the west they decided to veer northwards instead. However, that took them across a *chana* and open ground. Welman and his wingman flew their gunships there and quickly dealt with them.

Conditions on the ground deteriorated swiftly. An easterly wind had sprung up and fanned a succession of bush fires ignited by our bombs and tracers. The result was that Rabie and his troops were threatened from two directions—he had a raging veld fire, with flames reaching up to 10 metres or more, at his rear and a substantial guerrilla force ahead. The enemy might have been on the run, but they attacked just about everything in their path, Rabie's men included

In a sense, it was a perfect situation to control as there was no need to urge the troops to advance. The encroaching fire took care of that option. SWAPO troops, in turn, were aware by now that they wouldn't be able to escape towards the west and had started to put up a fierce resistance. Because of this, Rabie's momentum had been halted and some of his troops were burnt by the encroaching flames. In fact, by the time the fire had passed through both Rabie's and SWAPO lines and moved towards where the Parabats were operating, quite a few troops had virtually no uniform left intact as they had literally been burnt off their bodies and some of the men were left with serious burns. One section of the sweep-line had to turn tail and make a run for it to escape the flames.

Conditions had also deteriorated for the helicopter gunships. Smoke had enveloped the entire area and was so dense in places that the choppers were flying in IFR conditions. There were several near misses. At the same time, it was almost impossible to spot enemy troops on the ground, with the result that close air support couldn't happen and any kind of effective control of our sweep-lines became almost hopeless. SWAPO made good use of this mayhem and brought our circling choppers under intense fire.

Once the inferno had passed, the battle started again. By now, the two sweep-lines were working in close proximity but, in turn, giving each other even more problems. The men pushing forward were partially disorientated by what was going on around them—they were coming under enemy fire and there were more brush fires—and there was also some confusion along the lines because they were stymied by poor visibility. In fact, things became so bad at one stage that one of the officers trying to control the situation on the ground believed that there was a real danger of friendly fire casualties, especially since the encroaching lines were only about 30 metres apart. The problem was further compounded by the bush which, even after the fire had burnt away most of the undergrowth, was too thick for either of the two units to actually see each other; erratic radio communications did not help.

At one stage 32 Battalion's sweep-line believed they were under fire, which they were, as most of the Parabat rounds were ricocheting right past them and forcing the men to go to ground. A hasty tirade from Rabie over the radio on the open net put an end to that bit of mischief. Once that phase of the battle was over, all that remained was to sweep through the enemy camp and collect weapons and ammunition, destroy food and water supplies and collect documents that might be useful to the intelligence boffins.

During the troop uplift that followed, the seven Pumas, led by Captain Cor Greef, landed on open ground near the camp, with Anderson overhead providing top cover. Just as the Pumas took off, Anderson happened to see a small bunch of enemy troops lying partially hidden beneath one of the trees, their AKs trained on the lead Puma only 50 metres away. He shot them before they were able to do any damage, but said afterwards that had they actually opened fire at such short range they would almost certainly have caused serious damage.

Overall, the attack was a success. Own forces casualties were one dead and two wounded, all from 32 Battalion. The official body count of the enemy was over 100, although the actual figure must have been higher because it didn't take into account the many SWAPO troops who were killed in the bunkers during the bombing strikes. Quite a few weapons were recovered, together with huge quantities of ammunition. Events that day proved that the relatively flimsy little Alouette was deceptively rugged and, indeed, able to take a remarkable amount of punishment. With correct tactics and pilot tenacity, we proved that we could neutralize an anti-aircraft gun emplacement without taking undue casualties.

Before the South Africans finally vacated the area, Captain Tinus van Staden, also of 32 Battalion, was deployed with his company to ambush the camp area during the night. It was expected that the enemy would return at some stage to look for survivors and whatever weapons remained. However, this time things went awry. The enemy must have been aware that the troops were there because they hit the area with 122mm missiles from their B-10s. Fortunately, the troops had dug in for the night and there were no casualties.

The final week of Operation *Meebos* showed no evidence of a SWAPO presence and the 32 reconnaissance group commanded by Captain Willem Ratte was dispatched to an area near the Angolan town of Cuvelai in a bid to locate SWAPO's B Battalion, also known as the Socialist Unit. This was a large and, by reputation, aggressive fighting element which included the enemy's central and eastern area headquarter units.

Intelligence following our early successful attacks indicated that several fighting groups had merged. If this was true, we had to acknowledge that we would be up against a formidable force.

Each SWAPO element would consist of about 150 men, giving the enemy a force of approximately 600 soldiers, all well-armed and adequately trained. From our perspective, it also meant that there would probably be half a dozen, or more, anti-aircraft batteries. By my count, that would have given them a minimum of a dozen 14.5mm guns, plus scores more in the 12.7mm range.

Ratte and his group were due for uplift at midday but the previous evening he'd reported that he was fairly certain of B Battalion's location. He'd reported by radio that he had seen a suspicious vehicle and wanted to follow it through to where he thought the enemy might have concentrated their assets. However, his request for a 24-hour extension to clandestinely survey the area was refused, as headquarters felt that the enemy had either left the area or split into smaller units. Instead, it was decided to deploy troops to carry out area operations.

Troop deployment was scheduled for early afternoon that day. All our pilots attended the briefing and Captain Ratte suggested that, because of the anti-aircraft potential, the Pumas should avoid the area where he suspected the enemy might be encamped. Two Alouettes were tasked to give the larger helicopters top cover during the drop. Flown by Captain Mike Hill and Lieutenant Chris Louw, they would go straight in, hoping to pick up evidence of an enemy presence. Altogether, there were eight Pumas tasked, split into two groups of four each, with an adequate time gap allowed between each formation.

Then it happened; a catastrophe that was not altogether unexpected. 'What surprised me,' said Nellis a long time afterwards, 'was that it took so long in coming.'

At approximately 14h25 on that day, while routing into the area, the Pumas, loaded with troops, unwittingly flew over the *chana* where the long-looked-for SWAPO concentration had deployed their anti-aircraft guns. At first glance, it would appear that all the weapons had been gathered into an open clearing, but were positioned too close to one another, which would inhibit the crews manning them from firing all of them at the same time. The leader of the flight was Captain A. J. Botha. Captain Ian

Solomon was at the controls of another of the Pumas and he described what took place:

> We were following the Alouettes to the landing zone and my machine was in number three position, just behind that of Captain John Twaddle. As far as we were concerned, the main action was over, so we'd assumed a loose 'V' formation. Some of the choppers were over the *chana*, but my course overlapped some bush at its southern verge. Twaddle's flight course was straight down the *chana* itself.
>
> We purposely kept our profile low, just above the trees. Suddenly, I was surprised by a long tongue of flame and curtains of tracer emanating from the bush towards our left: we were obviously under some pretty heavy anti-aircraft and small arms fire. Then, quite unexpectedly, because I'd never seen anything like it before, I saw John's aircraft pitch up. For a moment or two, it assumed a nose-high attitude and then its tail boom separated and somersaulted through the air. Almost simultaneously the Puma rolled onto its back and dived nose first into the ground, after which it exploded.
>
> I recall that we were doing something like 160 knots, so it all happened very quickly: that was one of the reasons why I wasn't able to see what weapons were being fired at us. One moment John was there, the next he was gone.

The shooting down of a Puma, together with everybody in it, was an enormous loss to the South African forces. All the aircrew, Captain John Twaddle, Lieutenant Andre Pietersen and Flight Engineer Sergeant 'Grobbies' Grobbelaar, together with 12 National Servicemen, all paratroopers, were killed.

Hill and Louw immediately turned their gunships around and flew towards the area in the hope of rescuing survivors. Lieutenant Louw described what happened:

> While heading back to the LZ, we heard Cor Greef shout over the radio that number five in the formation had gone down. Mike

[Hill] immediately ordered us to turn around and fly to the crash area. There was no missing the crash site: a thick column of black smoke spiralled up from the area.

At this stage, we weren't sure why the Puma had gone down, or even whether it had been targeted. There was some conjecture that there might have been mechanical failure, or possibly pilot's error. I say that because until then there had been no obvious SWAPO presence.

We were still about a kilometre from the crash when Sergeant Major Thomas, my flight engineer, shouted over the intercom that he had the enemy visual, and that surprised me. I immediately put the chopper into a hard bank to the left to bring his gun in line, which was when, directly below us, I saw a group of about 30 guerrillas running towards the downed helicopter. Thomas didn't wait for orders and immediately began shooting at them.

During the turn, our chopper took a number of hits, which is when you tend to look at your instruments to see that everything is still working properly. It wasn't: the rotor RPM was winding down and I knew that I had to take immediate action before an engine cut. I told the crew to prepare for an emergency landing and started talking the machine down to force-land in the open area alongside a *chana* directly ahead.

Thomas, apart from being our gunner, was also the flight engineer and he came through on the mike to say that the engine was working perfectly. I could hear that his voice was tense as he urged me to get the hell out of there. But I was already in the flare and only a few feet above the ground. After taking power, I flew the Alouette close to the ground for some distance and headed past the wreck.

Any kind of inspection just then, with all that incoming, had to be cursory, but everybody on board was certain that nobody could have survived. Worse, there was already a large group of about 100 insurgents, elated at their success, dancing around the wreck. They were jumping up and down with their rifles held high above their heads and whooping, primitive style. Those on board who were closest to this spectacle started shooting as we sped past but, fortunately, possibly because of their elation, their return fire wasn't accurate. We weren't hit again. We cleared the area and Hill escorted us to the mini-HAG, which was about a dozen kilometres away. After we landed we inspected our own damage.

I believe there were two aspects that saved the lives of Thomas and me that day. The first, was that the flight engineer urged me to continue flying when I wanted to land, and the second was that, because of my inexperience, I flew so very low past the wreckage. There were some big guns in the immediate vicinity of the crash site but the enemy wasn't able to depress their guns sufficiently to target us. All the AAA had been assembled on a slight ridge to our right, and as we flew past, you couldn't miss their efforts to try to lower their barrels. They probably did in the end but we were gone in a flash.

A more experienced pilot would probably have gained a bit of height, and probably presented a better target and so also have become a casualty. But it was not to be.

As soon as word got back to the temporary helicopter base, Major Kiewiet Marais scrambled all the remaining gunships. Mike Hill refuelled, topped up on ammunition and also returned to the scene with an absurd hope that somebody might have lived through an experience that was clearly terminal. Hill was later awarded an Honoris Crux for bravery, while Louw got the Southern Cross Medal for his efforts in nursing his helicopter back to base.

When Nellis arrived in the area, he could see the wreck, but he also couldn't get close. Enemy 14.5s were firing in all directions and it was difficult to pin-point their positions as there was still a lot of smoke from the brush fires around and a subsequent fuel explosion from the downed Puma had made visual identification almost impossible.

Well aware that we would retaliate, most of the SWAPO guerrillas had dispersed, which meant that the South African choppers were at the receiving end of small arms fire several kilometres from the crash site. The enemy also seemed to have a hefty supply of MANPADS, mainly SAM-7s. Three F1 Mirages from Ondangua, armed with rockets, were tasked to provide close air support but, because of the low visibility, accurate forward air control wasn't possible. Neall takes over the story.

Somebody had to call closure pretty soon, I felt, because if things went on like this, we'd probably lose another aircraft as enemy ground fire had picked up markedly. For their part, the guerrillas had tasted blood and they wanted more. That was when I decided that all aircraft should return to base. I'd decided that we'd go into an immediate planning session for what was still regarded as a rescue attempt.

Time was running out. It didn't take long for the commanders to decide that it wouldn't be possible to deploy troops before last light. Instead, it was decided to leave Willem Ratte and his recce teams to observe conditions along the Colonga River in the hopes of perhaps detecting a SWAPO withdrawal. It was a typical SWAPO tactic to leave the area as soon as they had been compromised and it was likely that if they were not already heading north, they would soon be doing so.

A hopeful sign was that a number of the aviators had reported seeing a large herd of cattle near the contact area. We were aware that the guerrillas often took small herds of livestock with them as a mobile food source. Find the cattle, it was argued, and you'd find the enemy. Observation post elements still out in the field were tasked with keeping a wary lookout for any animals on the hoof.

We rose early the next day to be on standby just in case the remnants of the guerrilla force were observed. Among the men, both air crew and ground forces, there was a powerful groundswell of anger at the loss of the aircraft and its occupants. Revenge was very definitely on the cards.

Normally, the camp would take time to get its act together at the start of the day, but that was definitely not the case that morning. The reaction force troops were ready and waiting at the LZ just before first light, even though the Pumas weren't due for hours. I was tasked with a pair of gunships as escorts for a 08h00 take-off to get Pieterse to the crash site. His job was to coordinate his troops as well as a 61 Mechanised Brigade armoured unit advancing from the south.

We were flying low as we headed out to the area, when suddenly I picked up one of the 32 Battalion call signs on the radio. It was call sign 'CL', who reported that he had visual on a large herd of cattle moving in a northerly direction towards the Colonga River. I radioed Pieterse and told him that I was heading there to investigate. Without waiting for an acknowledgement, I flew down the length of the river in a westerly direction. As we passed a riverside position about 30km north of Cuvelai, I spotted movement out of the corner of my eye. I had just turned my head when the distinctive smoke trail of a SAM-7 passed straight through the middle of our loose 'V' formation about 800ft above the ground.

I immediately turned back and headed towards the launch site: Smoke from the missile launch still hung thickly on the ground and thus the action had started. I was still some distance away when the first rattle from the 'typing pool' began its clatter, but this time it was accompanied by a veritable wall of tracer fire. More disturbing, there were also the long pink flames of 14.5mm anti-aircraft fire together with blasts from RPGs. It was an awesome experience, and quite unusual for some of the crews because another four SAM-7s were launched in our direction, which was unheard of. They all missed.

We went into an orbit around the position and could now clearly see the AAA installations. Even though the sun was still quite low on the horizon, the dark shadows under the trees only accentuated the muzzle flashes. I counted at least a dozen positions, which meant that at least four detachments were moving together, which was a sizeable force in any war. I passed on the message that we had found the main SWAPO group and that they were attempting to escape towards the north. I also reported that they were bunched together, but even then, the entire group was spread over an area of about two kilometres square. If that first anti-aircraft missile hadn't been launched, we'd have flown over the detachments and not been any the wiser.

The remaining gunships were scrambled and ordered to head towards us. I also requested additional support from the squadrons of strike aircraft on standby at the air base. Unfortunately, the Pumas transporting the Parabats still had not arrived and I knew we wouldn't be able to contain this large a gathering of enemy troops once the contact had been initiated. In fact, the troopers with the Parabat stopper groups arrived on the scene only two hours after battle had been joined.

For once, the jets did a good job. In fact, they excelled. Between the Mirages and the gunships, all the enemy's anti-aircraft guns were taken out in just a few initial attacks. It was impressive watching the Mirages go in and launch their rockets and then, after pulling out of their dives, we'd sometimes see two SAM-7s hurtling at their exhausts.

At one stage, there seemed to be so many RPG bursts within our orbits that it became a cause for concern. I told the others that one of the helicopters would be hit sooner or later. To complicate matters, the RPG self-destruct air bursts were at the same height as our orbits, and that was unusual. It took me a little time to work out that the air bursts were not from RPGs, but from the self-destruct mechanisms in the 30mm shells fired by the Mirage F1s on the lead-up to their attacks. We were sitting at about 1,200ft to make it more difficult for the enemy gunners, yet our people were lobbing 30mm shells in our direction.

Once all the anti-aircraft fire had been silenced, we moved towards the main body of the enemy and started selecting individual targets. Sometimes, this would be groups of insurgents who had gathered in strength and were covering all approaches. At other times it would be two or three enemy troops who, although fleeing the scene desperately, were still not afraid to mix it with their pursuers. There were scores of these elements and because the survivors were desperate, these contacts soon became the most vicious exchanges of fire of the campaign so far. While the guerrillas might have been hurt in our attacks, there was still an awful lot of small arms fire on all sides, along with volleys of RPG rockets directed at the choppers.

The aviators and their gunners settled down quickly, especially after it became clear that none of the aircraft were taking strikes.

The SWAPO commanders must have realised that we were determined to avenge our losses so they were quite literally fighting for
their lives, which made them particularly aggressive.

Once the Pumas got there with the first wave of troops, these men
were dropped towards the west which seemed to be the direction the
remaining SWAPO cadres had taken for their breakout. Lieutenant Harry
Ferreira of 32 Battalion was dropped along the river and Lieutenant Tinus
van Staden was deposited, with his unit, to the north-west of the area. It
was the job of Major Jab Swart and his Parabats to cover the north-east
and they did so with meticulous aggression, in a bid to settle scores.
However, brush fires in the tinder-dry grass started to present problems
again. Some of Ferreira's men were trapped by flames towards the west
along the river and several men with serious burns had to be taken out by
chopper. Because of the proximity of the river, these grasslands were lush
and fertile, but also dry because it hadn't rained in a while, and in places
the flames were more than 10 metres high. Visibility also dropped as a
result of the fires, which meant that the choppers were forced to come
down to almost ground level in search of targets. Many enemy soldiers
were killed after they had sought shelter under bushes.

A particularly disturbing order came from headquarters later that
morning. During the course of the battle, the herd of cattle was found to
have been corralled in a *chana* to the north-east of the contact area. There
must have been almost 600 of these animals. Since SWAPO placed great
store on their mobile meat supply and, because of the lack of food in these
southern areas, their loss would obviously be a great blow. The gunships
were instructed to kill the cattle, every single one of them!

Some of the pilots refused. As Nellis explained afterwards, he understood where they were coming from so after killing or maiming about 100
of these poor creatures he gave the order to stop firing. He remembers that
it was an appalling scene down below.

In some cases, our 20mm shells had blown off legs and the animals, covered in blood and bellowing in severe pain, were hobbling
around with their shattered legs dragging behind. I asked Swart to
send a few of his men in to despatch the maimed animals so they

spent the best part of an afternoon running after wounded animals and delivering the *coup de grace*. When we finally uplifted the troops and returned to the TAC HQ the men were generally elated at the overall success of the battle but the cattle incident dampened spirits.

The final body count for that day was 116 SWAPO dead and two captured. Of particular satisfaction was the fact that we were able to capture quite a few enemy heavy weapons and a huge amount of ammunition. Our forces suffered no casualties, not a single man wounded. I made the point in the subsequent debrief that had we been able to get our men on the ground sooner, the real tally would have been closer to 400 of the enemy killed.

There was an incredible amount of chopper activity as the war dragged on. In fact, because the SAAF Mirages and Buccaneers were no match for the modern Soviet fighter aircraft that had been phased into the conflict by the Soviets, it was left to the Pumas and Alouettes to do much of the donkey work, sometimes at night. Without these helicopters, this guerrilla struggle would have taken a very different turn. Nellis comments:

Operating out of Ongongo in Western Ovamboland, there would usually be a pair of gunships deployed to a forward base and on standby for a Koevoet[1] call-out. Sometimes there would be certain areas partitioned off as 'no-go areas', such as the training area during Operation *Silver*, a Chief of Staff Intelligence effort to develop and train Dr Jonas Savimbi's Special Forces. However, as in any struggle, nothing on the ground remained static for long.

At one stage, intelligence came through of suspected insurgent movement in an area where nothing was supposed to be happening. I was flying back to base and spotted a group of more than a dozen people, obviously troops because they were armed and walking military-style, in single file. I radioed back to base, but they knew nothing of any deployment of either UNITA or other friendly forces in that area, so I checked again with headquarters: still nothing. I had no option but to go in on the attack. The men on the ground started running for cover but it was too late. They ended up taking a lot of casualties. I killed eight and wounded six, all seriously. It turned out that they were all UNITA troops. It was a catastrophe and a terrible price to pay for some desk jockey's laxity back at base.

Another time, working in South Angola with my wingman Bakkies Smit and gunner/engineer Lange Pretorius, we were called out after 32 Battalion had been involved in a serious firefight in the vicinity of Xangongo, one of the biggest towns on the Kunene River and a provincial capital during Portuguese colonial times.

It was already late afternoon and we were told to provide close air support but, as usual, being 32, they didn't give us the whole story. Had they done so the air force almost certainly wouldn't have allowed us to participate in an action that was heavily weighted against us. Not long after we arrived over the grid reference, we suddenly found ourselves circling a large enemy camp and picking up intense ground fire that included RPGs, 12.7s, 14.5s and AKs all at the same time. It was withering, intimidating and more than a little frightening. Of course, we retaliated but our machines were taking quite a few hits.

I'd just entered our second orbit when there was an immense blast right alongside the helicopter. Bakkies came through on the radio and said we were on fire. Looking at our shadow on the ground, with the sun directly overhead in a brilliant clear sky, there was no mistaking the huge plume of smoke emerging from our Alouette.

In those days I used to fly with no socks. It was desert boots (*veldskoene* in South African parlance) only. We had all been taught during training that if there was a fire on board, it would come through the hold at the base of the bulkhead behind us. However, I couldn't help sensing an imaginary heat around my ankles and was suddenly quite alarmed: we had flames *below* us. It didn't make sense, but then few things do when that sort of thing happens. So I wasted little time in auto-rotating down, which was when I saw a veritable army of black enemy troops careering across the country-side in our direction. They thought they had shot us down and were heading our way to claim their prize.

It was a macabre situation and I, along with the rest of the crew, wanted out of there. Therefore, I wound up the chopper once more and limped cross country for another 10 or 12 clicks, engine revs oscillating furiously, which was when I had to go into full auto-rotation. Our rotor cable had been nicked somewhere along the way and it snapped. We were pretty low by then and went into a couple of revolutions before hitting the ground.

It was pure luck that one of my standard operating procedures was always to call for fuel as soon as I was heading out: I had done that earlier because I knew we wouldn't have had enough get us back home again, all the way from Xangongo. Consequently, there was a pair of Pumas nearby with our drums and they took us on board. I was fine, but Lange had a hurt back, nothing serious though. The Alouette was recovered that evening, slung un-ceremoniously under a Puma all the way back to Ongongo. They techs counted 54 holes in my machine. The real damage had been caused by an RPG-7 grenade that exploded alongside the engine, cutting the oil line, causing it to spray onto the red-hot engine exhaust—hence the smoke and our belief that we were on fire.

I was ordered back to headquarters at Ondangua and, because it had been a pretty nasty experience, they wanted to evacuate me back to Pretoria. The base doctor maintained that I was in a state of 'traumatic shock', which was bullshit so I refused. Finally, I man-aged to convince the ops guys that I was 'all systems go' and that if the camp near Xangongo needed to be taken out, I'd personally lead the force in there to do the dirty deed. The other only notable event to emerge from that little scrape was that I never again flew without socks!

We had more fun and games during Operation *Protea* which launched in August 1981. I was on an operational conversion course in South Africa when an Alouette got shot down. I was immediately ordered back to Bloemfontein, from where I would leave for the operational area the next morning.

By the time I reached Ondangua again, most of the fireworks were over and the Angolan Army was in retreat, heading north and away from the South African threat. However, there were still lots of pockets of resistance about, especially around Xangongo again, where the main spans of the bridge across the Kunene had been dropped into the river.

On that sortie, I was flying on the far side of the river, towards Cahama, where I was able to destroy my first enemy tank. It wasn't one of the Soviet T-54/55s or T-62s, which were regarded as fairly sophisticated in those days, but was actually a German WWII-era T-34. I could see that it was armed with an 85mm gun and that it had company. There were a lot more Angolan tanks in the vicinity, all of which had taken up ambush positions. They were probably waiting either for a South African or a UNITA convoy to pass or for all our aircraft go home for the night so that they could escape northwards with their comrades.

We'd actually only spotted the T-34 after it had started to move, and I made my decision. I had to add a Soviet tank to my list of 'conquests'. Normally, the 20mm ammunition that we carried for our cannon was all high explosive, but I knew those charges would never penetrate the tank's armour, which was more than two inches thick in places, so I concocted something else. I'd always made a point, when working in remote areas, of taking on board a dozen or so rounds of ball ammo. Therefore, I instructed our flight engineer to remove all the HE rounds and use those hard points instead. I then told him to aim at the rear of the tank, where we could see black exhaust fumes and he fired the lot into the engine grill, disabling it.

At the end of it, Operation *Protea* was like many other strategic raids launched by the South African military into Angola during the 24-year war. As usual, the enemy suffered huge losses, substantial quantities of war booty were captured (and handed over to UNITA to use in their own efforts to gain ground against the Luanda regime), and the SADF—usually at the behest of angry American and UN protests—pulled back behind its own frontiers. Having achieved a bit of breathing space, Pretoria immediately started planning for the next season's war against SWAPO and its Angolan allies.

CHAPTER SEVEN

KOEVOET, NIGHT OPS AND A LIFE-CHANGING STAFF COURSE

'Gunship ... Gunship ... This is Zulu Sierra.' The call was urgent and authoritative.

Reply was immediate: 'Zulu Sierra go'.

'This is Zulu Sierra. We have spoor approximately 15 minutes old. Number in group ... five.'

'Roger Zulu Sierra ... We should be overhead in five minutes. Stand by to throw white phos.'

'This is Zulu Sierra. Standing by.'

'OK Zulu Sierra, you're visual . . . throw phosphorus *now*!'

'Confirmed', came the reply 'white phos on the ground.'

'Roger Zulu Sierra . . . I have your white phos visual. We're approximately two minutes out . . . you should be hearing our rotors any moment.'

'Gotcha gunship ... let's do it!'

The white phosphorous grenade exploded on the ground and the mission leader in the Alouette altered his heading to fly directly towards the cloud of white smoke rising above the trees. It marked the call sign's position. The scenario was typical of a call-out for chopper support from one of the most successful fighting forces used in the insurgent war along the Angolan border.

In South-West Africa, the Police Counter Insurgency[1] unit was called Koevoet, the Afrikaans word for crowbar. Loosely defined, a crowbar is a straight metal rod or bar of steel with one end flattened like a crow's foot which is used as a lever. Koevoet's declared role was to prise out insurgents sheltering among the local population.

Insurgents active in South-West Africa feared them as did FAPLA, especially whenever Koevoet units in their Casspir infantry fighting vehicles crossed the border to do battle with government forces. As a police unit, Koevoet was not supposed operate beyond the frontiers of the home state, but they did so, often.

In its everyday duties—either in the Operational Area or in the later stages of South Africa's domestic insurrection before Nelson Mandela was released from prison—Koevoet had acquired a reputation as an efficient, no-nonsense unit with a remarkable élan that usually only became evident when circumstances became tough.

The unit's role in the bush war—in contrast to its urban control in South Africa—was exemplary, largely because of its astonishing strike rate. Koevoet notched up more confirmed kills than any other unit, the South African Army included, for the duration of this two-decade conflict.

Comparatively small compared to other fighting groups, Koevoet operated largely as a Pseudo Unit. Apart from its white officers and NCOs, it was composed almost entirely of former guerrilla insurgents who, having been captured, usually in battle, were 'turned' to fight for their former enemies. Similar ploys were used by the British in Kenya against the Mau Mau and, before that, in the Malaysian Emergency of the 1950s and 1960s against what were referred to in news reports as 'Communist Terrorists' or, colloquially, CTs.

The unit had several additional strengths, including remarkable tracking skills. Their staying power in the field was regarded by those who spent time with them as phenomenal: kills were sometimes made days after the first set of tracks had been spotted in the dry, arid country adjoining Angola. This was not an unusual feature in time of war, but Koevoet's adversaries were young, strong, fit and able to keep on the move, usually at the double, sometimes for days at a stretch. However, Koevoet regulars proved equally resilient and more often than not were able to stay on their tracks, also on foot and also at the double.

Also, the Koevoet's officers, both commissioned and non-commissioned ranks, had the ability to 'talk' approaching Alouette gunships into the fray moments before a full-blown contact became imminent. In Nellis' view, this was helicopter warfare at its most effective and, as he likes to point out, the tactics employed are likely to be studied by protagonists of this form of counter-insurgency warfare for a long time to come. Certainly, the systems employed have an application today in some of the small wars with which the international community remains saddled in Africa, the Middle East and Asia.

As a thoroughly integrated black and white unit, with Africans in the majority, the combat unit in the field had few of the customary military trappings that one usually expected to find. During time spent with the Koevoet, both in Ovamboland and in the adjoining Kaokoveld region, where conditions on the ground were even more unforgiving, this author was regarded as little more than one of the gang. Scribblers embedded with military units usually enjoy certain perks, but not with this crowd. My food was the same as that of the rest of the team and so was my strap-up seat in the Casspir. My bedroll was also solely my responsibility.

The unit was formed in 1979, initially with a preponderance of white security policemen and black special constables. Its objective, when the call came, was to react quickly by vehicle to any intelligence that might have come in about SWAPO cadres operating in their deployment area. As the potential of the unit became more apparent, Koevoet was expanded to become a sizeable force with the acquisition of a number of 'tame insurgents', all the while maintaining its quick reaction capability.

Each call sign was manned by a mixture of policemen, consisting of a white team leader, white section leaders and approximately 40 black policemen. Most of the leadership group had originally worked as policemen in South Africa and were on extended tours of duty. The black component was almost entirely tribal Ovambo and the majority were trackers, some with outstanding follow-up ability under the most difficult semi-desert conditions. They could determine from a single spoor, the numbers of people involved, whether they were moving light or heavy, and follow it while on the run.

A typical Koevoet operational team would be equipped with four Casspir IFVs and a Blesbok logistic supply vehicle. All undercarriages were protected against landmines and the cabs were specially developed for Southern African bush conditions. Each vehicle carried its own armament and, depending on the 'negotiating skills' of its crew, those weapons might range from a 7.62mm light machine gun to a 20mm aircraft cannon adapted for vehicle use.

When information on an insurgent group was received, a team would deploy and, from intelligence gained from chatting to villagers in the suspect area, the squad, by a process of analysis and common sense, would try to establish where the insurgents might be hiding. That was when the unit's trackers came into their own; they would follow the tracks in the sand while jogging ahead of the Casspirs.

As soon as the guerrillas—invariably SWAPO insurgents, occasionally with a sprinkling of South African ANC or Angolan militants—were made aware that the unit was on their tracks, they would attempt to escape by moving swiftly to a safer area. Once the spoor or tracks of an insurgent group were found, the operational lifespan of the enemy unit would invariably be reduced to hours.

Tracking and attack patterns were similar each time a contact became likely. From the start, there would be regular radio comms with headquarters who, in turn, would advise the air force of developments. If a contact was likely, a pair of Alouette gunships might move towards a forward base and be placed on standby. That, basically, was the role of Neall Ellis and his chopper strike teams.

After the trackers reckoned they were 30 minutes or less behind an enemy group, the gunship crews would be alerted and the helicopters would move in for the final action, initially standing off a short distance from the ground team involved in the follow-up. By then, the helicopters would be in touch with the Koevoet commander and await his order to move in for the kill. In the final stages they would report:

'Gunships overhead.'

'Roger gunships . . . The terrs have bombshelled and we're following up on the tracks of a pair of them.'

'Roger Zulu Sierra . . . Number two, take the wide orbit and range up to four clicks ahead.'

The Alouettes, usually with Neall Ellis or Arthur Walker at the controls, would fly a set pattern during the initial stage of the search. This was basically two over-lapping, left-hand orbits, ranging ahead of the tracker teams as well as the vehicles on the ground. There was good reason for the left-hand orbit: the helicopter's cannon was mounted with its barrel pointing out of the left-hand door. It also ensured that the cannon was pointing downwards, which allowed for a quick reaction time should a threat materialize.

The lead gunship would fly a narrow kidney-shaped orbit, ranging up to 3km ahead of the Casspirs, and approximately 200ft above the trees. Number Two's orbit was considerably wider and usually flown between 600ft and 800ft above the ground. It would range from 2km up to 5km from the IFVs. While the narrower orbit was primarily to detect any evidence of a potential ambush, the more distant search was to prevent the enemy from bombshelling and speeding away from the follow-up.

One of the problems facing the air crews was the fairly constant threat of an air collision, especially once the shooting had started and attention was distracted elsewhere. As Nellis commented, 'it was always something that we had to be aware of during a follow-up operation . . . we had to watch very carefully for it . . . there were some close shaves in the early days'.

To prevent a collision, the two helicopters had to maintain height separation, with Number Two in the formation responsible for planning his orbit in such a way that he would keep clear of his leader's flight path.

'Gunships . . . this is Zulu Sierra. The fuckers are around here somewhere . . . we've found several spots in the bush where this bunch seems to have laid up . . . appears they are now taking cover under the trees . . . trackers estimate the group is 10 minutes ahead.'

'Roger Zulu Sierra . . . Number 2 . . . tighten up your orbit and come in a little closer . . . and you are clear to use flushing fire.'

The indication that the insurgents were taking cover in a copse of trees meant that they were now within the orbits of the two helicopters and, in all likelihood, had sighted the aircraft. The pilots and the men on the ground were aware that, with time, SWAPO insurgents had become adept at taking effective measures to avoid visual detection from the air. Thus, when an aircraft overflew their position, they would hide behind some of the heavier tree trunks, keeping the tree between them and the search team above. As soon as the threat had passed, even temporarily, the insurgents would dart across to the next tree and repeat the tactic, sometimes dozens of times over. Another ploy would be to crawl into a thick bush and remain prostrate for as long as possible until the aircraft was no longer in sight. To counter this tactic while in orbit, the gunner on board the chopper would continue searching towards the rear of the helicopter. If weight allowed, a member of the ground team would be picked up to provide an extra set of eyes for the search.

At some stage, the lead gunship pilot would tighten his orbit still further. If the gunner suddenly instructed the pilot to turn, it would usually suggest that he might have spotted something. Smiles would then abound on the faces of the ground troops, especially if there was the sound of stalling rotor blades. That would mean that the pilot was pushing his machine into a tight turn while being directed to the suspect position by the gunner.

'They know that when they hear our stalling blades, the prey is in sight and the "daka-daka" will soon be talking,' explained Nellis.

'Daka-daka' was the insurgent term for a machine gun, which is very similar to the Swahili, 'taka-taka-bom-bom'.

'Zulu Sierra . . . this is gunship . . . We have a terr visual and are firing'.

The ground troops would observe distance and ground cover and usually send their Casspirs into the chase immediately afterwards. According to Nellis, chopper operations with Koevoet teams usually meant that the flying was pretty demanding. Pilots had to concentrate continually on maintaining aircraft separation, make sure that the trackers were not walking into an ambush or that they, themselves, were not flying into something precarious. It was not unknown for SWAPO foray teams to be issued with SAM-7s. In addition, they had to try to project to ground forces the direction in which the escaping insurgents might be heading.

The early 1980s saw a dramatic development in operations, both along the southern Angolan border with South-West Africa and within Angola itself, where Pretoria's military forces were almost permanently at war.

Because the South Africans remained aggressive throughout much of
the region, with air strikes called out for anything suspicious that moved,
the insurgents were forced to revert to moving about at night rather than
during daylight hours. SWAPO's logistics problems were manifest because
they got little help from the Angolan Army. Consequently, their favoured
means of transportation were pick-up trucks, bicycles and donkeys. Occasionally, they would revert to having oxen pull wagons across the sandy
terrain.

Although a curfew was enforced, South African security forces found
it impossible to cover an area half the size of the United Kingdom and for
much of the time they were unable to curtail guerrilla night movements.
Consequently, in 1982, a decision was made by operational headquarters
at Oshakati to determine the efficacy of using Alouette gunships in a bid
to counter movements by civilians as well as SWAPO insurgents who
might be breaking the curfew. Other targets were enemy concentrations
picked up by security force spotter groups or observation posts.

There were limitations, of course, the most significant being the paucity of night flying instrumentation fitted to Alouette III helicopters. There
was no night vision equipment at this stage of the war (though obviously,
there should have been). As a result, the pilots had to fly unaided, with the
naked eye. A second problem was actually identifying the curfew breakers.
Much of Ovamboland was populated by civilians and movement between
villages and *kraals* after dark was as traditional as drinking beer. To intercept
and indiscriminately kill curfew breakers would do nothing to help the
ongoing Combined Operations 'Hearts and Minds' programme and, anyway, it was unethical. A third problem was the positioning of troops on
the ground to arrest curfew breakers and, if necessary, give medical aid to
any person who was injured or wounded during operations.

The first issue was overcome by restricting operations to nights where
there was sufficient moonlight for the pilots to have a visible horizon. There
was no question that moving an aircraft about in total darkness at inor-
dinately low levels—as was customary to avoid SAMs and anti-aircraft
fire—was demanding, especially if the pilot was flying without a horizon.
Disorientation could easily occur, and often did, with disastrous results.

To increase safety, only pilots with a minimum of 400 hours on Alouette III helicopters, 40 hours night flying experience (of which 15 hours

had to be on that type) and a healthy amount of experience in bush operations were considered. Flight engineer/gunners had to have a weapons delivery assessment of high average for gunnery work and not wear corrective lenses.

Preliminary tests showed that it was no problem to visually acquire vehicles travelling at night. However, as soon as the drivers or their passengers were made aware of choppers approaching, they would switch off their engine and stop. Ideally, the pilots should have had heat-sensing infrared detectors, but they didn't. Unfortunately, the Alouette could be heard from some distance and a blacked-out vehicle was almost impossible to find in the bush. To counter the problem, South African arms manufacturer Eloptro supplied locally manufactured sets of NVGs which were issued to flyers deployed on the border. This gave the aviators the advantage of visually acquiring and identifying their targets and within weeks of receiving them, they were creating havoc among the enemy.

To improve accuracy even more, a laser designator was mounted onto the helicopter's 20mm cannon. The gunner was able to see the beam through the NVGs and could also help to mark the target for a second aircraft in the formation. The custom throughout this war was for helicopters always to move about in pairs. This provided mutual support during contacts and assistance if a helicopter was downed. Because the threat of SAMs was a given, the helicopters would always fly without navigation lights. However, this presented the problem of possible mid-air collisions, so a rear tail light was allowed. All other illuminations were masked off.

Initially, to overcome the problem of deploying troops on the ground at night, Puma helicopters were considered. However, it was considered too dangerous to bring a large chopper onto a dusty landing zone at night, especially without lights. Even in daytime 'brown-outs' were a common feature in some areas and then, again, lights on any aircraft made it an easy target for insurgent groups lurking nearby. The problem was solved by positioning a vehicle reaction force at various points in the area of operations. They, in turn, would be in radio communication with the helicopters. Helicopter night operations using Alouette III helicopters eventually became so commonplace that they were dubbed 'Lunar Ops'. To stress to the locals that the curfew would to be more strictly enforced, a campaign was carried out by Combined Operations (COMOPS) where pamphlets were dropped from aircraft and warnings were broadcast on local commercial radio. Inhabitants were warned that if a helicopter circled their position, they were to stop and await the arrival of the ground troops.

Prior to night operations taking full effect, it was clear that the deployment of a land-bound reaction force was proving to be too time consuming and not as effective as required by base commanders. The reaction time was sometimes up to 20 minutes and by the time troops reached a suspicious area, the birds would have flown and all they would find was an abandoned vehicle. Another problem was that the helicopters could not orbit the area indefinitely. Because of fuel considerations, time aloft was limited, leaving the curfew-breakers unguarded.

Since ferrying troops in by helicopter at night was considered too dangerous, the next step in the evolution of 'Lunar Ops' was to drop squads of paratroopers from a DC-3 Dakota. 'Gooney Birds', as they were known to the Americans, although antiquated even then, were able to take up two sticks of ten paratroopers each. After take-off, the aircraft would orbit in a pre-arranged holding area and wait for the mission leader to call the drop. The lead helicopter always had the Parabat commander on board. He wore NVGs and his job was to control his troops on the ground after they had landed.

If the gunships were called out at night to engage an insurgent group, or to drop their airborne load, the pilots followed set procedures. The lead helicopter marked the target by dropping three lumi-sticks (luminous chemical light sticks) approximately 200 metres apart. The second helicopter would climb to an appropriate height and make radio contact with the Dakota, passing on the heading and distance to the drop. Concurrently, the mission leader and the army commander settled on a suitable drop zone. Three minutes out, the pilot would give a radio call and switch on his navigation lights, which was when the lead helicopter marked the DZ, usually with an 'instant light' hand grenade that burnt with an intense white light for approximately 45 seconds.

The army officer in charge in the lead gunship would then instruct the paratroopers to jump by calling out the requisite 'one minute', 'ten seconds' and finally 'green light', the order to go, which was when the 'Bats would jump into the night sky. To ensure that all ten paratroopers in the stick had exited the aircraft and would be visual to the lead helicopter, the first, fifth and tenth paratroopers had 'lumi-sticks' attached to their backs. Once these men had landed and established radio communications with the lead helicopter, they would form up into a sweep-line and advance to target. The 'lumi-sticks' attached to the backs of the three men were also used by the reaction force commander to control his troops while they moved forward.

Though 'Lunar Ops' in the South-West African Operational Area resulted in very few clashes with the enemy, the fact that they took place at all ultimately had the effect of curtailing SWAPO movements during the dark hours.

By all accounts, the inability of Puma helicopters to carry out night trooping during the war was a limiting factor for helicopter night operations. During the initial stages of conflict, Pumas were primarily tasked with the deployment of Special Forces behind enemy lines, sometimes hundreds of kilometres in. They would take off late in the afternoon, the idea being to deploy reconnaissance teams at last light, and the return flight would be in the dark. The reason for last-light deployment was to give the troops on the ground time to put as much distance as possible between the LZ and local inhabitants who might have observed the insertion as any nearby guerrilla groups could be informed quickly by runner. Also, there were few pilots willing to take their choppers into an LZ that had not already been cleared of insurgents by ground forces.

As the War developed, 19 Squadron, a Puma squadron based at Air Force Base Swartkops in Pretoria, was given the task of developing a strategic night flying capability in an extremely primitive African environment. A special night flying flight, called 'Alpha Flight' was initiated and, with intensive training, was to become an extremely successful unit. It wasn't long before the air force could claim that its Puma helicopters were capable of carrying out operations in the dark in almost all weather conditions.

Nellis had been involved in some of this work himself, planning for night operations which involved intensive map preparation since navigation in remote regions, such as those adjacent to Angola, could be difficult at night. He explained that all aviators are aware that the hazards associated with normal day-time flying, such as telephone and high-tension wires, are difficult, and often impossible, to distinguish at night. Night flying,

even in remote topography, required up-to-date intelligence, terrain details
and information about enemy and friendly force deployments.

Maps had to be clearly marked with the track to be flown, direction,
headings and all hazards that might be encountered along the way. Two
types of maps were used: the 1:250 000 scale chart for route planning and
navigation, and the 1:50 000 scale chart for navigation in the objective
area (within five to eight nautical miles of the target).

Because pilots preferred to 'hug the ground' while moving in unfamiliar areas, selecting the route had to be tactically sound and support accurate
navigation. Certain factors had to be taken into account, including avoiding brightly lit areas, population concentrations and almost all roads, as
even in the middle of the night vehicles could not miss the roar of a passing
helicopter and this information could be passed on. While negotiating
north–south valleys, it was essential to keep the machine on the lit side
with regard to the position of the moon. This would silhouette most terrain
features for navigation and avoid shadows.

As Neall Ellis always told the younger pilots, they should make a point
of avoiding routes that headed directly towards a low-rising or setting
moon. To which he would add: 'when selecting checkpoints for navigation
along the route, we tended to choose easily identifiable natural or man-
made features that could be visually acquired from a distance.'

All this experience eventually paid dividends. During Operations *Modular*, *Hooper* and *Packer* in 1987–1988, Puma helicopters were the only
aircraft able to fly after dark in southern Angola in all weather conditions.
Puma aircrews, often as a matter of great urgency, were required to haul
essential supplies, personnel and, more often than not, ammunition to forward elements. The wounded would be taken back to the rear on return
flights. The pilots would take off from Rundu airfield in northern South-
West Africa at last light and plan to cross back into South-West Africa at
first light. Aircrews would consequently fly up to eight hours at a stretch
and conditions could be both hazardous and demanding.

To avoid acquisition by enemy radar, the maximum height allowed
above ground level was 200–300ft. Moreover, the aviators flew without
night vision and sophisticated navigation equipment. The objectives were
almost always tiny clearings in the bush, usually marked with no more than
a few dozen coke tins that had been cut in half and filled with a combina-

tion of sand and paraffin—this mixture would burn with a small flame and mark the LZ.

At times, particularly during the summer months, there would be extreme weather in the region in which the Pumas were active. Tropical thunderstorms in Central Africa are not only intimidating, but can also be breathtakingly dangerous, especially during lightning strikes which sometimes go on for hours. Heavy rain would often restrict forward visibility through the cockpit Perspex, making the task of searching for a tiny LZ in that blackened quagmire even more difficult. Fortunately, these storms did keep enemy MiG fighters on the ground and friendly reception groups, usually UNITA troops, were able to send up flares as additional beacons, without fear of being rocketed or strafed.

One of the most consistent problems facing aircrews was the South Angolan bush, particularly some of the forests that stretched from one horizon to the other. It is a spectacularly beautiful and isolated region, almost all of it untouched by any kind of modern development. Indeed, it is so far from any sizeable towns or proper roads that it remains isolated, decades after the war has ended. As Nellis declares:

> Once you moved into the interior, the kind of trees you were likely to have below could easily average 10 metres in height and become fairly dense further north, near Cuito Cuanavale, where most of our forward elements operated. Also, the terrain wasn't as uniformly flat as it is further towards the arid south. Instead, it slowly became more undulating.
>
> On a dark night, the pilots would be unable to see the ground, and would monitor their radio altimeter needles oscillating wildly up and down. This indicated that the jungle was sometimes less than 10 or 15 metres below them. Under those conditions, clearly, emergency landings were not a consideration.
>
> Once, during a dark moon phase, a couple of Pumas were tasked to drop off a reconnaissance team at a point well behind enemy lines: an operation that was required to take place after midnight. The pilots were briefed to use their landing lights only in an emergency during the approach to landing and, of course, in the touch-down itself.

A Koevoet counter-insurgency group in their distinctive Casspir anti-mine vehicles in a routine patrol in an area adjacent to the Angolan border.
Author's photo

After successfully bringing the choppers down, without the use of lights, the formation leader felt uncomfortable. He risked flashing his landing light at the area ahead of him and, to his consternation, he discovered that the helicopters had carried out a successful approach and landing in a dry river bed. The river banks rose steeply more than 15 metres above their position and he hadn't seen any of it in the dark. Had he taken off, he would probably have flown into what could best be described as a steep embankment that towered 50 metres from the LZ.

There are countless such stories about missions flown in the dark, many of the situations seemingly impossible. Only because of good training and the thoroughly professional manner in which chopper aircrews tackled problems were more helicopters not lost.

During one of thxe many breaks from operational duties, Neall Ellis was finally selected to go to Pretoria on a staff course. An unlikely candidate, he never believed he would get past the flying stage, never mind make senior rank. As it happened, he did make the rank of colonel in the South African Air Force prior to moving on. He comments:

As in any job, things move on. Somebody in the rarefied atmosphere of defence headquarters in Pretoria must have thought I'd been doing a good job, which I suppose I had because I'd been decorated with a gong for bravery as a result of an action in Angola. Thus came the nomination for that dreaded staff course. However, what emerged during those few months completely changed both my perception of the war and what I felt about South African politics in general.

Orders that I was to attend the South African Air Force College at Swartkops came in the late 1980s while Operations *Modular, Hooper* and *Packer* were still going on. I was still pretty hyped up from the excitement of flying combat, but I was aware that if I wanted to get on with my career I'd have to at least go through the motions. It helped that I was the first among my contemporaries on my original pilot course to be invited.

Those who had been through the mill regarded the staff course as a fairly demanding nine-month effort. Also, as an air force major, I was at a disadvantage because, customarily, it was commandants [half-colonels] and above who were selected. The objective was to prepare candidates for the rank of brigadier and above. Suddenly, I saw my original objective of possibly making general's rank became a reality.

Things didn't start too well. My very good friend Gary Barron, who had gone from choppers to flying jets, was at headquarters at the time and was among our group as course leader. He began complaining of headaches within the first two weeks. It was obviously serious because none of the pain killers the docs gave him worked. Within three months he was dead of a brain tumour. He was young, fit and an extremely capable aviator so his death was one hell of a shock.

Of the 24 officers on the course, only four were pilots and it was clear from the start that there was an imbalance because we spoke English and the rest were all Afrikaans. Also, without making too fine a point of it, none of the other officers were blessed with the same level of mental preparedness for decisions and planning as were we four aviators, largely because it was part of our everyday job.

The staff course ended up being completely different from what I might have expected. We were required to tell the group about our lives, what we had done, our failures, what we were sorry about and a lot else. Frankly, I regarded that side of it as bullshit. I had never been one to elaborate on anything personal and wasn't about to start then.

Some of the guys would be in tears while recounting their experiences of life, but I went in the other direction. With my black sense of humour I would tell the group about recent battles, of killing people and of seeing blood and guts everywhere when we pulled out the casualties. That was real and had shaped the lives of those of us who were involved.

I recall one woman recoiling in horror during one of my particularly gory descriptions. Pete Vivier, one of my flying pals, in contrast, egged me on because, being a pilot too, he understood perfectly what I was talking about. He'd also been through that crap quite often. In the end we two weren't invited to take part in any more of these 'bleeding heart' discussions. I think they must have regarded us as crass. The consensus was that the majority in the group couldn't understand how anybody could sink to such a depth of depravity. 'Fuck! What was war all about?' I asked. But I never did get an answer.

It didn't take me long to appreciate the extent of the mismatch. I was amazed at the inability of the jam-stealers and technical people among us to appreciate a situation for what it was and to make a snap decision. There were some officers on the staff course who didn't know what the hell they were doing. Most were apprehensive when I was made a Syndicate Leader, largely because I didn't take myself all that seriously. I was perceived as simply too casual in my approach to things.

Then I started having second thoughts about the value of a staff course qualification. I couldn't help feeling that my processes of ratiocination were being downgraded to their level. Also, I deplored being conditioned to think the way they did and Pete and I went over this a couple of times. At one debriefing, I confronted the CDS on this issue. A Mirage pilot himself, he couldn't avoid agreeing with us. However, he also had his reservations. One of the purposes of the staff course, he declared, was that everybody was taught to think along the same lines. I replied that the real objective was that they wanted me to destroy my own individuality. It was like something out of George Orwell's novel *Nineteen Eighty-Four*.

Soon, my enthusiasm waned and I started coasting. I kept thinking about the higher staff echelons in the SADF. What was the thinking at the uppermost levels? For instance, some of the operations across the border in Angola were a nightmare because of a patent lack of cohesive planning. I ended up fairly disillusioned about the quality and capabilities of the majority of senior military commanders with whom I had come into contact. However, that didn't detract from my feelings about the really good ones with whom I'd worked and who were still very much around. My conclusion was that brilliant minds were being dragged back by a bunch of Neanderthals.

To cap it all, towards the end of the course, we were getting lectures on the geo-politics of the region. Some very controversial figures were invited to address us, including a number of bleeding-heart liberal types who were telling us that what we were doing in Angola was all wrong. They claimed, totally without justification because none of them had ever been near the place, that those Afrikaners with whom I was dealing believed they had a covenant with God that told them what they were doing with regard to people with other skin colour was right. It came as a bit of a shock to listen to them.

By the time I left Swartkops, about all that had been achieved was the complete undermining of all the confidence I'd ever had

One of the SAAF Pumas on the ground during Operation Super to bring in ammunition and take out casualties.
Photo: Neall Ellis Collection

in the political system. By realising that the apartheid politics that I had been so avidly supporting were totally wrong, I'd become a maverick. Curiously, it wasn't an overnight transition. It took quite a while to get me there.

That was when I started to rebel, subtly at first and then quite blatantly. I'd totally lost faith in the course and its purpose to create decision-makers and even began wearing my *veldskoene* with no socks, except when I was flying, even to quite important social events at the base. Also, I resented having to don suits on more formal occasions and it wasn't long before I was upbraided for my non-conformist attitude. I often wonder whether I would ever have moved up to staff rank after that fiasco. I doubt it.

The outcome was that I'd become a misfit. The war on the border continued and I went on working as one of the senior gunship pilots in the air force. Somehow though, I couldn't help feeling that somewhere along the way I'd lost the initiative, and when the opposing sides in Angola called it quits, I was actually quite happy.

These were difficult times for South Africa in other respects, but with the release of Nelson Mandela from prison and the abolition of apartheid, my spirits were heightened. I knew, too, that there were others out there who thought as I did. At the same time, a future in the SADF suddenly became sticky.

Gen Joep Joubert, a seasoned veteran of hostilities in Angola from the early days, who had been one of my mentors throughout my career, called me one day to say that for the time being all air force promotions were frozen. The order had gone as high as the Air Force Council. In short, he confided, there was no real future for me or anybody else like me in the SAAF. The air force wouldn't disappear, he said, but there would be no new commands, except dead-end jobs like flying desks. However, there was an option, he suggested: 'Take the package.' He was talking about the air force retirement package, which was actually quite lucrative for somebody like me who had served for so many years. That is what I did not very long afterwards, and for the first time in decades, at the age of 40, I was out of uniform and in Civvy Street.

CHAPTER EIGHT

NEW DIRECTIONS— DANGEROUS CHALLENGES

Leaving the air force was an enormous challenge. It was the only real life Neall knew. The men and women in uniform who had been part of his life for decades, almost since leaving school, were not only like family, they were his family.

> But I'd made the break and I knew that I couldn't go back. Anyway, I had good money in the bank, my entire pension. Unfortunately that didn't last because, like so many military people who had little experience of the world outside, I was soon persuaded to part with most of it by investing in a sharp-edged fishing venture and that was that—money all gone
>
> It was a catastrophe. I could see everything going wrong and there was nothing I could do about it, which was when I started getting panicky. Meanwhile Zelda, a nurse, had been working intermittently and at that time wasn't earning. She went back to her old nursing career, starting with a fairly good job in Hermanus. It took her away from home most of the time, although she would join me for weekends at the Arniston fishing village where we were living. Apart from what she earned, there was nothing else coming

in which complicated things somewhat because we had the two elder children at boarding school at Bredasdorp. Things were starting to get tough.

I was finally offered a job by Richard Devine, a friend from way back, who had made his packet in horse racing. He had a farm just outside Paarl exporting flowers and fruit to Europe. He also had seven or eight hectares of carrots, some of which became my responsibility. However, I wasn't earning much—R3,000 a month (about $700 at the time)—and it was difficult because the children still had to be educated. Somehow we managed though.

I'd see Pumas from the air force base at Ysterplaat flying over the valley where I lived, and my heart would leap. Still, I kept at it for about 18 months until Zelda asked me: 'why don't you go back to flying?'

With the war in the Balkans gathering pace, things were tense in Europe at the time and I'd been following events carefully. A couple of weeks after the NATO bombings of August 1995, Slade Healy, an old air force chopper pilot pal of mine, called and made me an offer I couldn't refuse. He said he'd been in the Balkans flying Mi-17 helicopters for a bunch of rebels in Bosnia and was looking for some willing hands to join him. The money was good—$6,000 up front with an additional $1,000 an hour flying time. Obviously there were risks, but then that was what it was all about, were his words. I spoke to Zelda about the prospect and she said I should go. It was what I wanted to do anyway. She declared she'd manage on her own until things were more settled. Richard arrived at the farm the following morning and I told him I was leaving. I was stagnating and just had to make the move, I stated, which was the truth.

Shortly after I'd spoken to Slade, I got the call from Johannesburg. 'How does flying for a crazy bunch of Islamic militants appeal to you?' asked a fellow named Mario, Slade's colleague. I'd worked with Mario in the past while flying combat in Angola and he was one of the most experienced pilots in the game. My reply was guarded: 'Depends on which bunch of Muslims.' I wasn't exactly hesitant, but I didn't want to sound overenthusiastic. After all, the Balkans had already acquired the kind of reputation that caused most freelancers to shy away, not only because of the lack of money but the word coming out of there was that most of the equipment was sub-standard and poorly maintained. Even worse was the fact that both sides had little regard for the fundamental ethics of combat. The Geneva Convention might have been a parlour game and everybody knew that you'd be fortunate to survive if you managed to live through being shot down and were taken prisoner. The odds were stacked against us. I was also testy because of the experiences of some of my friends who had volunteered to fly in the Balkans: some hadn't been paid, others were killed.

'There is a limit to what I will do for money', I told Mario.

'This is different, though', said the other man. 'You'll be working for Muslim separatists in Bosnia. They're a tough bunch and they're reliable.' Mario went on to describe the mission.

'Done!' replied Nellis, unequivocal because he trusted Mario, although they still hadn't discussed money.

'Where do you want me?' he asked.

'Jan Smuts, at four this afternoon', came the reply.

That was a tall order, since the main international airport in Johannesburg was a two-hour flight away, with another hour on the road to Cape Town's airport, and Nellis still had to make his booking. However, he got going anyway.

Mario had said that Nellis would be working with friends on the new assignment. Two of them, Jakes Jacobs and Jaco Klopper, were still serving members of the South African Air Force. They would have to take 'unofficial' leave and wouldn't be telling their bosses where they were heading or what they'd be doing. As in any regular force, flying combat for a foreign government was what the Americans like to call an effective career terminator. Others in the team were Phil Scott, Pete Minnaar, and Mike Hill, all veteran former SAAF chopper crews with years of combat experience. Hill had been a member of the team in one of the final phases of the war in Angola when Nellis was commanding the chopper wing.

The way Mario explained it, the men would be handling a pair of Bosnian Mi-8s in ground support roles in outlying areas such as Gorazde,

Bihac, and other enclaves. Since the Serbian Army had isolated most Islam-ic settlements from the world outside, either by laying siege or ambushing all the approaches, these people used helicopters to bring in supplies.

Although the South African pilots finally settled on the financial details and agreed to go, the assignment worried Nellis as it did the others, although Nellis did not discover this until they later discussed it. For a start, this was an unusually hazardous undertaking with a few twists to it. It would be winter by the time they arrived, and winters in Yugoslavia could be harsh. Because much of the flying would be over the mountains, the terrain would be difficult to traverse, especially when cloud cover obscured towns, which could happen for weeks at a time, and high ground constantly loomed over them.

Then came the bloody-minded Serbs, whose territory they would have to traverse in their aircraft and whose arsenal included some of the most sophisticated anti-aircraft weapons available. Only after they reached Bosnia were they to discover that the choppers had no navigational aids to speak of, and that almost all the flying was at night. It was a tough call!

Still, the pay was excellent and all the 'volunteers' were broke. Weather allowing, the men would be required to fly as many missions as they could, two a day if possible. They would get an extra $500 for each sortie com-pleted, and, as was agreed up front with Mario, operational flights would be in tandem with two Mi-8s to a mission, very much as they had operated in Africa. If one of the machines was forced down, the other could pick up survivors.

In Johannesburg, Nellis and the others were briefed by Slade Healy. He had just returned to South Africa, having flown for the Bosnians. It was his job to negotiate terms for this new group of aviators and he told them that his link in the Balkans was a fellow by the name of Zarif: a 'heavy Muslim political character from Zenica', were his words.

It was also Healy who warned Nellis and company at that first briefing that the job was not easy. He used the word 'precarious', emphasizing the threat by detailing his first flight from Zenica, a city north-west of Sarajevo. That mission had been planned to reach Gorazde, then completely sur-rounded by Serbian forces.

'Our chopper took some heavy ground fire, much of it sustained', Healy explained, adding that there was a lot more battle damage than they would have liked before they were able to make it safely into a landing zone in the mountains. Also, the crew had to fly in both directions using night vision goggles. 'This is going to be hard work', he declared. However, it seemed worth it, considering that South Africa was in a recession. Universally, this kind of freelance military activity was in short supply just then, so it was a welcome opportunity for them all.

Healy also cautioned the new arrivals about the machines they would be flying. Since none of them had piloted Mi-8s before, they wouldn't have time to conventionally convert to the Russian helicopters before going operational. It wasn't an ideal situation, he cautioned, but there wasn't any other way. He also hinted that if they didn't accept the contract, there would be others who would.

Arriving at Zagreb, the Croatian capital, was an experience for the men. Nellis recalled that it was the first time he'd been out of Africa, so he was excited at the prospect of something different.

The group was met on arrival by Zarif, a short, slim man with a moustache, and taken to a small, dismal hotel where he arranged dinner. He left them to spend the night on their own, and in Nellis' view this combination of events did not bode well for the future. The following morning they were driven to a Croatian Army military airfield on the outskirts of town, where they boarded an Mi-8MTV destined for Zenica. Once there, they would be taken to the Bosnian front line, said Zarif.

Along the way, their helicopter halted briefly in Banja Luka to pick up a couple of mysterious characters dressed totally in black. With their faces hidden behind balaclavas, they were obviously the local version of Special Forces. They didn't utter a greeting or a word throughout, which wasn't that unusual. Neall recalls that many of the troops the South Africans encountered in the following days were dressed in black and were uncommunicative. What really worried him was that these people didn't look or act like professionals, especially considering that this was a country at war. The men didn't have that seasoned military look about them, either in appearance or in the way they handled their weapons. For all that, wherever they landed there was a lot of military hardware about, including tanks and former Soviet APCs, 20mm cannon, 14.5mm heavy machine guns and 23mm quads (four-barrelled, heavy machine guns). Seeing all that made it really hit home that there was some really serious fighting going on.

While heading to their final destination, they were able to check out the terrain in which they would be operating. It was bleak and mountainous with little tree cover. Generally, recalls Nellis, it was all quite uninviting and not the kind of country that made hostilities easy.

The first afternoon after they arrived, after several stops along the way, the group landed at Zenica and were taken to a house by the river, a couple of kilometres from the local military headquarters. Zarif said that it would be their home for the duration. While there was a rumbling of artillery in the mountains, there was not much evidence of fighting around town, although most of the buildings were scarred by shell fire. Whenever a UN vehicle came past the people would shout abuse at their blue helmeted occupants and hurl rocks. Neall recalls that 'it was all pretty sinister, actually, especially since this was our first exposure to the world of Islam'.

It was also the first time he had sat at the controls of an Mi-8. Fortunately, Pete Minnaar had spent time with Executive Outcomes in Angola and was experienced on these helicopters. He ended up giving the crew the full technical conversion course in their kitchen. They were also briefed by Zarif and his military cronies on what they were going to be doing and exactly what was expected.

Nellis takes up the story:

Essentially, he said, our job was to ferry supplies into garrisons in the interior that were under attack by the Serbians. At that point somebody raised the issue of the promised second support chopper as we'd only seen one on the improvised flight line Suddenly he started back-pedalling. He said something about some Russians also flying for them and that they were using it but he couldn't, or rather wouldn't, tell us anything definite.

We also told Zarif that the chopper we'd seen on the pad wasn't the right colour for the kind of military operations he envisaged. The machine still had its original Aeroflot paint job, much of it blue and white, and we demanded that it be black all over. We'd be flying at night, we explained, and we didn't want to give the opposition the opportunity to shoot at something that would stand out like a neon sign should there be moonlight.

Zarif said he'd think about it, although he did produce a couple of Russian NVGs which he believed were OK. We thought they were not as streamlined as we were accustomed to and weighed too much. Fortunately, we'd brought with us some Litton NVGs from South Africa. We still had to adapt the helicopter's interior lighting system with green LEDs to make the cockpit as NVG compatible as possible, something that was tackled by Phil and Pete.

It didn't take the South Africans long to accept that while morale within the Bosnian Army was at a broadly acceptable level, discipline throughout was poor. Quite often, Nellis recalls, the soldiers would start shooting into the air for no reason or someone would throw a grenade or two because it was what he felt like doing. Nellis sensed that part of it might have been a reaction to the nightly bombardments to which the population was being subjected. The Serbs were using some heavy stuff, including 155mm guns, and Zenica was at the receiving end of artillery and mortar bombardments just about every night. Usually, the Serbian Army would fire five or six rounds and then there would be a lull. That could last minutes or even several hours, and then it would start all over again. While there was a steady flow of casualties, the city's inhabitants seemed to have become accustomed to rounds falling about their buildings.

Although the Bosnians demanded that the new arrivals be put through their paces on the Mi-8 'Hip' to demonstrate that they could actually fly the machine, Nellis didn't feel that he needed to disclose that he had never flown a Hip before. As he reckoned, he had a basic understanding of the chopper and although he tended to overshoot quite a lot at first, with some high-nose attitudes, it took only a couple of approaches to master the right speed. He did one 30-minute daytime flight and another after dark and it was quite exciting, he recalls

One of the immediate concerns among the newcomers was the acknowledged anti-aircraft capability of their adversaries, the Serbians. A series of sophisticated radar-guided SAM systems had been installed at vantage points in the mountains throughout the region and, by all accounts, there were a lot of them. Nellis had long been aware that SAM-

8s were one of the better Soviet anti-aircraft weapons systems, especially against low-flying aircraft. As he explained: 'We had seen what these missiles were capable of in Angola. We were familiar with the threat—the weapon was deadly, especially in the right hands.' He continued:

> Although the local people said they were still trying to get us another chopper, we split ourselves into two crews. I'd fly with Jakes, who was designated commander, and Phil Scott while the other crew would be Mike, Jaco and Piet.

Meanwhile, Jakes and Jaco approached Zarif again to discuss the support helicopter that had originally been promised, and they were adamant. They were still serving members of the South African Air Force and technically 'on vacation', they told him, so their concern about going down and being taken captive by the Serbs was real. Should that happen, it would be a huge embarrassment for them personally and, of course, for the South African government as well. For that reason alone, they declared, a second Mi-8 had to be produced if they were to go ahead with the contract. This development reflected some of their concerns about their role as a whole. It was obvious that the work involved was dangerous, critically so. That they accepted. However, they also felt that their hosts had to meet the criteria that had originally been agreed upon.

Their immediate problem with Zarif was that he had broken a cardinal promise on which the entire operation hinged. Before leaving Johannesburg, the team had been assured by Slade Healy that every flight would be a two-ship operation. On arriving in Zenica, however, that was countermanded by Zarif. He declared that it was not possible to have two helicopters airborne at the same time. He argued that his forces did not have the necessary resources to deploy two choppers for a single operation, which the South Africans felt was duplicitous. Further, he told the group that the matter was a *fait accompli*. The subject warranted no further discussion, he said bluntly.

'That was that,' recalls Nellis. 'The man had said his piece and we were obliged to accept. However, since we'd always been accustomed to flying in pairs, in some of the remotest corners of the globe, his backtracking on that vital issue caused our first real rift with our employers.'

However, that was not all that bothered the South Africans. The other matter they had raised, said Nellis, was that of the radio set. They had been assured that there was a High Frequency radio set at the apartment. The equipment was needed for the guys who stayed behind so that they could monitor flights to make sure there were no problems. The way they worked was that one team would go out and the other would keep track as things unfolded. However, the South Africans were given VHF equipment, which was limited to line-of-sight reception. Consequently, once the aircraft went into the hills the crew would have no communication with their people. That really bothered the pilots and they said as much. No radio set ever materialized.

The first flight was taken up by Mike, Jaco and Pete from a sports field in the heart of Zenica, late in September 1995. The weather wasn't kind. The helicopter was loaded with ammunition and medical supplies. However, they were hardly airborne before they had to return to base because of a powerful weather front that had closed in. They were stymied for the rest of the day and after dark a mist enveloped the hills. With winter almost upon them, bad flying conditions were inevitable, but this was a lot worse than they'd anticipated.

The next evening, things improved and they tried a second time. This time they made it to Gorazde, their destination. Although the flight was only about 35 minutes each way, with another 15 minutes or so on the ground for offloading, it was about as problematic as it gets. Things weren't helped by the fact that the LZ into which they were supposed to go was perched on the side of a hill. The reasoning behind this, as offered by their hosts, was something to do with protection against enemy snipers. Mike Hill recalled afterwards that it was a very difficult approach: 'We had ground fire coming up at us just about all the way . . . the chopper was hit several times but there was no serious damage. In the end, we brought out a batch of sick and wounded troops and some civilians.'

On touchdown back at Zenica, the South Africans became overnight celebrities: everybody wanted to pump their hands and, Islamic or not, buy them hefty shots of slivovitz. However, it was during their debriefing that they realized that their mission wasn't as straightforward as they might have hoped. In fact, it was a lot dodgier than any of them had anticipated because in getting to the target areas, they had to cross several rows of enemy lines, which stretched from the Yugoslavian border all the way to Sarajevo and beyond. Worse, nothing was in a straight line. Mike Hills said that they were required 'to fly a jagged, winding course that more or less followed the road from the border'. He continued:

A second, more persistent issue was the deployment of enemy forces around Gorazde itself. Once the helicopter had crossed the first hurdle, enemy troops dug into positions around Gorazde would have been told by radio that there was a helicopter heading their way, so the Serbs would be waiting for us, having been allowed about 15 minutes to prepare for our arrival. Consequently, there would be quite a volume of incoming fire heading for us as we approached.

Getting to the target LZ was only half the battle. Mike continued:

Whether that first leg of the sortie was successful or not, we still had to bring the chopper back to Zenica, our home base. So the chances of us getting hit whenever we took the machine out were just about a hundred per cent.

Because Serb defences around Gorazde were not as concentrated to the immediate west of the enclave, the crew thought that the best route on the return leg would be over the mountains towards the coast. Just then, however, the weather turned nasty again, so they had no alternative but to follow more or less the same flight path home that they had used on the way in. The other possibility was to go high and seek cloud cover, but that would have meant flying blind in the mountains and it just wasn't an option. Also, Serb radar would have picked them up in a jiffy and the Serbs would have been able to fire their SAMs.

It didn't take the South Africans long to accept that since there were no airfields or let-down facilities anywhere between Gorazde and Zenica, their options were constrained, severely, as it transpired. It was a hell of a way to be earning bucks, the guys joked afterwards. Writing about his experiences in the Balkans a few years later, Nellis said that the stark reality of almost certainly being shot down at some stage or other meant that some members of the group were seriously unhappy with the setup in the Balkans. He continued:

> Going into a strange country about which none of us knew shit and dealing with people who didn't speak English, made us decide very early on that if one of us was unhappy with the situation, then we'd all be unhappy. It wasn't an ideal solution, but it did create something of a common bond.

It was also agreed that if they couldn't sort things out, they would all leave. Obviously, it didn't help that they could not really trust their hosts because they had gone back on their word more than once. 'In fact,' he added, 'they'd lied fluently from the start, and we knew that in their eyes, we were expendable.'

Consequently, the mercenary group felt that if they stuck together, their chances of success would be better, especially if they had to make a dash for it. Nellis continues:

> A few nights after Mike's mission, it was our turn, with the crew consisting of me, Jakes and Phil. Again, Gorazde was our objective. This time the weather was perfect and we left for the helipad just before sundown. We'd already seen how these people operated so we decided to supervise the loading of the helicopter and do a proper pre-flight check ourselves before it became too dark.
>
> The helicopter had, meanwhile, been moved to a hilltop outside the town where it was out of sight of anyone who didn't need to know what was happening. However, intelligence was coming through that the Serbs were being informed by their own sources or, possibly, observation posts in the surrounding hills each time we lifted off. Consequently, nobody had to tell us that the bastards would open fire the moment we approached their positions.
>
> Leaving Zenica that night was an event. We were just about to cross the first line of Serb defences when we came under some really heavy fire. What was coming up at us wasn't just cursory, it was big stuff. We could hear the bird take hits, you couldn't miss

it. It was like somebody using a giant hammer on the fuselage. This was not the 'typing pool' clatter of AKs.

I felt a heavy thump underneath my seat accompanied by a loud bang. A moment later 'Natasha' started screeching.[1] We knew enough about cockpit warning systems to be aware that something was seriously wrong and, while we couldn't detect any immediate damage because all the instruments seemed in order, Jakes decided that it might be better to take her back. It was a sudden, impulsive move. Although we were flying a bit high, he turned and dived towards the ground. Luckily, there was a full moon and we couldn't miss the ground coming up at us. Once we'd levelled out, we stayed low to reduce the threat of incoming fire.

As it happened, Jakes' decision wasn't the best option facing the South Africans. What he'd done was turn the helicopter directly towards enemy gun emplacements. More rounds followed and after taking more punishment, the Hip finally moved out of range. Nellis takes up the story again:

Back at base, nobody was chuffed with this performance. We'd come back without completing a mission. An immediate result was that we got nothing for our efforts even though the flight was about as perilous as any that I'd experienced in my career. The passengers in the back were even more shaken by the time they emerged; they'd been sitting on three tons of explosive mortar and artillery rounds.

The team waited several days for the chopper to be repaired and then tried again.

We had just got to the LZ when the weather started to close in once more. This time Jakes told the Bosnians that neither he nor anybody else was prepared to take her up in those conditions and we were promptly taken back to the house.

Zarif was furious, and the pilots accepted that he probably had a right to be. In the four weeks that the crew had been in Bosnia, the South

Africans had notched up one successful flight. Apart from losing money, Zarif had also lost face with his own people.

At a confab later that night, Jakes decided that he wasn't prepared to go on. He told us that he wanted to return home and that was that. We had sensed it coming over the previous weeks because relations with Zarif had deteriorated to the point where he had become both obnoxious and aggressive. He insulted the men, once or twice in public. At one stage he threatened us with arrest if we didn't fly.

We stood by our earlier decision that if somebody decided to pull out, the rest would follow. I wasn't too happy with the idea because I needed the money, but once the decision had been made, that was it. Actually, I was desperate, but since none of the others were prepared to hang in there, and I didn't have the experience on type to try it alone, I ended up on the plane back to Zagreb with the rest of the gang.

CHAPTER NINE

EXECUTIVE OUTCOMES
IN WEST AFRICA

'It was November 1995 and the outlook couldn't have been bleaker', recalls Neall Ellis.

I had no job, no money, I didn't want to go back to work on the farm, the fishing issue was history and Zelda had left me and moved to Stellenbosch on her own. Frankly, I didn't have a clue what to do next. Then the 'phone rang.

The call that came from Ibis Air, the aviation component of Executive Outcomes (EO), was from somebody I knew from way back and who asked whether I was doing anything just then. I hesitated briefly so as not to appear over-eager and answered something about being busy, but what did he have in mind? He suggested that I get myself to Pretoria the next day and find out. I didn't have the money for the air fare, so I borrowed some cash from a neighbour and headed to Cape Town Airport.

In one respect, the approach puzzled me. Early on, while EO was still working in Angola, they had spoken to me about taking a contract to fly gunships against the guerrilla forces of Dr Jonas Savimbi. The UNITA leader was somebody I'd worked with in the past and whom I both liked and admired for the consistent stand he'd made against a government that had been a Soviet client-state from the first day they had taken over from the Portuguese. It was Moscow that had helped to bring the ruling MPLA political party to power, so in my eyes this was a puppet regime. As events have subsequently proved, I was right.

I couldn't help but refuse the EO offer, even though it was lucrative and money was short. I told EO that it would have meant going operational against somebody who had been a trusted ally in our Border War and, by my book, you don't just start killing your friends because somebody offers you the cash to do so. These were pretty harsh words and I never thought they'd actually approach me a second time. However, they did.

I was told that the new job had nothing to do with Savimbi or Angola. The deployment would be in Sierra Leone. I was obviously pleased because I wouldn't have to consider going against my conscience this time round.

Once Nellis arrived in Pretoria, it was explained to him that a particularly brutal bunch of rebels was in the process of murdering civilians in the tiny West African country of Sierra Leone. Moreover, they were doing so at an astounding rate and there didn't appear to anybody able or willing to stop them. 'Sierra Leone was remote, corrupt and inefficient,' Nellis declared, 'and from what I understood, everything centred around diamonds, which were abundant in the country'.

The EO contact told Nellis that although the UN had a large number of men there, the force was all but moribund. 'They couldn't organise a good crap if their lives depended on it', commented another of the men present at the meeting.

Sadly, as I was soon to discover, all this was true. The last time the UN had fought a decent war was in the Congo, and that was 30 years earlier. The EO personnel manager explained that if I were willing to leave for Sierra Leone almost immediately, they would offer me a contract to fly choppers there and to become part of a fairly large component of aviators already active against the rebels.

Ibis Air, the company running the aviation side of things—as opposed
to the mercenaries who were actually doing the ground work against the
rebel force—was British owned and, as Nellis was to discover, ran a pretty
tight ship.

Ibis' directors had acquired two practically new Boeing 737s from surplus stock in the United States for US$1 million. The only problem with
them was that their engines exceeded newly imposed FAA noise-limitation
regulations. That effectively resulted in both aircraft being put out to pasture. Ibis snapped them up for use in the African conflicts in which the
company was involved, both in Angola and Sierra Leone. The two passenger jets were used to move mercenaries and their supplies from South Africa
to the various operational areas to the north.

Ibis also bought a number of other planes for use in the various African
wars in which EO and its associates were involved, including at least one
King Air, four Mi-8 helicopters (two each for Angola and Sierra Leone), a
Cessna 337 for Sierra Leone, and a pair of former RAF Hawker Siddeley
Andover CC Mk2 twin-prop transports, previously operated by No. 32
Squadron for the Queen's Flight.

Ostensibly, the Andovers were for casualty evacuation and, indeed,
they did save lives. However, overall they did comparatively little work
because EO suffered minimal casualties. Most of the evacuations involved
men who went down with tropical diseases, malaria especially. One of the
Andovers was stationed at Luanda International Airport, which served the
Angolan capital, and the other sat at Lungi, outside Freetown.

Nellis says of that time: 'Of course, the deal I was offered was im-
mensely appealing because, money apart, I already knew quite a few of
the people associated with these ventures.' He added that it was a pleasure
renewing those old acquaintances.

It was then that I realised what I was missing when working with
men like Zarif. While I was attached to the Ibis crowd, we all spoke
English, enjoyed the same kind of food and beer and could get
things done without the bullshit to which we were subjected in
Bosnia.

Without more ado, I signed on the dotted line and was flown
to Freetown in one of the Boeings the next morning. There were

South African Air Force Alouette helicopter gunship hovering over defences at a military base adjacent to the Angolan frontier. The photo at left shows air force engineers servicing a Puma chopper at an improvised bush base.
Both photos author's collection

Left: Dead and dying insurgents brought back to base in South West Africa aboard a Puma helicopter. *Author's collection*

Center: The Soviet SAM-6 ('Gainful' in NATO parlance) was one of the deadliest Soviet 'command guidance' missiles in the war and accounted for several hits. Having been 'blooded' in the Middle East and South East Asia, its most telling advantage was that it was mobile, could be fired at a range of almost 35 kilometres and achieve altitudes of 50,000 ft. *Source: Pierre Victor*

Bottom: Soviet anti-aircraft missiles such as this sophisticated SAM-8 which was captured on the battlefield by South African forces were a regular threat to SAAF planes providing ground support during combat operations inside Angola. *Source: Pierre Victor*

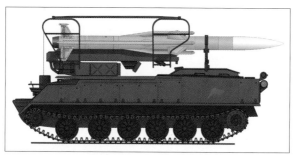

Above: Sukhoi Su-27. Because of its racially-dominated apartheid policies, the South Africans had no answer to sophisticated jet fighter/bombers such as this Sukhoi Su-27 which Moscow sold to the Angolans but which were flown either by Eastern Bloc pilots or by Cubans. *Source: Pierre Victor*

Below: South African Air Force Impala jet fighter/trainer of the type to which Neall Ellis converted during training. These planes played a useful ground-support role during the war. *Photo: courtesy of the late Herman Potgieter*

Left: Some of the munitions captured by the 32 Battalion strike force during Operation Super (see Chapter 4). Among items taken were large numbers of Soviet TM-57 anti-tank mines as well as batches of SAM-7 (Strela) supersonic hand-held anti-aircraft missiles, three of which were fired at Nellis' helicopter.
Author's collection

Neall Ellis prior to take-off on Operation Super, which he controlled from the air.
Author's collection

Above: South African Air Force Puma helicopter about to touch down in barren country adjacent to the Angolan border.
Author's collection

Right: Troops attached to Koevoet—the police counter-terrorism unit—prepare their weapons prior to an operation in Ovamboland.
Author's collection

Above: South African Air Force Puma and Alouette helicopters at a temporary base inside Angola.
Author's collection

Left: Combat casualty brought back to base out of Angola by chopper.
Author's collection

Above: A well-shorn Neall Ellis and his Mi-24 'office' at Cockerill Barracks, Freetown, Sierra Leone. *Photo: Neall Ellis*

Below: The cause of the guerrilla struggle in Sierra Leone was overwhelming government corruption and nepotism, but diamonds ended up playing a seminal role in the struggle. Open air diamondiferous diggings such as these were to be found just about everywhere we flew operationally. With the first rains, the holes would be filled with water. *Photo: Neall Ellis*

Members of the Ethiopian technical team—sometimes with good Russian support—kept at least one of the gunships in the air most of the time. Repairs were done piecemeal and—in spite of tropical conditions—in the open. *Both photos: Neall Ellis*

Above: Neall Ellis' Mi-24 helicopter gunship on the helipad at Freetown's Aberdeen military base preparing for take-off during counter-insurgency operations. *Author's collection*

Below: Nellis with Hind crew members and ground staff at military headquarters, Freetown. *Author's collection*

Left: Nellis served for a time with the South African mercenary group Executive Outcomes: one of the EO troops with grenade launcher mounted on a vehicle in Freetown. *Author's collection*

Below: Chopper pilot's eye view of Freetown, one of the largest cities in the region. *Author's collection*

Above: Air-to-ground rockets being loaded onto pods attached to Mi-24 winglets at the Freetown helipad. *Author's collection*
Below: While Nellis' gunship dominated Sierra Leone air space, Executive Outcomes troops cleared rebels from their positions throughout much of the country. Sierra Leone was an extremely difficult country in which to fight a war. *Author's collection*

Left: Wounded Sierra Leone soldiers ferried back to Freetown in Nellis' Mi-24.
Author's collection

Below: View from one of the Hind's port-side windows while on operations in Sierra Leone. One of the chopper's two rocket pods can be seen, below left.
Author's collection

Right: British forces enter a suspect village in Sierra Leone.
Author's collection

Below: Author Al Venter flew combat missions in Sierra Leone while spending time with mercenary forces in Sierra Leone, gathering material for Britain's Jane's Information Group. He is seen here, prior to take-off, in the gunner's seat on board the only serviceable Mi-24 helicopter gunship in Sierra Leone at the time.
Photo: Neall Ellis

Above: Civilians massacred, raped, killed and disfigured by RUF rebel cadres, one of many senseless killings that took place during the war. *Photo: Cobus Claassens*

Below: Neall Ellis' Soviet-built Mi-24 being prepared for an operational flight at Cockerill Barracks. Conditions were primitive, with one of the Hinds often having to provide parts for the other to maintain a strike capability. *Photo: Neall Ellis*

Top: In January 2004, Nellis had to teach himself to fly this Westland Sikorsky Commando MkIIC originally donated to Sierra Leone by the Emir of Qatar to President Kabbah for advice given on a border dispute with one of the Qatar neighbours. It is seen here taking off from Freetown docks.
Photo: Neall Ellis

Center photos: One of Sierra Leone's Mi-24s flown by former SAAF pilot Cassie Nel going up in flames after it had crashed. One of its engines exploded: pieces of shattered turbine blades went through the hot turbine section and caused the good engine also to burn. Nel was able to auto-rotate and carry out an emergency landing, but a female British soldier in the monitoring force died when a shattered turbine blade passed through the cabin roof and entered her cranium. Afterwards, all that was left of the once-proud Russian Mi-24 helicopter were these charred ashes.
Photos: Cassie Nel

Bottom: Nellis' favourite 'workhorse' on the helipad at Cockerill, on the outskirts of Freetown.
Author's collection

One of four Royal Air Force Chinook HC2 helicopters deployed to West Africa at the start of Operation Palliser early 2000 under command of then Brigadier (today General) Sir David Richards. This official picture shows the chopper dispensing anti-rocket flares during an operation in thick jungle in the interior of the country. *Photo: Courtesy of the Boeing Corporation*

more revelations after we arrived at Lungi. We were billeted in one of the better Freetown suburbs—not that it made much difference, because the city had already been thoroughly trashed by the rebels—and stayed in what had once been an executive villa. It had high ceilings, tiled floors and walls that were concrete and all of 18 inches thick, which would have been comforting had there been anybody hurling rockets or mortars at us. Also, our doors were great hulks of steel and wood and were bulletproof. In the end though, while living in Freetown we never actually became targets, not then, anyway.

There were almost 20 of us living at the house and, as I was to discover, this little entourage was one great big, happy family, with a minor army of servants, cooks, cleaners, gardeners and others. They would arrive at dawn each morning, including Sundays, to attend to our needs.

The aircraft engineers in charge of keeping the helicopters operational were all American-trained Ethiopians, so they knew the business. They'd been recruited in Addis Ababa by one of Ibis' managers, Paddy Mackay, who kept a beady eye on everybody in his fiefdom. An original, pint-high, crazy Irishman, who spoke with a thick brogue, his saving grace was that he was a pilot himself and he would tell people that he lived for his flying and that the Cessna was his 'babe'.

The rest of the air crews were mainly South African, but there were some British and New Zealand nationals. One of the New Zealanders would sit on the old colonial veranda, arms outstretched, and toast the sunset with the comment: 'God, I do love Africa!'

Those early days, just after EO had first arrived in Sierra Leone, were difficult. In initial discussions with the mercenary group, Chairman Valentine Strasser's government promised the South African mercenaries everything they asked for, but, as it transpired, almost nothing was forthcoming. Consequently, to make things work, EO had to improvise and it did so very effectively. The purchase of the two Boeings was all part of said improvisation.

EO had its own ideas about what it had to do once it got to Freetown because hostilities were escalating at an alarming rate. Led by Foday

Sankoh, a former Sierra Leonean Army NCO (he'd been trained in signals by the colonial army), the Revolutionary United Front (RUF) wasn't so much an effective military force as one able to strike terror into the hearts of the populace.

The situation became so bad before the South Africans arrived that if the word went out that the RUF was heading somewhere, everybody there would grab their things and try to flee. Those who did not get away often had their arms or legs chopped off with machetes. Ordinary people suffered shocking privations at the hands of groups of pubescents who appeared to take great delight in savagery. Some of the innocents had their eyes gouged out and this author was shown a little girl of 18 months at the Murraytown Amputee Centre in a Freetown suburb who had had one of her arms sliced off in what was termed 'a show of force' by the rebel commander responsible for the atrocity.

Stories that emerged after EO arrived were macabre, sometimes horribly so. Others were too gut-wrenching to repeat. However, one deserves to go on record. A group of juvenile RUF rebels, having slit open the stomachs of two pregnant women in a remote bush village, made the victims boil the foetuses and eat them. They were told that if they did not, they would be killed. They were murdered anyway.

An EO patrol came upon this horrible spectre shortly afterwards and they were appalled. Totally incensed at this barbarism, for that is what it was, the squad set off on its own and went looking for the perpetrators. They tracked them down a short while later as they were taking a break at a stream and killed every last one of them.

Under the auspices of their British contacts, some senior EO executives had already visited Sierra Leone and met the youthful Chairman Strasser who had originally come to power at the age of 26. He was the youngest head of state in the world at the time. Former British SAS operator, Tony Buckingham, who had originally put together EO's contract in Angola, had been looking for other opportunities and took it upon himself to introduce Strasser to EO's directors. Meanwhile, he and his friends provided assessments of their own, based on reports gleaned from contacts in British Intelligence and elsewhere.

The situation, EO was told prior to their involvement, was critical. The organization would have to move quickly to have any hope of countering rebel advances. They went ahead anyway because promises of excellent returns, which included diamond mining concessions, were good.

Meanwhile, back in South Africa, Eeben Barlow, chief executive of EO, and his directors put together a team and in no time at all produced a working blueprint for the operation. This was rushed to London and Freetown just in time, as already the first elements of an RUF advance guard were on the outskirts of the capital.

Until EO arrived, nobody had a complete picture of what was going on in the interior of Sierra Leone. The South Africans had to assess the situation for themselves and this they could only do after having been active for a while because none of the men brought in by EO had been further than Freetown's city limits. Part of the problem lay with the already desperate Valentine Strasser, who was hardly likely to level with the newcomers about what was really going on as he wouldn't have wanted to frighten them off. However, he was not aware of what the South Africans were made of: almost all EO personnel sent north to quell the rebel insurrection in Angola and Sierra Leone had served time in their country's Special Forces.[1]

Fred Marafono, an illustrious, larger-than-life, former British SAS operative who had been living in Freetown had offered his services to the mercenary force around the time they delivered their blueprint for action. Married to a local girl, he was an ideal choice because he had good local knowledge and the kind of West African connections the company desired. Without prevarication, EO took him up on his offer after the company financial director, Michael Grunberg, had checked his background.

Marafono was not only familiar with what was going on in his adopted country, he'd been living on the periphery of some of the earlier fighting. At one stage, he'd recruited a group of his military pals and struck out deep into the interior to bring his in-laws to safety. In the process, he'd killed a number of rebels. From then on, the RUF were wary of this seasoned veteran and for very good reason. Before Foday Sankoh's disciples were beaten, he killed scores of them.

What he told EO about the rebel force was sobering. The situation had all the ingredients of a long-term guerrilla struggle, he declared. Being ex-Special Forces himself, and having been faced with this kind of insurrection for a good part of his professional career, it was agreed that if anybody knew what was going on, he did. As a result, EO director Lafras

Luitingh immediately formed two combat groups—a Mobile Group and a Fire force Group. Instructions were passed to his field commanders to prepare for action.

Heading EO's mission in Freetown was Bert Sachse, a former Rhodesian SAS and Selous Scouts veteran who, until approached by EO to run the Sierra Leone mission, was a serving officer with the Recces. As he says today, 'I didn't even think about it. I'd made colonel and when the offer came, I wasted no time and took six weeks leave from the army'. A couple of days later, Sachse was heading for the west coast of Africa. He returned to South Africa after that brief session to resign his commission in the SADF and immediately went back to Freetown to take command of all mercenary operations in Sierra Leone.

Sachse was an obvious choice as field commander, not only because he was an experienced bush warrior, but also because he'd seen a good deal of fighting in his day. As a senior operations officer in Angola during the Border War period, he'd crossed swords with Soviet- and Cuban-backed battle groups numerous times and invariably came out on top, although in his last encounter with Castro's forces in the Cuando region, a shell fired by a T-54/55 tank exploded in a tree above his IFV and he took a hefty chunk of shrapnel in his back. He conceded years later that he was lucky to be alive.

For all that, Bert Sachse had always been the thinking man's soldier. His vision was never clouded by immediate demands and his views came across as clear and dispassionate. He had the ability to view conditions from every perspective, blemishes and all, and if he gave an order he expected it to be expedited immediately.

By the time Neall Ellis arrived in the country, EO forces had driven the rebels back into the interior and had also managed to retake the diamond fields at Kono, which EO then used as their main base in the interior.

> I started my flying along the west coast of Africa in one of the EO Mi-8s with Mark von Zorgenvrei, an oversized, very jovial colleague who had served with me in the South African Air Force. Initially, while Mark put me through the conversion, I served as his co-pilot, but a few days later I took over as flight commander,

in part, because I was already familiar with these machines.

Meanwhile, the war in Angola had been all but won so large numbers of EO troops were surplus to requirements. Most of these men were transferred northwards to Freetown at short notice, which meant that the majority of the time we were deploying those troops out into the interior.

My initial contract was worked on the basis of four weeks in and two weeks out, all of it on full pay. This was made easy by the Boeing's bi-weekly visits. The terms were different from those of most private military or security companies, where the money stops when you're on leave.

EO had suddenly started picking up problems from the Sierra Leonean government and the word was out that EO's Sierra Leone contract was coming unstuck. 'The company hadn't been paid for months and, as with this sort of thing, you can only carry your principles for so long', he commented.

'By March 1996, our pilot strength had been cut from an initial nine to four. With one of the aviators on leave at any one time, that didn't leave us with a full crew each time we were called out', commented Nellis. He explained that some of the small-scale stuff like reconnaissance and pin-pointing the positions of enemy camps was left to the Cessna 337 fixed wing, which he also started flying when time allowed. He would go up after dark with some of his people in the back wearing NVGs and search for enemy camp sites, which would often be found because of their fires. Other times there would be a prominent glimmering in the jungle where something was going on below the triple canopy, all of which the aviators would pinpoint with their GPS.

The following morning we'd load up a pair of choppers with a fighting group, together with mortars and bombs, and take them into a landing zone near to where we had reconnoitred the previous night; then we'd take off again and watch the action from above. If the guys on the ground needed us to lay down any covering fire, the side gunners would oblige. When it was all over, we'd count the dead, load up everybody again, return to base and head off to Paddy's for a couple of beers, or more. It was all fairly mundane, but at least we were achieving results.

Nellis' helicopters were based at Cockerill Barracks on the eastern fringes of Freetown, an ideal position, he reckoned, because there was a huge swamp around three sides of it. However, although this headquarters was arguably the most important military base in the country, the only people who observed any kind of martial routine were the South Africans based there.

Each morning at about eight, after all the EO personnel had mustered for the day, Sierra Leone's military forces would be lounging around sipping their Pega-Packs of locally brewed gin and getting doped-up. There was usually quite a lot of drugs around as well. It was hardly a satisfactory situation because you couldn't miss the acrid smell of ganja that hung over the camp as if somebody had aerial sprayed the base.

Obviously, we weren't happy. We were sharing the same space and would sometimes feel vulnerable in front of these hyped-up troops, as we could never be sure if they were going to pull a weapon and start shooting. That meant that most of us avoided moving around Cockerill earlier in the day if we could help it.

We also had a disparate bunch of Russians to contend with. Hired to fly the country's lone Mi-24 gunship, they were perpetually drunk. I recall that one of their ground crew members, who seemed to act like a political commissar from Soviet times, was constantly arguing and full of hooch. It eventually became a fairly serious problem both for us and the government.

Looking back to when they arrived in Sierra Leone in 1995, one of the first tasks facing the South Africans had been to train the Sierra Leonean troops who were detached to work with them. They were an unruly, unprofessional lot, but were rated by their officers, most of whom weren't much better, as 'the best of our best'.

Sierra Leonean troops at the base were very cautious at first as they were wary of these people from 'down south'. While the civilian population was ecstatic about the new arrivals, the soldiers of the Republic of Sierra Leone Military Forces (RSLMF) weren't so sure. It took the tough South African veterans about a day to quash any doubts about their ability. Sachse commented:

> The guys who came from Angola were more than useful. They not only looked fit and strong, nobody who had anything to do with them could dispute that this was one capable bunch of fighters: you could see it in their mién and by the way they handled their weapons.

Things took a turn for the better when their hosts discovered that the men had been fighting Savimbi for a year. Moreover, it had become clear to the South Africans that Foday Sankoh's men were not in the same league as many of UNITA's seasoned guerrillas who, when really pressed, could remain on the trot for a day or more at a stretch. 'We should know. It was our guys who'd originally trained Savimbi's special units', Sachse declared.

In the original agreement with EO, the Sierra Leonean Government had promised that there would be vehicles at EO's disposal at Cockerill. However, these did not materialise. Undeterred, Sachse commandeered a handful of Land Rovers. Among them were four that had been shipped out of the UK for use by a mining subsidiary linked to EO. He also 'acquired' a couple of heavier trucks from the Sierra Leonean armed forces and some of the men did what was needed to make them ready for ops. Others were sent to scout around town for spare parts. More vehicles were expected, he explained, but since they were coming by sea, it would be a month or more before they got there.

Sachse went on:

> What they did have was a pair of not-so-new Soviet BMP-2 infantry fighting vehicles that were a part of the original army inventory. There were two more guarding Valentine's residence and we couldn't touch them. Like everything else, all those machines had done a lot of time without maintenance . . . the tracks on one were pretty worn, while the other 'was sort of OK', although neither of

the turrets would turn. Also, the guns looked like they'd never been cleaned and their electrics were totally defunct.

That meant that if EO intended using these IFVs operationally, almost everything on board would have to be manually controlled, which would include physically cranking the turret to bring it to bear. Jos Grobelaar, a tough EO veteran and former Koevoet combatant who liked to double as a technician, got to work and sorted out some of the problems. In the end, quite a few of the others helped because they had all worked with BMPs in Angola and had mastered the weapon's idiosyncrasies. Also, they'd quickly learnt to keep them mobile, sometimes while the fighting raged all round them.

One of Colonel Sachse's deputies was another old Angolan hand, Colonel Duncan Rykaart, who had been with the company almost since its inception. One of his first jobs was to create an effective intelligence unit together with an operations room, complete with operatives in the field. Using his vast experience of this kind of combat, gained while serving in the South African military, he told senior Sierra Leonean Army officers, with whom he was in daily contact, that they needed to train and integrate interpreters and analysts. It was an essential part of the war, he explained, although he shouldn't have had any need to. It took him no time at all to appreciate that hardly any of the indigenous senior staff with whom he was dealing had the vaguest idea what he was talking about because, for most, it was something they had never seen done before. Nonetheless, he kept at it and an 'Int' network gradually started to take shape.

Conditions at Cockerill Barracks, where most of the 80-strong EO contingent lived, were appalling. Accommodation that had been promised never materialized. On the contrary, living conditions, if anything, deteriorated: the place was inundated by rats because the men also ate their food there; there was also no air conditioning, which, because of mosquitoes, made sleep difficult; and since the men had no place to secure their personal belongings, pilfering became a problem.

There was a lot more that wasn't up to scratch. A single tap serviced the entire garrison, together with two modest-sized bathrooms: all for 80 men. Rations weren't much better. The bulk consisted of homemade parcels that had been flown out from South Africa, a lot of it commercial packs of sugar, coffee and other perishables that had been bought in supermarkets and bundled into manageable 'kits' by wives. The most notable problem in Freetown was its humidity, which can be both clinging and fetid, and which meant that everything quickly deteriorated because it was packed in paper bags. Within a week, for instance, a half-pound of coffee became a lump of brown rock. The same happened to sugar.

According to Nellis, much of the time he spent with EO in Sierra Leone was occupied with putting local troops through their paces at a training barracks outside Freetown. It was his job to teach them helicopter trooping drills.

> One day, we had a bunch of them arrive, almost all with their heads shaven and unceremoniously decorated by little plaster adhesive dressings, like those used for a cut finger. It was unusual, so we asked the EO sergeant major what it was about and he laughed. He called them 'battle wounds', and explained that that when the trainee troops didn't listen to orders, they were given a sharp crack across the head. 'Which is why we carry these sticks', he said, pointing to bulky shillelagh tucked under his arm. 'We can see very quickly who's performing well and who is not' he jocularly explained.

As it turned out, the EO training programme was tough. It was also uncompromising. However, in the end the South Africans turned out a small group of competent, trustworthy and reliable soldiers. Two of them served as side gunners on board Nellis' Mi-17 and both proved to be outstanding fighters. Those trainees who could not, or would not shape up, were sent back to their original units.

In spite of problems with the government, which were dealt with as they arose, usually with a measure of compromise and adaptation, things generally seemed to work themselves out in the customary African way and the offensive against the RUF proceeded steadily. The rebels, meanwhile, were made very aware that they were facing some extremely determined

opposition from small EO units who, with gunship back-up, ranged well
into the interior.

Very early on in the campaign, EO commanders had demonstrated a
ruthless brutality in the implementation of their pacifying programme.
Moreover, they only took prisoners if they believed they might be useful.
Neall Ellis explained:

> We began an extensive offensive against the RUF in September
> 1996, downriver from Kenema, where we'd discovered they'd
> established their first headquarters in that region. For a while we'd
> experimented with additional firepower on all the aircraft, and
> finally fitted a 12.7mm heavy machine gun into the side door of
> the Hip. It was the first time we'd done so on an Mi-8, and it
> worked very well because we flew with the doors off anyway and
> were able to give close air support to our ground units using HE
> instead of ball ammunition.

As Nellis was to recall, driving the rebels into the interior after EO's
first series of battles in Sierra Leone had a significant effect not only on
Freetown, but on much of the rest of the country. As the word spread, the
people felt that they could breathe again. Also, it stymied Sankoh's hopes
of occupying the capital, although it was not the last time that he would
try his luck.

Meanwhile, the South Africans were hailed as heroes wherever they
went in the city. Never mind that they had come from a country steeped
in racial discrimination, they had put their lives on the line in an African
state and saved the day for everybody. The job was never easy and some of
the men were killed while fulfilling their obligations, but they did what
they had been paid to do and felt good.

However, the war was far from over. Sankoh's RUF still had a sizeable
force in the hills around the capital and one group after another was dealt
with in the weeks that followed EO's success. Also, for the first time, usable
intelligence was coming in which eased things considerably for the gunships.

On a personal level, Nellis recalls, it was impossible not to get involved
in the plight of the people of Sierra Leone. One of the victims was a lovely

young woman: 'She'd been crowned Miss Sierra Leone a short while before and had a can of paraffin thrown over her by her boyfriend because he was jealous of all the attention she was getting. The poor soul was terribly burned. I tried to raise funds to bring her back to South Africa for treatment, but that was in vain. She died soon afterwards.' The tragedy affected Nellis so deeply that once the fighting in Sierra Leone had subsided, one of his dreams was to establish a burns care unit there.

Back in South Africa not long afterwards, Nellis once more found himself without work. One of his EO associates from East London offered him a job as manager of a Freetown supermarket, but Nellis felt that the $1,000 a month that came with the deal simply wasn't worth it. 'Just as well I refused', he recalls. 'Had I been in Sierra Leone, he would probably have asked me to fly the planeload of marijuana he'd organised to England. He flew it himself in the end. However, the Brits were onto him and when the aircraft landed somewhere in Cornwall, the cops were waiting. He ended up in prison for several years.'

CHAPTER TEN

INTO THE CONGO'S CAULDRON

Neall Ellis was introduced to Pretoria businessman-cum-lawyer-cum-intelligence agent Harold Muller when Sakkie van Zyl, a former security policeman and Koevoet Special forces operator, contacted him at his home in the Cape in November, 1996.

It was the same old story as before: they wanted to see me, like yesterday. I was in my garden when Van Zyl called and asked whether I'd drop everything and fly to Johannesburg that same day. They had something interesting on offer, he confided, and it was all going on in the Congo of old, then calling itself the Republic of Zaire. Van Zyl added that this new development wasn't only an interesting proposition, but it had enormous potential and could ultimately be worth a tidy fortune to them all.

Naturally, I acquiesced, got myself ready and rushed to the airport. Once on the ground at Jan Smuts, Van Zyl and Harold Muller were there to greet me. I met Mauritz Le Roux, the third member of the team, the following day and, frankly, I wasn't impressed. He came across as a little naïve. However, as I discovered, he was anything but. He'd formerly served as an engineer with 32 Battalion and was a founder member of the South African mercenary group Executive Outcomes.

Once he started talking about the project, I realized there was more to him than I'd originally thought. He went on to brief me about how he had been approached by the Zaire Embassy to form a unit to assist Mobutu defeat the rebel advance.

Thus was Stability Control Agencies (Stabilco) formed, with Muller and Le Roux as the directors, and registered in the Isle of Man. The company did not survive the Congolese debacle and Le Roux eventually went on to create Safenet (later, OSSI-Safenet) one of the largest private security companies in Iraq. Before moving on to do similar work in Afghanistan, it had more than 4,000 people in its employ.

Once our little team had gathered in Pretoria, the party went into a huddle and everybody was briefed on what was going on in Central Africa. Basically, President Mobutu Sese Seko's Zaire Republic was involved in a major civil war that had been festering for years. There was nothing new about this because, ever since independence in the 1960s, the country had been teetering on the verge of anarchy. There had been a continual spate of hostilities, if not amongst its own people then with its overly belligerent neighbours. As Chris Munnion of London's *Daily Telegraph* once suggested: 'somebody was always getting killed in the old Congo, sometimes by the hundreds and occasionally by the thousands, and nobody cared a whit.'

One wag described it as Africa's first real 'non-event' even though two or three million Congolese war victims died of famine or disease or were slaughtered during this period. The problem in late 1996 was that Mobutu was about to be toppled and the country was in the process of fragmenting. Enter Muller and Le Roux, who were going to 'save' it. Nellis comments:

I knew a bit about Africa by then, and I couldn't help voicing a little scepticism: I'd heard this 'last gasp' kind of thing before and in modern-day Africa, it has never really worked. In the end I wasn't wrong, but there was money on the table and it was good, so I asked them to count me in.

I was asked to find another pilot and hire a couple of flight engineers: we would be flying choppers, they reckoned. I called my pal Ryan Hogan in Durban, who had served with me in the

SAAF, and he immediately agreed. Between us, we settled on Grant Williams and Phil Scott as our engineers and, once approached, they threw their hats into the ring. Like me, they all had to get themselves to Johannesburg in a hurry.

So we came together the following morning, got ourselves kitted out with tropical gear, and a couple of extras we thought we would need, and headed out to Lanseria Airport where Le Roux had leased a Lear jet to take us north. There were problems about getting clearances to fly to Zaire, so we slept on the floor of the offices of the people from whom we had leased the plane.

After filing a flight plan to Kinshasa via Malawi, the six-man team quietly slipped away early the following morning. It was a pretty tight fit in the Lear with all their stuff, but somehow they managed. Van Zyl had work to do in South Africa, so he didn't go along. Nellis carries on:

At Ndjili Airport, the country's biggest international airport on the outskirts of the capital, we were met by the representatives of the ranking Zairean security minister, all senior people and very well dressed with polished ostrich skin leather shoes and expensive suits. I remember thinking that if the country was on the verge of revolt, these people certainly weren't showing it.

Instead of leading us through normal immigration and customs channels, which at Ndjili can be quite severe, they took our passports, had them stamped and hustled us, and our baggage, past the guards to a pair of luxury four-wheel-drive vehicles. I thought it was all great until we were unceremoniously dumped at what was probably one of Kinshasa's dingiest two-star hotels. It was inappropriately called the Christmas Hotel, which was a misnomer because there was nothing white or festive about the place. Instead, it was dark and dingy with sombre wooden panelling in the lobby which matched its dark linen bedding and its equally depressing restaurant. At least the concierge was happy to see us because most of his business was based on transients like us who had hopes of doing business with the government.

Even the menu was limited, although we did have several

options. There was steak and chips (fries), chicken and chips, fish and chips, vegetables and chips and a meat that was as tough as leather and, being quite small, I felt might have once been something feline (that dish also came with chips). One of the group thought that it was not impossible that one of the embassies in Zaire was missing its cat. To add further insult to all the gore, all the dishes were covered in grease.

Meanwhile, Le Roux and Muller, with a considerable effort, were able to get to see General Kpama Baramoto, Mobutu's security chief who was in command of the Civil Guard. One of the most feared men of the regime, he would be responsible for dealing with what we had to offer. The meeting over, they went on to meet a host of other government officials including General Nzimbi, who headed the Presidential Guard, and General Baruti, an exuberant man who was in charge of the Zairean Air Force. Finally, they were able to put forward something of a plan, which relied on Ryan, me and the engineers being able to make enough of the remaining Congolese Air Force aircraft airworthy to create a helicopter strike force.

We reasoned that the best tactic would be to approach Mobutu with the offer of a couple of squadrons of gunships, with our chaps in charge of course. With such a force, we could argue pretty persuasively that the revolutionary advance could be stopped. Also, we had history on our side because it had been done before, very recently in Angola and subsequently in Sierra Leone. Both times, EO was involved.

However, Stabilco's founder still had to persuade the dictator's henchmen that the proposals were realistic and attainable and could be implemented with a modicum of effort and outlay. That was the difficult part because, although there was a lot of money around, the people in government weren't too eager to part with any of it, even though it was obvious that we offered them salvation. We needed to act quickly because the enemy was on the last stretch of road leading to Kinshasa, the final objective and, as we were to learn soon enough, Mobutu's much-depleted army wasn't doing much to stop them. One of the reasons for their inaction was that most of the soldiers hadn't been paid for months—their officers had simply pocketed all the money.

What was more unsettling, thought Nellis at the time, was that some of Mobutu's senior men, including a handful of generals, sensing the inevitable, had already defected to the revolutionaries. This hugely diverse bunch of Congolese, Rwandan and Burundi nationals were better known by their initials, AFDL, than by their proper name, *Alliance des Forces Démocratiques pour la Libération du Congo-Zaïre*.

Meanwhile, General Baramoto arranged for the South Africans to be taken to several air force bases around Kinshasa and they were perturbed at what they found. It didn't take them long to appreciate that although Mobutu remained the Congo's head of state, in reality a hopeless inter-regnum prevailed. Instability, and the uneasy lassitude that resulted, had pervaded the entire community in a country already stultified by corruption. However, even with all its problems, Zaire still seemed to attract just about every charlatan known to Interpol, as well as many others that weren't.

Among those who arrived were some gritty, fast-talking arms dealers from both sides of what had once been the Iron Curtain, as well as numerous dubious characters from France, Israel, Yugoslavia, South Africa and elsewhere. Also poking about in the embers were all manner of 'financiers' and hopeful mercenary groups. It was truly a congregation of opportunists, each one of them believing that he could cut a deal. They had good reason for this belief. Despite the war, there was still a lot of good money about. The mines around Mbuji-Mayi in Kasai Province never stopped churning out diamonds, with more being smuggled into Zaire by UNITA's rebels from Angola and, of course, there was widespread corruption. Often when there was a shortage of real money, gemstones would replace greenbacks. Two or three tiers down the economic ladder were a myriad of smaller operators, among them Neall Ellis and his group of freebooters.

A couple of days after they arrived, Le Roux and Muller were ushered into Baramoto's Kinshasa residence. Le Roux's initial presentation in Baramoto's plush offices was both forceful and disarmingly simple. Apart from the heli-force, he told the general, he and his associates could muster about

500 ground troops within weeks. These would mostly be former EO veterans with experience in conventional as well as counter-insurgency operations. He stressed that many had been blooded in Angola.

Le Roux also told the general that he had any number of helicopter pilots on call, all professionals who were immediately available for deployment on the Zaire Air Force gunships that would be used to stunt the Kabila offensive. That done, he suggested that his people would set about training indigenous aviators so that the next time Zaire was faced with an emergency, foreigners wouldn't have to be hired.

Having persuaded General Baramoto that Stabilco's contribution might be the cure-all that he sought for the country's ills, the South Africans were taken to the office of another close military associate of the president, Special Forces commander General Ngbale Nzimbi. After that it was the turn of the Minister of Defence, Admiral Mudima Mavua.[1]

One of Nellis' first jobs on arriving in Kinshasa was to try and assess the situation with regard to military aircraft assets. He needed to find out whether Mobutu actually had any aircraft that could fly and whether there was any kind of strike capability that could be used against Kabila's rebels. It was a hard task as everything was cloaked in secrecy. However, despite this, it didn't take Neall long to discover that there were almost no airworthy helicopters. The machines had been bought, but most of them were in the crates in which they'd arrived and hadn't even been unpacked. Many critical elements, such as electronics or something applicable to rotor operation, would be missing. Often, they would have been sold so that the requisite rake-off could be passed on to the responsible minister or general after the order had been placed. Occasionally, one of the Mi-24s that could still lift-off would go out on a sortie, but ammunition and fuel were limited. In a tight spot, the Hinds could be used for ferrying troops, but that was only a stopgap measure.

As Neall recalls, they'd insisted on seeing all of the country's aviation assets, and they were eventually taken to a local air force base where they found a C-130 transport plane, minus three of its engines. Otherwise, it was in excellent shape, having been refurbished by the Atlas Aircraft Corporation in Johannesburg the year before, at a cost of millions. It was only discovered years later that General Baruti, the man responsible for the planes, had sold the engines to a local trader, together with an export permit to get them out of the country.

Also at the base was a Canadian-built Caribou showing serious signs of wear and the lack of adequate service. There were also 20 Sia-Marchetti 260s, the majority in reasonable shape but not flyable. Although these prop-driven trainers were light, they could be fitted with machine guns and under-wing rocket-pods (very much as the Pilatus PC-7s had been fielded against UNITA forces in Angola). These planes could then be deployed against Kabila's rebel force as ground-attack aircraft and with good tactical direction, could cause a lot of damage.

Nellis commented about the obvious lack of care and attention given to all these aviation assets. He told the generals that in Zaire's tropical climate, more sophisticated equipment had to be looked after or it would deteriorate very quickly, and that included aircraft. Many of the trainers had been abandoned in the rain, their cockpit hatches left open. There was a Puma helicopter, also inoperable because it had been stripped of some of its parts, which had been sold.

'In fact,' Neall recalls, 'there was an enormous amount of stuff, but nothing that would actually work properly, never mind that we might be able to use it if we were to go to war. . . .' It was Baruti's view, he recalls, that if they could get somebody to repair these aircraft and somehow buy weapons for the Sia-Marchettis, all would be well.

Others must have thought along similar lines before, probably several times, I told myself . . . so why hadn't anybody done something about it? More to the point, these generals were not short of the money needed to do the necessary as there wasn't one among them who was not a multi-millionaire.

I came up with something of a solution and said that we could fit 20mm cannons onto the three Gazelle SA-342 choppers (which the Zaireans had originally stolen from Rwanda when that country imploded). The next day I walked into the armoury attached to the base and spotted five 20mm MG-151 cannons, the same guns the South African Air Force fitted to their Alouette gunships. All were ex-factory stock from Lyttleton Engineering outside Pretoria. Although a couple were badly rusted and beyond repair—they'd probably also been left in the rain—three were still in their original grease and had never been used. They were literally 'out of the box'.

I scratched around a bit more and even found some of their ammunition, but none of it looked reliable. They said they had some newer stuff, and I left it at that.

A few days later, Nellis and the rest of the group were flown in a Zaire Air Force turbo-prop Cessna to Kindu, a large town to the east of Kinshasa. It was regarded locally as a minor hop, but it still took four or five hours to get there, which was when Neall said he realised how big Zaire really was:

What amazed me was the extent of the forests that we flew over: they literally stretched from one horizon to another, almost without a break. For hours there was no evidence of habitation.

We landed at a fairly big airport at Kindu and were told that the rebels weren't far away. We were taken to the three choppers that were parked, untended and unguarded, looking pretty forlorn, in a field not far away. Our flight engineers looked the Gazelles over, found them in good nick and, under the circumstances, quite well maintained considering that we were standing way out in the bush.

Satisfied that they were operable, the South African pilots took each of them up in turn and came back pleased. The rest of the time in Kindu was spent quite pleasantly, Neall remembers:

We ended up spending the night in Kindu, lavishly entertained by the general in charge of the region, French champagne and all. For all that, we couldn't miss the poverty about us. The town itself was incredibly dilapidated—there were almost no private vehicles (nor any fuel for them, anyway) and certainly no electricity. Meanwhile, the military at the local base lived like proverbial regents of old. It was almost medieval.

While the South African mercenaries were all made very welcome by the officers and never felt any animosity, Nellis felt there was a distinct reluctance to provide any kind of information about the war, even though it was literally around the corner. They flew back to Kinshasa the next morning and reported that the Gazelles could be gunned up and sent into action almost immediately, and that Ryan and Nellis would fly them. 'But to do that, I stressed, the three choppers had to be brought through to Kinshasa from Kindu without any delay', said Neall. There was still a lot of work to do on the machines, including fitting firepower, he told air force General Baruti. However, the matter simply died a natural death, and Neall doubts whether those helicopters were ever flown again. They're probably still in Kindu, what's left of them.

In his personal dealings with the mercenaries, General Baramoto was both courteous and friendly. Socially, he was scrupulously correct. Nellis remembers him as a tall man with greyish hair and spectacles and, unlike many of his colleagues, not too heavy for his height. Also, he projected a confidence that reflected power. Whether in uniform, in traditional African dress or in a formal suit, he was always impeccably turned out. A non-smoker, he liked a good whisky, especially a good single malt, but he didn't overdo it, at least not in the presence of the South Africans.

Although he understood English, Baramoto confided to one of the South Africans that he felt he could express himself better in French. Consequently, there was usually an interpreter in attendance, although the man was more than a good linguist. He had large bulges under both arms and, judging from what the other generals used for protection, Nellis believed that they were possibly something from the Heckler and Koch range.

Baramoto's house was a single-storied villa in Kinshasa surrounded by high walls and bougainvillea. It wasn't as flamboyant as might have been expected, especially since Mauritz Le Roux, on first arriving there, had been shown a room piled almost to the ceiling with bundles of cash, mostly large-denomination U.S. dollar bills, although there were also piles of Sterling, French francs, Deutschmarks and Japanese yen. Some of the stacks of cash were metres tall.

Another distinctive feature, Nellis recalls, was a SAM-14 ground-to-air launcher, complete with a missile in the tube, propped up precariously against a wall in the entrance hall. It seemed to be a permanent fixture because nobody ever moved it and, as he mentioned to Le Roux, had it been accidentally detonated, it might have demolished the entire building. He recalls making a mental note that if there was one, it was likely that there would be more.

Furnishings at the Baramoto home were sumptuous and included several leather-covered lounge suites in the sitting room, set against some magnificent silk drapes. Although Nellis never met any of the general's wives, the pilot was introduced to two of his daughters: 'they were quite lovely girls . . . very well dressed in chic European clothing that seemed to be mostly designer', he remembers.

Baramoto's taste in cars was 'orthodox oligarch': the inevitable black Mercedes limo with tinted windows, of which there were several, together with a couple of top-of-the-range land cruisers.

There was always a crowd of soldiers and civilians hanging about the place including a contingent of guards who must have been as well kitted out and efficient as any in the country. Those troops were always present, resplendent in their smartly pressed camouflage uniforms. Most sported shiny AK-47s and there was always a clutch of RPGs nearby. There were also quite a few Toyota pick-ups, some with 12.7mm heavy machine guns mounted on the back, usually with somebody standing by in the driver's seat.

Nellis could see that these troops knew what was expected of them, and they kept a wary eye on everything going on in the vicinity, which included monitoring passing traffic. Some of these soldiers were South African trained. A couple actually recognized one of the former Recce commando officers who arrived with Le Roux one morning and the 'reunion' ended up being quite emotional, with big smiles all round, Baramoto included. This minister's ties with South Africa's apartheid leaders were once referred to by an American diplomat as 'all but intimate'.

Most meetings took place late, as if Baramoto and his generals were almost afraid of being seen in public with white people. At the same time, warned Nellis, while you were with the man, you couldn't help sensing that under the brittle crust of his amicability lay a magma of paranoia.

Once Neall Ellis and co. became better acquainted with the generals, they spent a lot of time chewing the fat at the home of General Likunia, the

Congolese Minister of Defence, or they would pop along to General
Mahele's place. It was similar to Baramoto's but seriously needed to be
painted. As Chief of the Armed Forces, Mahele preferred to do his enter-
taining in the garden, usually under an Oriental pagoda, left behind by
some forgotten colonial functionary, which seemed to have weathered well
in the tropics.

There would be endless talk about the best way to tackle Kabila and
his 'thugs'. Nellis would choose his moment and try to swing the conversation around to the subject of helicopters: after all, he would say, it was
his reason for being there. He very much wanted to create a chopper gunship wing so that he could prove his worth. With time, the issue became
more difficult to broach, if only because he had to keep going over the
same imponderables: the war; the lack of resistance on the part of government forces; the inability of the air force to make headway and so on. There
was a solution to it all, he would urge for the umpteenth time, 'there was
an immediate way of turning the war around!'

He would get everybody's attention for about 40 seconds. Brows would
furrow, the generals would stop what they were doing and, for a few
moments, they'd listen. However, Neall admits that the degree of interest
was usually directly proportionate to the amount of grog that had been
drunk as one of them would usually make some inane comment and everybody would laugh. With that, the party would go on as before, more drinks
would be called for and Kinshasa's deceptive fog of war would envelop
them all as they ignored the harsh reality of their situation.

The reality was that the military situation had become precarious in
the month or so that Nellis and his group had been in the country. At that
stage, already, Kinshasa was well within Kabila's sights. What's more, everybody in the city knew it.

One of Zaire's key problems was the army's pay hiatus, a situation
which nobody, least of all the generals with whom the South Africans
socialized, was prepared to remedy. They had money in abundance; in fact
any one of the generals could have paid the army's monthly salary bill a
hundred times over, but none of them was prepared to part with any of it.
Not that there was any great deal of cash involved. The average *Forces
Armées Zaïroises* (FAZ) soldier's basic wage was about $2 a month, in a
country where a pack of local cigarettes cost half that. With government

forces estimated at about 100,000 men, the sum required to keep them happy and loyal was modest compared to the millions that were being squandered by autocrats on the most absurd luxuries.

For instance, flowers for all of Mobutu's residences, which numbered about a dozen, large and small, were still being flown in daily from Europe, as was fresh dairy produce and container-loads of milk-fed veal, some of it from Japan. This was all in a country where the majority of the population had almost nothing.

It seems illogical that all this money would be spent on such excesses when it could have been used to fight successfully against the insurrection. 'Looking back, none of it makes sense', Nellis says today. 'The security, the longevity of all of these people was at risk, but nobody bothered to challenge the system, probably because they feared for their lives if they did so'. What seemed to matter most to the majority of the people in control was that their moveable assets had already been stashed abroad. At the time of his death, Mobutu was estimated to be worth somewhere between five and eight billion dollars.

A few days before Christmas, Le Roux suggested that everybody should head home for Christmas. Baramoto had gone silent and there were rumours that he had fallen out of favour with Mobutu. When they got back to Pretoria, Nellis and the others met a group of former Special Forces operators to plan the Zairean operation. Nellis comments:

> What we didn't know yet was that after we had put forward a figure of 500 troops and airmen needed for the rescue, it was first whittled down to 300 men and then to a miserable 30, which was crazy for a country four times the size of France. In the end, numbers didn't seem to matter anymore.

Roelf van Heerden, an old friend from the SADF and EO in Sierra Leone, was put forward as the man who should command Stabilco's ground forces. He had led a very successful campaign as a mercenary in Angola, his squad having cleared the area around the diamond city of Saurimo, in the east of the country.

A slender fellow with long, scraggy hair, a moustache and small

rimmed glasses, he hardly looked the archetypal bush fighter but he seemed
to fit the bill as far as Le Roux was concerned. Van Heerden and Nellis
were offered directorships in Stabilco. A week later, on New Year's Day
1997, they headed back to Kinshasa with Muller. The rest of the gang
followed a few days later to assist with planning. Muller had several
meetings with government officials and suddenly things looked good.

The figure that was put forward for the six-month contract plus the
equipment required was U.S. $90 million. This included all vehicles, light
and heavy weapons and both Mi-8 and Mi-24 helicopters. Included in the
deal would be strike jet aircraft and food and salaries for the 500 men the
directors believed would be necessary to make it all work.

The generals didn't argue, but insisted that the South Africans sort out
any equipment already in the country that might be of use. However, after
a quick look and dismal report-back, it was clear that it would be quicker
and easier to buy all the stuff new from overseas suppliers, but first they
needed money to be able to do that.

Then Captain Atembina suddenly appeared on the scene. Although it
was never clear what his job actually was, he eventually arranged a meeting
with General Mahele, who immediately came across as a more professional
soldier than the usual military opportunist the South Africans had dealt
with so far. Mahele was surprisingly candid in admitting that his people
were simply not up to the job and that he and his colleagues needed help.
He was also concerned about Stabilco's ability to put men on the ground
as soon as possible, but stressed that he would not be able to provide assistance with equipment. Nellis comments:

> This was clearly a problem. Our men, all 500 of them still waiting
> back home, were ready to roll but we needed the equipment to
> make things work. That, in turn, relied on the money that needed
> to be paid up front. We told him that buying military hardware
> wasn't something that happened overnight. Some of the stuff was
> 'on the shelf', but most of it was not. There were international
> laws and obligations in place to prevent the illegal sales of weapons
> to rogue nations which included the need for End User Certifi-
> cates. Also necessary were authorisations for the aircraft ferrying
> the arms to Zaire to overfly the countries en route. Getting over

these hurdles took time. The governments doing the selling had to satisfy themselves that the arms would not be passed on to another country. In a sense, it was bureaucracy gone mad, but these were things that had to be taken account of.

It was immediately clear to us all that things had become bogged down again. Moreover, it would take a massive effort to arrange it all, and that was before factoring in the extreme level of corruption that we would have to deal with. On top of that, Kabila and his rebel army were making significant progress in the east. Time, obviously, was of the essence.

General Mahele quickly tasked us to produce a plan, which he wanted to present to Mobutu a few days later. Meanwhile, we needed an office from which to work, so Captain Atembina introduced us to George Kiriakos, a Greek businessman in Kinshasa. George, the ultimate dealer, broker, entrepreneur and outrageous speculator, was one of those charming quasi-colonial characters you find all over Africa, even today. He allowed us access to his office where, he said, we could put the plan together. Obviously, nothing was free and he and Atembina wanted their cut from any deal that was ultimately brokered: 30 per cent of it, and that on top of the original figure! It was an enormous add-on, he agreed, but as he said, who cared, as long as the government was prepared to pay and Le Roux and the rest of us got our share. We couldn't argue with that kind of logic, so we let it roll.

George appeared to have financial interests in many corners of Africa. After dealing with him, we became aware that he was involved in the war in Angola. He had actually been dealing with the Angolan rebel movement UNITA, buying and selling coffee and timber from the eastern part of that country. Diamonds were clearly a part of it, but he couldn't be drawn on that issue. We decided soon enough that George Kiriakos was playing both sides and that we had to be circumspect about how much we told him. It was entirely possible that he had links with Kabila and his henchmen.

Because of the impasse that gradually took shape—the government was seriously dragging its feet—Harold and the rest of the group returned to South Africa, leaving me and Roelf to hang in there and hope that something would develop. We ran short of cash and, to cut a long story short, we went through difficult weeks when we sometimes didn't even have enough money to eat, never mind buy beer.

The food issue gradually developed into a major problem. Roelf and I eventually had to resort to buying a loaf of bread and a tin of pilchards each day simply to keep us alive. Because there was no money left over for transport, we walked wherever we needed to go, which wasn't easy because Kinshasa is a pretty big place. One day, while walking alone down one of the avenues, I was surrounded by a group of young thugs who demanded money. They pointed to my watch and it was clear they meant business.

I tried to reason with them, telling them that I was as broke as they were and that there was no way I was going to give them anything. They suddenly turned aggressive and started the usual strong-arm stuff, pushing and manhandling me. That was when I decided that the only way out was to show them that I wasn't the usual passive tourist, and I hauled out my only means of protection.

Normally, in these primitive countries I like to carry a knife, so out came my Spyderco, a pretty mean-looking blade shaped like the claw of an eagle. It was actually quite vicious. Frustrated as hell, I lunged at the leader and it was clear to everybody that I had serious intent. Obviously, I might have ended up in one of Zaire's notorious prisons had I actually stabbed the man, but all I could think then was 'fuck the consequences'. With that, this brave bunch of muggers fled. Nobody was robbed or stabbed that day, but I certainly felt a lot better for it afterwards. At least I'd managed to work off some of my frustrations.

Then, from nowhere, Captain Atembina pitched up at the dreaded Christmas Hotel and told us to get our things together. He loaded us into his vehicle and took us across town to the Intercontinental Hotel, where, with a flourish that you might have expected from somebody who is spending a lot of his own money, he checked us in at the government's expense. Night had suddenly become day.

The hotel was remarkable, the best in Central Africa. Moreover, we could eat and drink as much as we liked and didn't need to pay: we could sign for all of it. Our hotel room even had its own fridge, which was kept well stocked, and we had CNN on TV.

Roelf and I tended to keep a low profile, in part because the Belgian woman running the hotel with her Jordanian husband mentioned that there were Kabila supporters in residence. She wouldn't say who they were, except that there were quite a few of them. There were also three Frenchmen staying there, and they liked to make a nuisance of themselves by routinely getting drunk at the bar.

A man calling himself JJ Fuentes, or simply 'JJ' for short, claimed to be a French Air Force fighter pilot. He also said he had Special Forces training, which sounded bogus. Another man in his little francophone coterie was a rather big fellow who had served in the French Foreign Legion, or so he said, and the third, the quiet one, maintained that he had history with the French Army. In fact, it didn't take us very long to work out that this was another group of hopefuls trying to secure a contract for French mercenaries, probably under the auspices of the legendary Bob Denard.

We sent word back to Pretoria and told them that things were looking up, especially since we were now happily ensconced in five-star luxury and all the trappings that went with it. All the while, we were waiting for Captain Atembina to take us to visit General Mahele because, from what we gathered, it seemed that the elusive money was finally to be made available for a smaller contract for just over 300 men instead of the original 500. This was a bit of a blow because even 3,000 men wouldn't have been nearly adequate in a country of this size.

Towards the end of March the situation in the country became critical. The rebels had taken Kisangani and the Serb mercenary group, which was supposed to be holding the city, retreated to Gbadolite in the north. There were also political demonstrations in Kinshasa which turned violent.

Suddenly, it wasn't even safe to walk in the streets around the hotel, so accepting good advice, Nellis stopped heading out for his early morning jogs.

The demonstrations could be quite violent and were dealt with severely by the police, with the army also getting involved from time to time. Just about every day guns could be heard being fired, especially if there were demonstrators involved. The authorities were ruthless. They would fire live rounds and people who stood their ground and shouted abuse were shot dead. Nellis remembers:

> Sometimes these demonstrations would take place within sight of the Intercontinental and Roelf and I would take up grandstand positions on our balcony and watch running battles and, more often than not, see some of the demonstrators being felled. The rounds fired by the cops would sometimes pass quite close to where we were perched and we'd be reminded of the old 'tikking' sound as bullets flashed past. It was certainly a diversion from watching CNN.

Overall, the two men couldn't miss the fact that conditions in Kinshasa had become quite nasty. The government was crumbling and, as the saying goes, the rats were jumping ship, furiously so.

Many local people and expatriates had already left the country for Brazzaville across the Congo River and Nellis and Roelf would keep a check on the hotel guest list at reception as the numbers dwindled. They were aware too that it was almost impossible to get a seat on a plane leaving Kinshasa's Ndjili Airport. Nellis has distinct memories of that time:

> And then, when even the journalists started to leave and only the die-hard hacks remained, we had to accept that the end was not far off. On 1st June, we were told that rebel forces were only 200km from Kinshasa and, obviously, that late in the day the government wasn't going to be forthcoming with a contract that would end up costing more than $100 million. Roelf and I talked endlessly about it and there was no escaping the fact that it was almost time for us to leave as well.

We'd just started lunch at the hotel when Captain Atembina

called the next day and told me to get ready. The acting president of Zaire wanted to see me in person, he disclosed. The Congo Army captain was actually quite excited and he said that the portents looked good. I'd met General Likunya previously, while having discussions with the other generals on the prospect for the contract, and he seemed to be a reasonable man who had certainly shown himself in favour of hiring mercenaries to save his country.

When I eventually got to his office, he asked me to sit down and said that the government had decided to award us the contract immediately. Trying to maintain as dignified a pose as possible, I was elated. He didn't waste time with words, but immediately set about describing a situation that was not only bad but, in his own words, could be equated with 'a state of emergency'.

Could we help? His brow was pinched when he asked.

Of course we could, I replied. We now had a contract and we would immediately set to work.

CHAPTER ELEVEN

ON THE RUN ACROSS THE CONGO RIVER

It could be said that what happened next was entirely predictable. By the time Kabila's forces began to close in on Kinshasa, no trained pilots could be found to man the Hinds. There was a persistent fear within Zaire's military command that its pilots couldn't be trusted and some generals felt that there might be rebels among them who would take their gunships into combat and end up behind enemy lines. In reality, that would be tantamount to committing suicide as any government asset approaching enemy lines automatically became a target.

Nellis was of the opinion that had it been possible, one or two of the pilots might have been crazy enough to do just that, especially once the situation became critical. However, in the final months of the conflict there was only a single operational Puma and some combat-ready Gazelles.

Nellis takes up events as they happened:

> After the meeting, I phoned Mauritz and told him we had the contract and that he needed to get the guys to Kinshasa as soon as possible. That was a priority, I stressed, because Likunya wanted us to deploy to Gbadolite the next day. Mauritz was good to his word, and arrived in the Zairean capital by private jet with a couple of pilots and ground personnel. After a short discussion, Juba, one of the South African pilots who had flown with us in Sierra Leone

162

agreed to stay. JJ Fuentes, the French pilot who had made such a nuisance of himself in the Intercontinental Hotel, agreed to travel with us to Gbadolite as well. He made no mention of what had happened to his two pals.

Initially, the plan was for Juba and Nellis to ferry two of the Mi-24 gunships to Kinshasa. JJ would bring one of the serviceable ground strike jets down and they would then start operations against the rebels.

In checking things over, the pilots found that the Hinds were not in very good shape. In fact, most of the gunships were unserviceable, although a pair of them looked like they could be used in combat, even if there were no spare parts and little ammunition. Juba decided to test fly the one chopper that looked better than the rest, but once airborne it began vibrating so intensely that he thought he wouldn't make it back onto the ground. Fortunately, he and Nellis were able to land. They then test-flew the second helicopter, which seemed to be relatively serviceable. Nellis commented:

> The decision was made that we would try to operate the one Mi-24 until we could get one of the Russian technicians to make some repairs. We realised then that the Yugoslavian crews who had been based there before we arrived had deliberately sabotaged the aircraft. Only weeks previously, when Roelf van Heerden and I visited Kisangani, we had seen them in operation.
>
> While we were flying, Mobutu's son visited the airfield and spoke to JJ. He assured the Frenchman that we would get all the support we needed from his father and that if we stayed to fight, we would be handsomely paid. He also declared that if there were to be a sudden extraction of his father and family, he would ensure that we would be on the aircraft, and that he would get us out of the country to safety. In the meantime, we should let him have a list of logistical requirements which would be dealt with immediately. Ammunition for the gunships was our priority, we told him.
>
> Our plan was to leave as soon as possible for Kinshasa. Mobutu's son said that everything would be arranged. Unfortunately, that was the last we saw or heard of the man.

While there are conflicting views about what went on during those final days of Mobutu's rule, much seemed to stem from the inability of the country's military to communicate internally. It was a fundamental issue, with staff officers alienated from the main body of the armed forces. More significantly, the generals who should have been prosecuting hostilities would sit comfortably on their backsides in the capital and hope that the next day would bring better news.

In their befuddled minds, said Nellis, there was little that prompted urgent attention: 'it's out there in the bush somewhere . . . doesn't matter now . . . perhaps later', one of them was heard to say after a few drinks with the South Africans.

To the majority of these senior military men, Kabila's rebellion did not appear to warrant any kind of radical action. It was impossible for them to grasp that a crass and untutored clown like Kabila could win a single battle, never mind lead a revolutionary army to victory.

For years Mobutu's intelligence services, which were immense, utterly intimidating and intrusive, had been downplaying the threat. It got to the point where opportunities arose to assassinate Kabila (twice by poison), but the idea was scotched on the basis of better the devil you know. There was no rationale for any of it, especially the failure of the Zairean High Command to do what was expected of it.

Despite the horrendous hardships suffered by their troops, who had been holding the line in the interior for more than a year by then, these sycophants went on living the good life as if it would never end. Their staff officers would sometimes come back to Kinshasa and try to argue that disaster was only a step away, but it made no difference. For a major or a colonel to infer that his boss wasn't doing his job wouldn't have been worth his life. The last person to be made aware of any of it was *le grande patron* himself. Nobody had the courage to suggest to a visibly ailing Mobutu that things were falling apart in his beloved country. One member of Kinshasa's peripatetic diplomatic corps commented: 'You needed a really big pair of balls to bring any sort of bad news to the old man.'

When they finally did get things going towards the end, recalls Nellis, they rushed about like proverbial chickens without heads and achieved even less. 'And that was already late November, with everybody looking after their own interests and fuck the country', was his wry comment. 'It certainly didn't appear to work that way with the rebels,' he said, 'they just came headlong at us and nothing seemed to stop them.' By then, Kabila's main force was perhaps a few weeks march south of Kinshasa. Nellis remembers:

> We all knew that Mobutu could have bought ten squadrons of modern Russian fighter jets with his small change alone. Had he done that, he could have ended the war in a month. The best helicopter gunships were available to him on the international arms market and no government would have minded a jot, not even if he acquired foreign pilots to fly them. To begin with, Moscow would have seized the opportunity and scored billions of dollars in arms sales.
>
> All that stuff was ready and waiting: surplus stocks that lay rotting in dozens of abandoned former Soviet bases in Siberia. The only thing that Mobutu had to do was get hold of some of Kinshasa's resident *biznesmeni* and they would have sold him their grandmothers if they thought they could have scored.

It was also a reality that most nations trading with the Congo were desperate for Mobutu to reach some sort of accord with his enemies. As well as exporting diamonds and precious metals, for more than half a century the Congo had been a major producer of about two dozen essential metals, including copper, uranium and cobalt. Zaire alone owned half the world's reserves of coltan (short for columbite-tantalite—a heat-resistant compound used in electronics to make things like mobile telephones and Sony PlayStations).

Obviously, as the war dragged on the insecurity that resulted from the impasse suited nobody. It was also certain that none of the major powers would have stood in his way, no matter what he did, even if he hired mercenaries. Executive Outcomes had already very successfully established the concept of the private military company, so that precedent was in place. That the country topped the international list in human rights atrocities was no longer an issue. Instead, peace, at any price, was.

As Nellis reviewed the situation facing him after his tiny group arrived in Gbadolite, he saw that there were two options, and both were immediate.

The Hinds could be stripped down and taken to Kinshasa in a couple of support planes. However, Jet A1 fuel would have to be freighted in as, by then, Ndjili International Airport was down to its final reserves and being avoided by all the foreign airlines that usually called.

Alternatively, if necessary clearances could be obtained, the Mi-24s could be routed through Congo (Brazza) and from there, flown across the river to Kinshasa. That option went down when an American military advisory group in Brazzaville commandeered all available aircraft fuel in the state. The Yanks put out the word that permission for the Hinds to transit was, as they liked to phrase it, no longer viable.

The situation in Gbadolite itself was discouraging. The MiG fighter jets were there all right, but they were still in kit form. Russian technicians were assembling them, but that could take weeks. Also, special oils and greases, ordered from Moscow to complete the task, never arrived. Then there were some battery problems. There were none for the MiGs, which meant that even if they were able to fly, it would have been impossible to start the engines. Issues were further compounded when it was discovered that the Jastrebs' batteries were missing and that there was only one serviceable Mi-24 battery (whereas two are needed for an internal start). It was a shambles.

The crunch came when Nellis was told by Rudi, a Russian technician in charge of the air force base at Gbadolite who spoke passable English, that the ground power units that had been sold to Mobutu's people didn't have the correct fittings needed to plug into the aircraft, so they were useless too. Hands in the air, the normally unflappable Nellis asked what else could go askew. Lots, he was to discover. On top of everything, neither the aircraft technicians nor the unit armourer had arrived at Gbadolite, as had been instructed by the head of the air force.

The following day, Friday 16 May 1997, President Mobutu arrived at Gbadolite in his presidential jet. He had a huge throng of family, ministers, wives and children in tow—easily more than 100 people. Kabila was on the verge of taking Kinshasa. Later that afternoon, Rudi quietly cornered the South Africans in one of the hangars and said that he'd had a call from friends. 'Things are really bad', he told them. If the government hadn't already collapsed, it was about to do so.

The news didn't exactly come as a shock, but Nellis hadn't expected things to move quite so fast. Most worrying was the prospect of being stuck in one of the darkest reaches of central Africa. An hour later they got word that rebel units were moving towards Gbadolite itself, and that their vanguard might even be there the next day.

Meanwhile, Rudi whispered that he'd heard that Mobutu was intending to leave the country that night on an Ilyushin Il-76. The plane was expected to arrive at Gbadolite in the early evening and the remainder of the ZAF mobile missile systems still positioned around the airfield were scheduled to be removed and returned to Moscow. They should all be sure to be on that aircraft when it left, the Russian warned. If they weren't, he shrugged and made the symbolic cut across the throat.

Nellis and Juba Joubert met Mobutu later that afternoon and it came as a surprise when the old and obviously ill leader started ambling around the airport with a couple of bodyguards. He stopped to talk to the two South Africans. Nellis was impressed, especially since there were no shared experiences to stoke a conversation. Even at that late stage Mobutu asked them in a quiet, dignified voice what they needed. When they told him what the problems were with the Hinds, he said that everything would be delivered the next day. He confided, too, that he was expecting several arms shipments from Libya. His manner reflected confidence, recalls Nellis.

The relief flights were part of a done deal, Mobutu told them. Therefore, there was no reason to doubt the man, Nellis recalls, although at that late stage, he would have liked to believe just about anything. Mobutu did warn the crew not to return to Kinshasa, and promised that if he had to leave, he'd take them with him. With that he shook hands and moved on.

A short while later they heard that their old friend General Mahele, by then appointed Commander of the Army and Minister of Defence, had been shot by one of Mobutu's sons, an army colonel. The story was that Mahele had intended to defect to Kabila, or at least that was what a Kinshasa radio bulletin suggested. Perhaps he had, it was an excellent option, although the South Africans doubted it. Everybody was aware that Mahele was professional to his fingertips and perhaps he had been perceived a threat to members of the Mobutu family who were still in Kinshasa. The turncoat general had been 'dealt with', Kinshasa Radio crowed shortly afterwards and Nellis thought it was a great pity. Mahele was the only real soldier he'd met during his six-month stint in the country.

Unknown to the South Africans, Mauritz Le Roux at that moment was in the air in a chartered Lear heading towards Gbadolite. He'd told his wife that he intended to pull the two men out, even though he believed he might be too late. When he arrived at Brazzaville, he was not only denied fuel but arrested and his plane was impounded. Having been allowed to refuel the following morning, Le Roux and his flight crew were warned that if they ever returned, they would be jailed. They had no option but to head back to South Africa.

That evening, taking stock of what had suddenly become a critical issue, the three pilots worked out something of a contingency plan should they be left on their own or if Kabila's army should suddenly arrive. Nellis recalled:

> Obviously, we could not get away, although we thought that morning might offer a few more options. Because of our air force training, Juba and I were thoroughly conversant with the essentials of escape and evasion, but we realized it was not the sort of thing to do after dark, certainly not in a heavily forested environment secreting a multitude of threats. In contrast, JJ was all for leaving Gbadolite immediately, but in the end we prevailed.
>
> We were staying in Baramoto's country house in Gbadolite. A couple of hours after sunset, one of Baramoto's female servants, who had been friendly to us, poked her head around the door and warned us that we were in the gravest danger. They knew we were at the house, she said, and it was only a matter of time before some of the troops, who by now had mutinied, would come looking for the *mercenaires*. We settled on the unlikely story that we were all Air Zaire pilots who were stranded there, but it was obvious that we'd already been spotted tinkering with the gunships and the other aircraft.

At about two in the morning, the same night that legions of mosquitoes were devouring Le Roux in the one of Africa's filthiest jails, Nellis was awakened by the sound of a passenger aircraft gunning its engines. He didn't have to be told that Mobutu and his entourage were fleeing. A couple of hours later, the thumps of heavy explosions and continuing small arms fire reached the house. The noise came from the edge of town and seemed to intensify as a dismal grey dawn approached.

The two South Africans grabbed their clothes and went outside. The first hint of light had barely begun to appear over the jungle when strings of tracers arched across the sky. There were troops shooting everywhere, seemingly not at any specific target, but in all directions at once. It was impossible to tell whether it was a rebel attack or FAZ troops on the rampage. When they checked the guards at the compound gates, they discovered that they too had disappeared, as had all the Russians.

By now JJ had joined them outside and there they stood, the last three white men in a region almost 1,000km from the nearest civilization, in a country that was coming apart at the seams. Nellis recalls:

> There wasn't an officer in sight. The only troops we saw were on the rampage, many of them drunk and firing their weapons at anything that moved, their own people included. Some were as aggressive as hell, furious at having been abandoned by their leaders, others on liquor and drugs were just going berserk. All we knew was that we had to get our butts out of there, but how to do so? So we got our heads together.

The tiny group had very few options left open to them. At first they believed that they had a remote chance of getting to the remaining Mi-24 at the airfield. While the gunship wasn't altogether airworthy, Juba said that it had enough fuel to get them into the Central African Republic. The only alternative would be to make for the border on foot. The first idea was discarded when firing picked up again, as this time there was some heavy automatic stuff coming from the direction of the airport. Clearly, had they gone that way it would have been obvious to everybody what they were trying to do and they would almost certainly have been shot.

Having been in those parts before, Nellis knew that the closest border post was at Mobayi-Mbongo, about 60km away. However, that was along a road that would have been packed with Zairean refugees, as well as government soldiers, who were also fleeing Kabila's people.

The army had mutinied, and already there were reports of soldiers going berserk. Some of the mutineers, including a few who had already discarded their uniforms, had come by the house earlier that day and most were already high. While not hostile towards the mercenaries, they certainly were not their usual smiling selves. If the shooting continued, Nellis realized that things could only get worse.

There was one other possibility, JJ suggested. He was aware of a bush track that led straight north from Gbadolite to the frontier. He'd spotted it in the past when he'd circled the area prior to landing. Although there was no border post at the end of it, the route could be their salvation because it headed in a straight line for the river. The Central African Republic (CAR) lay just beyond.

They made their decision immediately. Meanwhile, Nellis used his satellite phone to call home and tell Zelda of their plans and JJ spoke to friends in Paris. His contacts there said they would advise the Ministry of Defence about their predicament. Also, he was assured that French Army units in the CAR would be watching for them. As it was, in anticipation of a full-scale rebellion in Zaire, France had already deployed troops along the CAR's north bank of the Congo. At this point, some Zairean soldiers who had stayed behind came into the house, forced open the general's cellar, and began the party in earnest. More soldiers arrived with a truck shortly afterwards and began loading furniture, drapes, TVs, kitchenware and mattresses. One of them even ripped a bidet from the bathroom floor and carried it outside on his head.

One of the women in the general's compound then came forwards and said that she was worried for the safety of the three whites. She told them that the word had gone out on the local radio for the army to be on the lookout for three white mercenaries who had infiltrated Gbadolite and suggested that they take refuge in her shack. It was well away from the main house and at least they'd be safe there until the main body of soldiers left.

Also, she promised to divert the attention of anybody who came looking for them. They were in serious danger, she warned, words that were echoed by a priest who arrived shortly afterwards. They would be dead within hours if they didn't get away, he said

Nellis' flight from Zaire into the CAR with Juba and JJ, all of it on foot except for the final leg, which was undertaken in a leaking dugout canoe, lasted two days. Along the way they were beaten, spat upon, robbed, shot at and pistol-whipped. They hadn't even got to the far side of town before they were grabbed by some troops and told that they should prepare themselves for execution. Even today Nellis is not certain why it didn't happen because 'the bastards seemed pretty set on it'. Hardly a religious man, he admits to having prayed more in those 48 hours than in all the previous years of his life.

Initially, the woman who had befriended the men instructed her son to guide them out of the town, and they started their escape. Although the firing in the town had calmed down a little, there were groups of soldiers, hyped up on marijuana and alcohol, walking around. Nellis said:

> Then they saw us and, guns pointed at our torsos, they stopped and interrogated us. Systematically, they stole any articles of value they found while doing the search: cash, watches, cameras, everything they fancied. That was basically it, as we progressed from one group of thuggish troops to another. They even forced us to remove our clothes and left the others in their underpants. I don't wear jockeys, so I was allowed to keep my trousers. Fortunately, JJ was able to talk to them in French and calm them down. However, he ended up losing $11,000 and I had $3,000 taken from me, while Juba lost his last $1,000.
>
> Then we ran into a bunch of troops who were totally out of control. After some argument, they instructed JJ to leave and told Juba and me to walk down the road and keep our arms high above our heads. After about 20 paces, they shouted for us to stop and then told us to turn around. Once we were facing them, three of them opened fire with their AK-47s. Fortunately, they were so high on drugs and booze, the rounds weren't accurate and went over our heads or hit the ground in front of us.
>
> Juba took some shrapnel and fragments of stone in his legs and face. A couple of women who'd been watching this impromptu firing squad with some amusement started shouting at the soldiers, which distracted their attention. I said to Juba, 'Run', and we bolted off between some houses on the edge of the road. The

guide—the son of the woman who had taken us in tow when we left Baramoto's house—led us to a building where we met up with JJ and some of the general's soldiers who hadn't taken part in the looting.

Our troubles weren't yet over. Although Baramoto's soldiers were friendly, we didn't trust them so we slept in an outhouse, ready to run at the first sign of danger. That night we could hear plenty of firing from drunken troops, and vehicles driving around town with the occupants calling for '*mercenaires blancs*' to surrender. Fat chance of that happening!

We eventually reached the border between Zaire and the Central African Republic, which was demarcated by the Oubangui River. The only way to cross was by pirogue, and we managed to find an old man who owned one and was prepared to take us to a police post in the neighbouring state, some way down the river. He demanded cash as payment, but as we had none he initially refused to take us.

However, with hostile troops following, he immediately agreed to let us board his boat and when he saw them approach he powered up the motor. Within minutes he'd put distance between us and those drunken louts.

How the three men ultimately managed to escape from Zaire remains a mystery to Nellis. The odds were so heavily stacked against them that they'd all written off the possibility of ever seeing their families again.

After a couple of hours on the river, the men reached a police post in the Central African Republic where local police took them in and gave them food and a place to sleep. Nellis recalls:

As I mentioned earlier, before we'd left the house in Gbadolite, JJ had managed to contact one of his friends in the French security services who, in turn, had managed to inform the French authorities in CAR of our probable arrival. The police at the post were expecting us, so for the first time in a couple of days we were able to relax.

The following morning, we were uplifted by a French Army

Puma helicopter and flown to Bangui, where we were confined to the French Army Barracks while our story was pieced together. JJ was flown out of Bangui to France that same evening, while we stayed with the French military for another two days before Mauritz made arrangements to fly us to Brazzaville, the Congolese capital.

Once the French security authorities had established that the two South Africans were who they said they were, the men were looked after quite well.

They were actually very friendly towards us, but we weren't allowed out of the building in which we were billeted. Two days later, we were put on a flight to Brazzaville, where we were secreted in what I can best describe as 'a safe hotel', while Mauritz arranged for us to be flown back to South Africa. Our time in Brazzaville was quite traumatic because the individual appointed by Mauritz to handle our affairs during the stay kept on telling us that Kabila's people were searching for us. He warned us that we shouldn't leave the hotel.

We stayed put for three days, each night waiting for someone to barge through the door and kill us. It didn't help our state of mind that some of the people living there with us were actually refugees from Mobutu's Zaire, and sympathetic towards Kabila. It was an immense relief when we were finally taken to Brazzaville Airport and able to board a plane to South Africa.

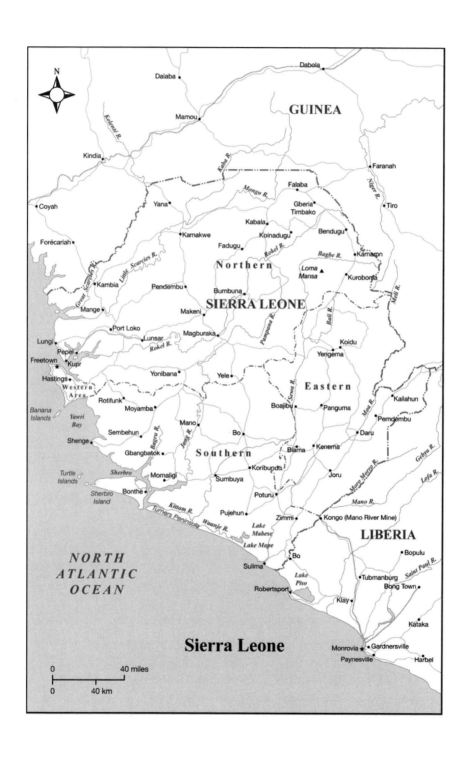

CHAPTER TWELVE

BACK TO SIERRA LEONE— THE SANDLINE DEBACLE

In early February 1998, Neall Ellis was back home again when he got a call from one of his old friends from EO. He asked whether Neall would look at working in Sierra Leone again. Neall remembers:

> The money was good and once more I was broke. The company I would be working for was Sandline International, which was run by Lieutenant-Colonel Tim Spicer OBE, a former British Army officer. There was a specific demand and should I be interested, I was to be in Johannesburg 'within hours' to talk, which tells you that nothing really changes in this business.
>
> I'd already heard of Spicer and the private military company for which he worked. He'd emerged from the Falklands War as one of Britain's leading battalion commanders, having fought in battles such as the Battle of Mount Tumbledown.

The offer from Spicer represented a much-needed lifeline for Nellis and a day later he was heading for Conakry, the capital of the Republic of Guinea, Sierra Leone's nearest neighbour on the far west coast of Africa. From there, he was told, he would be flown to Freetown by the company. He remembers:

Obviously the question of visas did arise at some point, but nobody thought it important enough to examine the matter in detail. We thought Sandline would take care of all that. However, we thought wrong and when I arrived at Conakry, sans visa, I was put straight back on the plane and returned to South Africa. What it meant for me was the inconvenience of a journey of more than 12,000km and all the dubious African travel crap that went with it—bad food, sleepless nights, mosquito-infested airport terminals and, of course, the obfuscations of legions of what can best be termed as 'Little Hitlers', each one of them wishing to impose their will on us transients just wanting to board our planes and move on.

When Nellis did eventually get to Freetown it was on an Embraer that was in such bad shape that he believed it should never have been allowed out of the hangar, never mind carry passengers. He was met at Lungi International Airport by former EO senior officer Bert Sachse, the Country Manager, and his old pal 'Juba' Joubert, with whom he had escaped from Zaire. Nellis takes up the story:

My first impression of Sierra Leone was that not much had changed, except that Freetown was more run down than before and was showing its scars. There was evidence of the serious fighting at the airfield the previous year, when the RUF rebels had been ensconced on one side of the airport and the Nigerian Army on the other. It had apparently been a classic showdown and the Lagos team won, with the 'home side' forced to evacuate their positions and flee into the jungle.

Once formalities were over, I was taken to a house that had originally been commandeered by the Nigerians and offered to Sandline as a temporary base. It was a big place, and was eventually turned into the Mahera Beach Hotel. However, when I was there it was blessed with neither power nor water. Since the crew wouldn't have been able to manage without cold beer, a generator had been installed to keep the fridge working and that kept the guys content. Beds and bedding came with the deal, but no air conditioning so I slept on the wide veranda, which faced the bay and enjoyed the nightly onshore breeze that also tended to keep malaria at bay.

Our water problem was solved by a group of locals who would hoist 20-litre containers onto the roof and fill the tank so that at least we were able to shower. It wouldn't have done to drink from that tank because it also contained water drained off the roof when it rained. Said roof was populated by half a dozen vultures that did their bit by picking at the cadavers littering the fields in the vicinity.

Nellis discovered that, in keeping with what was clearly a strong British Army tradition, Tim Spicer ran an exceptionally thorough military-type operation. He ran the company with Bernie McCabe, an American. Ostensibly, their objective was to recover the mineral interests, ergo diamond concessions, that had been given to another EO subsidiary and to protect the Sierra Rutile, an oxide mineral used in the production of titanium metal.

To achieve this, Sandline needed to be loosely linked to the local Nigerian head of ECOMOG[1], Colonel Maxwell Kholbe, and the Deputy Minister of Defence in the government of President Ahmad Tejan Kabbah, Chief Hinga Norman. These two men coordinated the activities of the Kamajors, a tribal group from the jungle that was arguably the best fighting unit in the country. They had been brought in to replace EO as the principal anti-rebel reactionary force and it was left to Sandline to train the Kamajor combatants in some of the fundamentals of counter-insurgency warfare. Nellis comments:

By the time I arrived, Juba was already flying the Sandline Mi-17, dubbed 'Bokkie', and had an Ethiopian ground crew led by Sindaba Meri. Sindaba was to become one of the most valuable members of our team and after Sandline had been forced out of the country, he basically kept our chopper flying.

They also had former SAS operative Fred Marafono as a side gunner, loader, observer, advisor, 'bruiser at the door to stop unwanted people from entering' and general factotum who knew more about Sierra Leone than most. Originally from Fiji, he was one of those traditional fighting men who bowed to nobody, and feared nothing. While with the Regiment, he had been awarded a gong by Queen Elizabeth for the role he played in freeing hostages taken prisoners at the Iranian Embassy at Princess Gate, South Kensington, in April, 1980.

As Nellis recalls, their basic task in Sierra Leone was to fly in support of ECOMOG forces that were mainly based in Monrovia in Liberia, although there was a small detachment of two or three battalions in Freetown itself. They also flew support missions for the Kamajors operating in the interior.

> Initially, we were regularly tasked to fly the Freetown–Monrovia leg, taking ECOMOG troops on R&R and returning with supplies for those soldiers who were operating against the rebels. It wasn't easy. Freetown was in a state of war and every soldier tried to make money by bringing in something to sell in local markets, which meant that we were sometimes so overweight on take-off that we couldn't get off the ground. Then Fred would go to the back and, virtually at gunpoint, hurl some of the 'cargoes' out of the open hatch.
>
> At the time, we were working in and out of an open field at the ECOMOG base in Monrovia, but we weren't allowed to go into the city itself because Charles Taylor, the local oligarch, had put a bounty on the heads of all us helicopter crews, with a bonus if somebody could knock 'Bokkie' out of the supply equation. The reason for this was simple. Taylor was not only in cahoots with the rebels, but he was also supplying Sankoh and his RUF with all the weapons and ammunition they needed, the idea being that he would eventually get a stake in the Sierra Leonean diamond fields.
>
> I recall some of those take-offs from the football field inside the military camp where we would land. Juba was a brilliant pilot who had spent a lot of his professional career flying chopper gunships in Angola and elsewhere. Self-taught, he'd learned to fly the Mi-17 very well indeed. He ended up teaching me a trick or two, which I applied to my work in other contract areas when we

were overweight on take-off or there weren't any decent runways or areas for take-off.

He demonstrated a technique for taking off from a field the size of a football pitch that could be surrounded by high-tension wires, 20 metres high. He'd go into the hover using ground cushion and then slowly reverse back to the furthest point downwind of the field, where he'd initiate a positive move forward. He'd go on doing that to the point where we lost the ground cushion effect and translational lift and that would effectively allow the Hip to descend. At the same time, he'd pull maximum collective and would allow downward movement to the ground to continue. Together with forward speed, he would compress the oleos, which would cause the helicopter to bounce back into the air and, at the same time, pass through transition. The helicopter would accelerate while climbing out of the LZ and clear the wires.

It was all very hairy the first couple of times, because once committed nothing would prevent the chopper from striking any of the obstacles if all that didn't succeed. However, once mastered, the technique was sometimes the only way to clear confined areas safely, albeit with a small margin, without sacrificing load. We never considered the possibility of an engine cut during the take-off—after all, we were supposed to be immortal.

As Nellis recalled, Juba would never head directly to Freetown as that would have meant flying over the jungle. Apparently, he was paranoid about being shot down by a SAM missile because, in the Cafunfo raid in Eastern Angola, his Mi-17, with John Viera as co-pilot, had actually taken a strike by a SAM-7 fired by rebel troops. The hit should have destroyed the machine but it didn't. Consequently, he was able to auto-rotate and land without too much damage to the helicopter.[2] 'At least they were able to walk out of the downed machine alive', Nellis commented with a nod of his head.

Clearly, Juba's fear of being blown away by SAMs was well founded, but it did make for much longer journeys between Monrovia and Freetown because, as Nellis remembers, sometimes they would head out as much as 50km to sea before heading back towards Sierra Leone again.

Neall Ellis prepares for take-off at Cockerill Barracks. He often flew two sorties a day single-handed, sometimes three. During his Sierra Leone war he rarely had the support of a regular co-pilot. *Author's photo)*

When I asked him why he went so far out into the ocean, he would say something about enemy gunboats, which might have SAMs on board. Of course, everybody on the chopper worried about what would happen if we had to ditch in the ocean. The water was often brilliantly clear, and we sometimes saw really big sharks. Then you'd find a lone fisherman perhaps 60 clicks out to sea in his little wooden dugout canoe and you'd think he was crazy.

Heading out of Monrovia, the Mi-17 would sometimes go into a remote area to supply Kamajor fighting units at Base Zero, in the wetlands southeast of the small town of Matru. Nellis recalls:

It was completely isolated in some pretty heavy swampland, the kind of terrain that made it difficult for the rebels to attack with vehicles. We were always very impressed by the level of organisation of these otherwise primitive bush people but, of course, they were headed by Chief Hinga Norman, the only minister in the government who stayed on in Sierra Leone to fight Foday Sankoh's RUF after the coup d'état. By the time Hinga was done, he'd organised the Kamajors into a very professional strike force that was able to do a lot of damage. We would watch them doing their thing and you couldn't miss the fact that, unlike the Sierra Leonean Army, they were quite well disciplined and very good at their job.

At the time, Colonel Kholbe thought that the Kamajors were a group of upstarts and hardly worth regarding as an asset in his anti-rebel push; not that there was very much 'pushing' being done by the Nigerians in any event. He doubted whether they would match up to Hinga Norman's claims.

Norman arranged for us to fly Kholbe and some of his senior command, along with the Sandline management including Bert Sachse, to witness a live-fire demonstration at one of the camps in the interior. There followed a useful demonstration of fire and movement, and the initiation of each of the men by a shaman or witchdoctor where the Kamajor combatants were 'anointed' by one of their high priests to make them 'immune from bullets'. Norman then urged Kholbe to produce one of his best marksmen to actually shoot one of his soldiers.

'Shoot my man', Norman urged, but Kholbe refused, so Norman said to the Nigerian, 'then let us bring a chicken and shoot that'. Again Kholbe refused. The incident ended up badly souring relations between Kholbe and the Kamajor movement and there was really no reason for it. In the end, we thought it was something to do with ju ju or black magic, because there was certainly distrust on Kholbe's part.

Hostilities against the rebels in Sierra Leone continued to intensify and Sandline ended up spending a couple of million dollars on weapons and equipment for the Kamajors. In Spicer's view, it was money well spent as the Kamajors were committed, ruthless and totally opposed to the barbarians who had murdered scores of their people. Much smaller than the ECOMOG force, they were actually causing a lot more damage to the enemy than the entire Nigerian Army, which was immense by comparison.

After the weapons had been delivered by air to Lungi, Kholbe stepped in and confiscated the lot. The Sandline administration was accused of breaking sanctions. In the end, the Nigerian dribbled small quantities of equipment to the Kamajors.

From a shipment that filled an aircraft with military hardware, which was to be used to fight the rebels, the Kamajors ended up with five PKMs and a couple of dozen AK-47s (each with one magazine and five rounds of ammunition), which was not only absurd, but an insult to the prowess of an outstanding fighting unit. Also passed on by Kholbe were rimless GPMG cartridges for the PKMs. Kholbe's actions were viewed as a deliberate attempt to sabotage the Kamajor movement.

As Nellis recalled, after he and his compadres realised that Kholbe was not interested in helping the Kamajors fight the common enemy, they would steal Kalashnikovs and ammunition from the Nigerians and hand them to the bush fighters.

> Also, when we flew the bodies of the ECOMOG soldiers who had been killed in action back to Freetown, we'd carefully secrete their weapons in some of the nooks and crannies on board and hand them over to Hinga Norman's people the next time we made contact with them . . . we'd sometimes use our own money to buy rifles and ammo for them.

Whatever his faults, Colonel Kholbe had been a good professional soldier who, in most other respects, knew where his responsibilities lay. He certainly looked after the Sandline staff, the air crews in particular. During the ECOMOG intervention, he was seriously wounded in a firefight in the jungle, having taken a shard of shrapnel in his side, and it was Juba who evacuated him in extremely bad weather to Lungi for treatment. Had that not happened, Kholbe would almost certainly have died of septicaemia.

Thereafter, he arranged to have Sandline's aircrew stay at the Cape Sierra Hotel for the next two years. Although ECOMOG was supposed to have picked up the tab, says Nellis, 'I don't believe anybody paid our bills in the end'.

Meanwhile, the country had no effective ruler because the Kabbah government had been brought down in 1997 by a combination of factors including the destabilisation of its army, the Republic of Sierra Leone Armed Force (RSLAF). The collapse was almost certainly aided by strongmen elements within the bloated bureaucracy that was put in place after EO had been forced out. Thereafter, working with the Nigerians in a series of private deals, Sandline played an invaluable role in bringing

President Kabbah back into power in February 1998.

Ironically, even though it was a mercenary-based group, Colonel Spicer's organisation was a lot more transparent in its affairs than the then government of Nigeria, with the latter being responsible for numerous human rights abuses and criminal activities. Indeed, the lack of any real authority in Sierra Leone prompted Nigeria to regard the country as a base from which to expand its interests into other parts of West Africa, and this was a matter of concern to both Whitehall and Washington

Consequently, when President Kabbah returned to Sierra Leone from Conakry in April 1998, there was a welcoming parade through the streets of Freetown. The people were not only pleased to have him back in power, but it was hoped that he would blunt Nigeria's quasi-colonial aspirations. Interestingly, the Nigerian head of state, Sani Abacha, seized the opportunity and ensured that he was also on hand at the welcoming ceremony, which turned into a momentous occasion.

The other notable event that took place that day happened when President Abacha stepped out of his presidential jet moments before joining Sierra Leone's President Kabbah on the dais. Very publicly, the Nigerian leader called for the South African pilot Juba Joubert to step forward. He thanked him for what he had done for Sierra Leone and for ECOMOG. It obviously had to do with Juba's saving the life of Colonel Kholbe. After thanking Juba, he continued to the dais and joined Kabbah to address the crowd. Nellis remembers the day well:

> The welcoming crowd, who saw all this, went wild with adulation for this 'whitey' hero of the day, after which it was left to us to fly the presidential entourage to the football stadium in the heart of the capital in our dilapidated old 'Bokkie'.
>
> I'll never forget President Kabbah's wife, Patricia, who had been diagnosed with terminal cancer not long before. She was obviously very sick and in a lot of pain. However, she summoned the strength to get up from her seat and wave to crowds as though there was nothing wrong with her. After the parade we took her back to State House and almost had to carry her to the chopper. She collapsed on board and died only months later. She was a great lady!

Meanwhile, things in Freetown were falling apart. There was no piped water and no electricity in the city, yet whenever Nellis and his group went to talk to members of the ECOMOG Junta at their residences, they couldn't miss their opulent furnishings, expensive cars and Land Rovers, all which had been 'confiscated' in the interests of the ongoing struggle. Nellis said:

> All that stuff was later shipped to Nigeria, at government expense, of course, which was one of the reasons why the Nigerians soon got a deserved reputation of being extremely efficient looters. They were exceptional at what was termed 'the distribution of wealth'.

Things weren't going too well with the company either. John Farr, an ex-SAS major who was working for Sandline, approached Nellis and his team mid-August and said that they were pulling out. That was when the team was made an offer they couldn't refuse. The company could either pay them all their salaries and bonuses owing, plus their air tickets home, or they could have the helicopter 'Bokkie' in lieu, as a measure of recompense.

> There was no argument, recalled Nellis. There were no salaries for that final month but we accepted our beloved 'Bokkie' for sever-ance, which, together with the radios, tooling and other equipment left behind by Sandline, set Juba, Fred Marafono and me up in business doing freelance chopper work. We eventually netted about $1 million in the process, many times more than we would have been paid had we accepted the initial offer.

Because of Juba's friendship with Kholbe, he was able to negotiate a contract with the Nigerians to use 'Bokkie' for the resupply of their troops even though it was Sierra Leonean Government cash involved. Nellis recalls:

> It was of no concern to us where the money came from as long as we were paid at the end of each month, even though any payment would be minus the inevitable backhander. Said backhander was

roughly 10 per cent of all our earnings, which went to Kholbe and his senior officers. From then on we started flying quite a bit because everybody was scoring.

We were in a bar on the beach one evening when I heard this loud French accent talking. I turned to Juba and said something about that sounding just like our old pal JJ Fuentes from Zaire, and indeed it was. We never really thought we'd see him again but there he stood, spouting the same old brash bullshit. This time he was with another young Frenchman, Matthieu Chaissang, who soon became one of our most valued operators until he left Sierra Leone in January 1999 when the rebels overran Freetown.

Both men were in Freetown 'looking for opportunities', they told us and they couldn't have arrived at a better time. We were looking for somebody who could fly our fixed-wing Partanavia, which we used for transporting various generals and for reconnaissance purposes. Juba spoke to Kholbe and Hinga Norman and gave them the background, and it was agreed that we could take them on. We now had two French nationals on our team.

It was during this period that the notorious incident involving 'Bokkie' and the Royal Navy Type 23 frigate HMS *Norfolk* occurred.

The warship had recently berthed in Freetown after rescuing dozens of refugees at sea. One of the windows in 'Bokkie's' cockpit had been smashed in a bird strike and Nellis asked one of the ship's officers to give the crew a hand. No problem, he was told, and the helicopter was flown to the harbour and landed alongside the frigate, while RN engineers on board fixed the damage. They had no Perspex or Mi-8 windows to replace the broken one, as Nellis recalls, so this intrepid bunch of sailors pop-riveted a sheet plate of aluminium to the frame as a substitute.

Meanwhile, we'd been invited on board by the RN flight crew; we even had a small party on the frigate. What we didn't know was that somebody on the ship had taken a photo of 'Bokkie' parked alongside the frigate and leaked news to the *Sunday Times*. The story carried by that newspaper was that the Royal Navy was assisting a bunch of mercenaries and it didn't have to state that they were a cut-throat bunch of bastards; that much was inferred.

It was a cruel, unthinking piece of journalism and in its wake, after Sandline had been pushed out of the country due to pressure from Westminster, hundreds of thousands more people were killed in the hostilities that followed. Those responsible for the disclosure, which involved quite an innocuous event, have a lot of innocent blood on their hands!

After the proverbial shit hit the fan and questions were asked of the Ministry of Defence, the captain of HMS *Norfolk* was relieved of his command.

There is no doubt that British Intelligence was more than casually interested in what Sandline was doing in Sierra Leone. Colonel Bert Sachse told a visiting American journalist that everybody knew that diamonds from the country's rich alluvial deposits around Kono were being used by terrorist groups around the world to fund their operations against the West. These groups included radical Muslim groups, such as Hizbollah in Lebanon, as well as the RUF.

'This is a totally different ballgame,' Sachse declared. 'In this game, one doesn't ask a lot of questions. But I can tell you that as an ex-colony, the UK felt something of a responsibility to take an interest in where the diamonds went, the merchants who were marketing them, terrorist involvement and, as a consequence, the need to stop that flow. We went into Sierra Leone in our own interests. I think we could have handled the whole thing ourselves', Sachse declared.

He went on: 'As I said, we are not mercenaries but think of ourselves more as "privateers," and we went in where no government was prepared to go. I know the Yanks don't like losing guys for nothing. The Brits made it easier by turning a blind eye, seeing how far things would go.'

Asked why the Sandline operation wasn't stopped sooner, Colonel Sachse was candid: 'One must assume there is a link between Sandline and British Intelligence', were his words.

CHAPTER THIRTEEN

TAKING THE WAR TO THE REBELS IN SIERRA LEONE

Washington was clearly disturbed by the downturn of events in Sierra Leone and it wasn't long before there were some new faces—most of them American—at Cockerill Barracks. The first to arrive was a Californian company, the Pacific Architects and Engineers (PAE), who were instructed by the U.S. State Department to help the ECOMOG war effort. For its air operations in Sierra Leone, PAE hired another American company, International Charter Incorporated (ICI) of Oregon, which had a rather distinct U.S. Government footprint. This raised quite a few eyebrows.

ICI's helicopters were Russian and were painted white and blue all over, with large American flags prominently displayed on both sides of the fuselage. Flown by Russian pilots and protected by 'retired' U.S. Special Forces personnel, these helicopters provided the beans and bullets for ECOMOG forces fighting the war. Like Nellis' 'Bokkie' they would also remove the wounded and dead, bring in fuel supplies and ferry the occasional VIP about the country, usually some American congressmen trying to score points with his electorate.

ICI's presence in the country was a useful adjunct to what Nellis and his team were trying to achieve, and also a fairly effective distraction from direct British involvement in the war. In fact, very few people were aware that the command-and-control centre at Cockerill Barracks was run by senior British officers and included SAS personnel who, strictly against the orders of the Minister of Defence in London, Nellis would take on reconnaissance or fact finding missions.

Support personnel on board the ICI choppers were a mixed bunch. By all accounts, they were comfortable mixing it with the rebels, and more often than not took the initiative when they 'encountered' Foday Sankoh's people along the way.

Among the more prominent was Mykel Hawke, a Special Forces reserve operative who, when not with his unit in Iraq or Afghanistan, did this sort of thing for fun. He saved Nellis' bacon on more than one occasion. Hawke sometimes provided the Air Wing, as Nellis and his team were known, with logistical support in the field, including fuel drops in remote places so that 'Bokkie' could get home. Interestingly, he has since gone on to make a name for himself by hosting several television series on *The Discovery Channel*.

In an assessment of the situation much later, Nellis said that he and the others soon got the impression that the American Government had instructed PAE to help them where they could:

> including paying our fuel account so that we could remain active
> . . . in other respects they would invite us for the occasional meal
> or give us some of their surplus flying kit, which came in handy
> because we were almost in rags. Then we started working together
> and flew cross-country in three-ship formations. Sometimes we
> would move troops, other times food and ammunition for the soldiers in the field, who were having a really tough time against a
> much better equipped and motivated enemy.

With Sandline abruptly departed and no extraneous security elements in place, the rebels started making substantial advances against Freetown. In a sense, Nellis said, 'they'd already smelt blood and wanted more'.

On the chopper side, recalls Nellis:

> It didn't always work the way we intended it to because the Russian

pilots liked to fly at about 1,000ft, while we hugged the deck. We warned them about SAMs and they said we were crazy. They would insist that there were none, maintaining that being Russian, they would be the first to know. They changed their minds after they had been shot at a few times and started to think like we did.

There were some interesting contrasts in the mix. While the Americans would fly in full combat kit, with flak jackets, army boots and their M-16s, the Russians preferred to don white shirts and slacks for their flying duties, much as they did in peacetime.

Towards the end of November 1998, it was clear that the rebels had embarked on a serious anti-Nigerian offensive. They started to concentrate their assets in the north-east, around the diamond fields, and the intent was clear. The initiative, apparently, came from Charles Taylor who wanted to control Kono and have all its precious stones for himself.

On the domestic front, Juba had all but stopped flying because of his lunchtime meetings with friends at Paddy's Bar and Alex's Restaurant so most of the time it was just Nellis and his Ethiopian engineer, Sindaba, in the cockpit. That suited him fine, he recalls today, because he was steadily building up his hours and gaining more experience on machines which, until a short while before, had been quite new to him.

I recall going into Kono one morning and chatting to a Nigerian Army captain I'd met at the Cape Sierra Hotel a few weeks before. He told me that he was worried that Kono would come under serious attack sometime soon. He was right, because the RUF launched a major frontal assault two days later and captured him.

They literally ripped him apart. After he had been suspended between two vehicles, which tore off his arms and legs, they disembowelled him. I was obviously shocked when I heard the news because I was aware that he had recently married a Sierra Leonean woman and when we talked at the airfield, he mentioned missing the love of his life.

It disturbed Nellis that the ECOMOG High Command in Freetown didn't appear to be unduly concerned at the possibility of losing the diamond fields. Kholbe, by then promoted to brigadier-general, was in his office when Nellis called to talk. Nellis told him that he'd got a mid-morning call from the squad from Lifeguard who said they were under siege and couldn't hold out much longer.

He and I both knew that the majority of these people were private military contractors from South Africa, and quite a few were formerly with EO. He was also aware that Lifeguard was integral to his defence structure and that the squad, and the Nigerian troops in the area, were desperately short of ammunition. He caught me a bit off-guard by sending me to his second-in-charge, Colonel Garba, who was also Nigerian. I mentioned that Lifeguard had 82mm mortars and a couple of 12.7mms and that they badly needed ammo. He was aware that they were holed up on Monkey Mountain, where the mine was.

Instead of doing something positive, the idiot sent me on a ration run. I was tasked to deliver food to a Sierra Leonean Army base about 80km from Freetown, manned by a bunch of hooligan riff-raff who were still loyal to the government and under no threat at all. Barely an hour later, I got a call on the radio from Lifeguard and was told that the Nigerian lines had started to crumble. The gist of it was that the rebels had overwhelmed some of their positions, including those of two battalions of Kholbe's soldiers. They were all about to be annihilated and were running away from their positions.

My priority just then was to work out a way of helping the Lifeguard unit. I was able to get through to them again on the radio and they said that they had started to move to a stronger point about 15km away. They asked for immediate extraction.

Since this was the kind of emergency that one always fears—the fellows were not only desperate, they were cut off and their ammunition was drying up—I went to look for Juba. I found him at the base and told him that because of bad visibility, the rescue attempt should be a two-pilot operation. I also mentioned that because of the Harmattan wind, visibility was likely to be down to 1,000 metres. Laden with fine Saharan sand and enveloping much of West Africa, the annual phenomenon can make navigation difficult.

Juba refused outright. I should go on my own, he scoffed. With that, he was off into town for another lunch meeting with the Frenchman JJ.

There were five of them in the Mi-17 when they lifted off from Cockerill Barracks. The crew included the engineer Sindaba, Fred Marafono and two side gunners in the rear, with Nellis as pilot. Nellis tells what happened next:

> One of the gunners was Mohammed, a Nigerian soldier seconded to us who had proved useful in some of the tight spots we'd found ourselves in.
>
> When I arrived at the GPS position that Lifeguard had given me, I found the place deserted. All I could do was set a course for Kono. However, this time I flew a little higher, aware that if the guys heard me coming, they'd call on the radio. Throughout, I tried to raise them, but got no reaction. I was very much aware that we were within sight of rebel positions and were picking up a bit of ground fire, some of it quite heavy. That's when Fred came forward to the cockpit and said the bastards were using 12.7mms and 14.5mms against us, which was cheery. Finally, we were able to talk to the men who, by then, I regarded as 'our people'.

When Nellis finally managed to connect, the men trapped on the ground said they were only a couple of kilometres away, but because there was a heavy enemy presence, they'd hidden in a gulley. According to Nellis, this meant more problems because it was a particularly hot day and there were 16 of them. With their weapons and kit, he had a real fear that they might be too heavy for take-off. From past experience, he knew that when ground forces actually ask for a hot extraction, it is usually almost too late.

> But they were friends and allies and we simply had to extricate them from a situation that was obviously critical.
>
> Once I had visual on them, I landed as fast as possible, took

Road to Makeni, where Nellis launched his ambush against many members of the rebel command structure. *Author's photo*

everybody on board and attempted to lift off. I knew it was not going to be easy, but the alternative was too ghastly to contemplate. Sindaba was looking at me, wide-eyed and shaking his head, which was when I knew we were in trouble.

Having come down in the secluded gulley and quickly familiarised myself with the environment, I could see that the depression had its advantages. For a start, we were in dead ground, the rebels weren't in sight and their fire passed harmlessly overhead. However, that advantage was soon lost because, when I pulled power, the effect of the long grass and up-slopes of the gulley caused a marked recirculation of the rotor wash, with a consequent loss of main rotor blade effectiveness.

So even before attempting to move forward through transition, the rotor revs were already on the minimum of 92 per cent. I prayed for a nice flat area where I could nurse the chopper through transition but, had there been one, more likely than not we would have been full of holes as it was the defilade protecting us.

Obviously, the thought of asking some of the guys to disembark crossed my mind, but that would have been suicide. Enough of them might have been able to hold out for a while, but the prospect of coming back to fetch them was not appealing as the area had suddenly become very hot indeed.

Nellis had made his decision. It was an all or nothing situation, so he decided to give it a go. 'We'd all get out of this shit or we'd perish together in the process if we were unsuccessful.'

He didn't give much thought to the negative side of it all, he admitted afterwards. He was determined to make it happen.

I pulled collective, the revs dropped to 88 per cent and the red lights over the temperature panel on the engine started flashing. By then it was a matter of life or death, so I thought fuck the consequences which included the loss of our auto-pilot and electrics.

In the process 'Natasha' was screeching blue murder, so I eased the power up slightly and we just managed to clear the lip of the gulley. Fortunately, there was a slight incline downwards so, using the curvature of the earth and the bounce technique—to the accompaniment of a volume of enemy small arms fire—we managed to stagger through transition and gain enough flying speed to maintain forward momentum and eventually shudder our way back in the direction of Freetown.

Once out of the crap, a minute or two later, everybody on board was giggling like a bunch of schoolgirls. The elation of getting out of that mess intact, and picking up speed as we sped over huge clumps of jungle immediately below the fuselage, was incredible.

We were in Freetown an hour later and the guys were ecstatic. Instead of being eaten by the rebels that night, they joked, they would be doing the eating. The beers flowed continuously in the hotel bar that night, which meant that by morning there wasn't a man among us who didn't suffer from the effects of our 'gyros toppling'.

Nellis and his crew were ordered back to Kono early the next day to try to extricate the remnants of those who had survived the night. However, as he recalls, it was hopeless.

> We spotted some of the troops escaping along the road but most had disappeared into the bush, only to reappear in Freetown weeks later, having walked all the way. As I approached Yengema, the bodies of dead soldiers were everywhere, which meant that we were well behind the rebel lines. It was pointless trying to find survivors at the ECOMOG headquarters in the town as they would certainly all be dead by then.
>
> I had become friendly with one of the Nigerian Amy majors based at Yengema. He was a quiet, competent fellow who was one of the few who was quite committed to his job. I was to hear later from some of the survivors that, shortly before turning in for the night, he'd wandered off into the dark on the perimeter of the base, probably to have a piss, when he was captured by a rebel scouting group.
>
> The poor fellow was taken a short distance from the Nigerian camp and his colleagues could hear his screams as the rebels dismembered his body while he was still alive. He was subjected to the most gruesome rituals, which went on for several hours as they cut away chunks of his flesh and roasted them over an open fire before eating them while he watched.
>
> Africa can be kind, someone once commented, and it is axiomatic that it can also be barbarously cruel.

Had this happened to an officer from a British or American unit, Nellis believes there would have been no shortage of volunteers to head out immediately to end the carnage. Executive Outcomes operatives wouldn't even have had to think about it, he added.

> What disturbed me and the others about all this, was that the Nigerian commanders did very little to help their troops. One couldn't help but get the impression that their senior officers weren't overly worried about the fact that they had lost so many of their soldiers, but then the Nigerians usually march to the beat

of a different drum. It came as no surprise to hear shortly after-wards that their military structure had totally collapsed.

A couple of days later, I spoke to Kholbe and asked why he hadn't bothered to send some of his vehicles out to bring in the stragglers. His retort was something about not being able to afford to lose any more vehicles.

Not long afterwards, some ECOMOG officers still in Sierra Leone were evacuated to Conakry, in Guinea. However, the majority decided to stay and fight the rebel advance. There was only one serviceable helicopter at that time—'Bokkie'. All the others, PAE and ICI ones included, had left the country. By now Juba and JJ had also disappeared, the two men having decided that the Freetown was about to fall to the rebels. To give him his due, Juba had malaria and did need medical attention, 'though I think that JJ was just shit scared', was Nellis' comment.

A couple of days after Yengema and the diamond areas around Kono had been taken by the rebels, we had reports that the ECO-MOG garrison at Makeni was under concentrated attack and that there were heavy casualties in the Nigerian ranks. We were also aware that their ammunition supplies were critically low.

The day before Christmas, I was called to a meeting by Kholbe, who requested that we make a run to Makeni to deliver ammunition and uplift whatever casualties we could. Of course, according to him, the garrison was not under attack, and the fight-ing was on the outskirts of the town, which was not what we had heard. However, we were there to provide a service and also to help out buddies. We loaded the ammo at Cockerill Barracks, and took minimum fuel for the task.

On the way to Makeni, there were signs of serious fighting everywhere. The town itself was on fire and the huge volume of smoke made visibility difficult. I elected to skirt around the outskirts of the town and stay as low as possible so our approach to the garrison was from the north-east. The flight in was quiet enough and we weren't fired upon, which meant that our approach to the landing areas was normal and tactical.

We'd been there before, so we knew that landing zone was in a small clearing just outside the camp perimeter. The trouble was that it was pretty exposed on the northern side. As soon as we landed, Fred jumped out to supervise the unloading but nobody came from the camp to assist. As Fred alighted from the chopper, I couldn't miss the little puffs of dirt that were exploding on the ground directly in front of us, sending him scuttling back to the chopper and what should have been safety. We were being fired upon, but nothing had hit the helicopter yet.

Meanwhile, with all that ammunition still on board, there was no chance of pulling out, as we were too heavy to clear the trees in front of us. Fred and Mohammed climbed out of the chopper and, assisted by Sindaba, started to offload the ammo. I stayed at the controls, rotors running.

Soon after, some of the soldiers did arrive to assist and gradually their numbers increased. However, it wasn't long before Fred came to the cockpit and said we had to leave. The Nigerian troops, seeing a rapidly emptying helicopter, had decided that this was the way out to safety and they were all going to remain on board. I couldn't argue because RPG rounds were detonating all around us and in the surrounding trees.

I knew too, that if too many of the Nigerian troops became aware of what their brothers were doing, we would have more people on board than the helicopter could carry. We could easily suffer the same fate as 'Bokkie's' sister ship 'Daisy'. She was lost when large numbers of Sierra Leonean troops had tried to escape from the battlefield by swamping the departing helicopter with their bodies. South African pilot 'Tati' Tate had no option but to abandon his chopper because it was too heavy for take-off.

Fortunately, Juba was flying 'Bokkie' that day and was able to rescue the crew and get them away to safety. All the troops who had attempted to desert were killed by the rebels, who torched 'Daisy' the next day. These were pretty sobering considerations just then, especially since we were the only helicopter flying and there would be no rescue effort if we were overwhelmed by a bunch of mutinying Nigerian soldiers. I told Fred to get back inside, shut the doors and prepare for take-off. It didn't matter that we still had some unloaded ammo on board, and it was even tougher that we'd have to leave the casualties behind. However, just then the situation was out of control, and worse, the Nigerian troops already on board would not disembark.

Fred came through over the intercom 'Go, for fucks sake, go!' he screamed. I asked whether the rear doors were closed, but he just called for me to get the hell out of there. When I pulled power, I suddenly realized that we were heavy, extremely so, but we did have enough power to clear the trees and head out to Freetown. There was quite a lot of smoke ahead of us, so visibility was restricted.

Soon after take-off, we started receiving volumes of concentrated small arms fire as we flew over the town, so I kept the machine as low as possible over the houses, desperately hoping that we wouldn't have a wire strike. What was more unnerving was the tracer fire coming at us, masses of it. It is one thing to be shot at but, when you can actually observe tracer heading directly at you, the psychological effect is unnerving. There were also different, heavier sounds and that could only have meant that we were being targeted by a 12.7mm or 14.5mm heavy machine gun.

On the way out, I noticed one of the rebel troops standing in a clearing in between the houses. He had an RPG launcher on his shoulder and seemed to be aiming directly at my cockpit. Here we go, I thought, but the next moment his chest erupted as Fred opened up on him with his GPMG and the guy crumpled to the ground, dead.

For all the problems in Sierra Leone, there was hope. We knew the government had been trying to buy two Mi-24 Hinds, but we were also aware that if they didn't arrive within weeks, Freetown would fall.

By early January, we heard that the first groups of rebels had arrived in the nearby town of Waterloo, a medium-sized town with its own airport. This, in itself, was ominous because the RUF would be able to create an air bridge to Monrovia. We had also been made uncomfortably aware that there were RUF elements already starting to infiltrate the outer suburbs of Freetown. Worse, there was nothing anybody could do to stop them.

We'd observed many new faces in the central areas of the city, young men and boys, who were obviously out of place, standing on the street corners watching us as we drove past. They were all rebels of course. We saw the way they looked at us when we passed in our vehicles; the aggression on their faces was naked and uncompromising. Of course they wanted us dead. However, we went nowhere without our requisite stock of firearms, which included a little Czech fold-up stock sub-machine gun under the dashboard and an AK-47 next to the seat.

We finally decided to evacuate our house in the military officers' quarters on the outskirts of the Freetown. The house stood on a back road that led to Regent and Waterloo so we decided the best move would be to return to the Cape Sierra Hotel.

A day after the move I got a call in the middle of the night from the duty Nigerian officer at the ECOMOG headquarters. I knew the man quite well and appreciated the warning. The rebels were on their way to Aberdeen and Cockerill Barracks, he warned. I walked outside on the veranda of my room and could hear the sound of gunfire coming from the town. I woke up my guys and told them all to pack and get ready to leave. It was still too dark to fly so we left the hotel, which was already frantic with activity, at first light.

As we approached the barracks, I could see that things were not right. We hit the first of several roadblocks and were stopped. We were within sight of the main office block and some of the Sierra Leonean officers were screaming at the guards to let us through. 'They're pilots!' they shouted, over and over again, but it made no difference. Finally, Commodore Medani, one of the few Sierra Leonean general staff still around at Cockerill, came down and let us through.

We found conditions at Cockerill to be tense and the place was pretty much deserted. Most of the troops who had been guarding the barracks were out fighting, only too aware that if they were overrun, they would all be slaughtered. Walking about the base you couldn't help but get the impression that the prevailing atmosphere was that the war had already been lost. However, I accepted that if we were to survive, there was a job to do.

At this point I went to my helicopter, sat in my usual pilot's seat but didn't switch on the engines. Instead, I got on the radio and spoke to Brigadier General Kholbe. After a few brief preliminaries, I asked him whether we should go up and have a look. I reckoned we'd be able to assess from the fighting how deep into Freetown Sankoh's men had penetrated. He gave me the go-ahead and minutes later we were in the air, taking serious fire almost immediately.

I took the helicopter up to about 1,000ft but the firing continued. It was mostly small arms but there were barrages of RPGs as well. Fortunately, there was no heavy stuff. I was still worried about the prospect of Sam-7s, though.

We could see almost immediately that most of the rebel movement was coming from the eastern side of town but what made things difficult was that both sides were wearing almost identical uniforms. Also, both forces were walking in the same direction—towards Cockerill Barracks. We searched for targets but, in the end, it was Fred who suggested that we get the hell out of there because we were taking an inordinate number of hits. Fred had a point; it was time to give up and return another day

What we did establish, as I was able to tell Kholbe, was that the rebels were within a couple of kilometres of Cockerill Barracks. Moreover, they weren't static, but moving forward at a steady pace. I also said that it was pointless staying there, and that we'd take 'Bokkie' across the bay to Lungi International Airport. We packed our gear, landed alongside the hotel to fetch our things and then took off again.

At Lungi we were able to check on damage and it was worse than we'd anticipated. A round had gone through one of the helicopter's rotor blades and punctured the titanium spar, releasing the nitrogen inside. Anything bigger and the rotor would have separated: we'd been lucky.

Fortunately, Sindaba was able to recover a blade from one of the American government choppers with similar weights and 'delta angle', but it took him the rest of the day to fix it, so there was no more flying until the following morning. One of the problems to subsequently emerge from the repair was that the blades were not from the same set, and we ended up experiencing vibrations, which became worse with time.

The situation deteriorated steadily from them on. We were aware that there were thousands of Lebanese nationals trapped behind enemy lines. Most of these people had been traders or miners, involved in the diamond trade or professional people. While the rebels killed quite a few of them, they hadn't yet become a prime target.

Almost overnight, Freetown had become traumatised. There was no food and all water had suddenly become suspect. There were many incidents of Lebanese women and their daughters being raped. Everybody wanted out, and for the next few weeks, we were out there bringing groups of people across the bay to safety from where they were flown by international groups to Conakry.

We'd been joined by Hassan Delbani, who was Lebanese and until then had been working with Juba. An enterprising young man, he was pretty adroit with an AK and a good organiser. I was pleased that he had decided to stay with us in Freetown. Between us, Hassan and I worked out a pattern. We would take the Hip into a target area where we had been told there were civilians (mainly Lebanese) still trapped behind rebel lines. I would put down in a relatively secure position and Hassan and his hand-picked Kamajor fighters would go out into the night, find these people and lead them back to the chopper in the dark. Such operations sometimes lasted hours and were conducted always under considerable threat from the rebels. There were many shoot-outs in these outlying villages and many rebels killed, with not a single prisoner taken. Hassan was usually at the vanguard of these operations. He was quite fearless and on his own he must have killed scores of the enemy.

To keep our heads above water, we charged a flat rate of $25 per person—the only other helicopter still operating belonged to another private company called Soros and they asked $100. The result was that once the fighting was over and the city was able to revert to normal, the people we rescued never forgot what we had had done for them.

In order not to conflict with ECOMOG's objectives, we were able to negotiate a deal whereby we would have free rein for two hours a day. During those hours we could bring out refugees and get them to Lungi. It became standard procedure: we would do our thing every day from noon until two in the afternoon and we never turned anybody away. Those who couldn't pay because they had lost everything, or simply had no money left, were never stopped from boarding. In the end, things got so bad that almost nobody had cash and we flew them all for nothing anyway.

Operating out of Lungi, away from the drama taking place in almost all of Freetown, should have given us a respite from what was going on in the country. However, it wasn't long before conditions deteriorated there as well. There was no power or water at the international airport and it wasn't long before nobody had any food either.

We stayed free at the Lungi Hotel but we had to haul water up to our rooms. For food we'd go onto the streets looking for sidewalk vendors who still had the occasional can of sardines for sale. Bread was an almost unheard of luxury, although rescue aircraft coming through from Conakry would sometimes bring in supplies.

That situation prevailed for 10 days, after which things started to improve following the entry of troops from the Republic of Guinea into the war. Guinea had been observing things across its southern border since the start of hostilities and it was clear that if the rebels won that war a domino effect might occur and they might be next. Therefore, they sent in troops, to prop up the collapsing Freetown hierarchy, together with a sizeable force of armour. Once that happened, we returned to Cockerill and were really back in the saddle again and flying constantly.

The Guinean Army entered the country in the north, through the town of Kambia. Initial elements included some tanks and BM-21 Katyusha multiple rocket launchers (MRLs). Nellis recalls flying out ammunition to the new arrivals shortly afterwards.

> Then we got reports in at Cockerill about the rebels having overrun a position that had been held by the Guinean Army and having captured one of the rocket launch vehicles, which was serious. Headquarters did a bit of scratching on its own and soon discovered that the BM-21 hadn't been taken by force, but instead it had been sold to the rebels for diamonds. The sad part about this was that the MRL was then used to good effect against the same Guinean troops who had entered the country on a rescue mission.

One of the worst experiences that Nellis and his people lived through took place in January 1999. That was a time when the rebels were making a concerted push towards Freetown.

Their advance parties had already reached Waterloo, and if they were able to achieve a breakthrough there, there would have been very little between them and Freetown because ECOMOG and the Sierra Leonean Army—or what was left of it—were already overextended.

It was touch and go for several days, recalled Nellis. The extent of the fighting, which covered a large front, could be gauged from the fact that an army contingent from the Republic of Guinea, attached to the ECO-MOG force, had deployed a squadron of Russian-built T-55 tanks, and they were almost overrun at one stage. From the start it was a tough, tenuous fight to maintain positions in strength, and both sides took heavy casualties.

Then Nellis was called on to do a re-supply flight, bringing in ammunition to the Guinean battalion who were north of Freetown, not far from the border with Guinea. It meant taking the Hind into a situation that was not only uncertain, but also speculative from a safety point of view. Added to that, he could speak no French and the Guineans couldn't, or rather wouldn't, understand any English. He recalls: 'I'd asked for a sitrep on their status and what the rebels were doing. They came back on the radio and

Executive Outcomes started their Sierra Leone operations from the military headquarters at Cockerill Barracks: conditions were primitive from the start. *Author's photo*

said that all was "Charlie Charlie"—in other words, cool and calm.'
At this point Nellis laughed. He explained:

> My experience in that war was that whenever anybody reported that conditions were cool and calm, it meant that their faces were cool from the wind while running away from battle. The calm aspect would emerge after whoever was doing the reporting got to an area where there was no fighting!

Nellis explained that under normal circumstances, the Hind would have had one of the Guinean Army liaison officers on board, a man called Benson who spoke good English and who accompanied the chopper whenever they re-supplied positions held by Guinean soldiers. However, on that day, for some reason, Benson suddenly found half a dozen excuses for not flying when the South African suggested he go up with them. Nellis recalls:

Obviously, I couldn't help but smell a rat . . . I certainly sensed that something untoward was happening. So we took off. As usual, the Hind was loaded to the max with ammunition, but I couldn't shake the nagging suspicion that there was something wrong. Still, the men on the ground where we were heading said that all was fine and, who knows, perhaps it was.

However, we were acutely conscious of the fact that quite often government or ECOMOG troops in the interior wouldn't tell us when they were under attack. It was a logical reaction, I suppose, because they felt we might not bring in the supplies they urgently needed. They would act this way in order to get what they had asked for, and most of the time they were pretty desperate because almost always there was a shortage of ammo.

Nellis was circumspect about any such deception. It was his view that he and the crew were exposed to real danger on just about every flight and that it wasn't necessary to compound the issue by lying about the situation. In this case, though, the trip was a short hop across the hills and he had been into that LZ before. He reckoned they'd be in and out before anybody knew they'd arrived.

However, there was a problem with getting to the LZ at Waterloo. It lay between two rows of hills, which meant that there was only one route in and out of the place, which was over the town itself. If the rebels were in the area, as they were, everybody on board was aware that there would be a tough reception.

An interesting sideline to the sortie was that the crew had recently had to fork out some of their own money to buy new flying helmets. These were state-of-the-art pieces of kit and had come in a barter deal from ICI. Nellis found that while the helmets were the best things since sliced bread, they did tend to deaden external noise, especially the crack of bullets passing close to the helicopter.

On that mission, just as I came into the flare for the landing, I heard a variety of noises coming towards us. All were very loud and it was obvious the helicopter was taking some serious fire. Just then, though, I was committed to land and there was no going back, especially with three tons of ammo on board. So it was a question of ignoring the incoming fire and concentrating on getting our wheels on the ground.

As Nellis tells it, the surface of the LZ had been in regular use by both helicopters and vehicles for several weeks and had been churned into a fine powder. The presence of a squadron of Guinean tanks didn't help either. Therefore, just as the helicopter came into the hover, its rotors caused the entire area to be enveloped in a brownout, which was just as well, he thought, because the enemy couldn't see what they were shooting at either.

However, once down, it seemed as if all the ground troops had either taken cover or were exchanging fire so there was nobody to help offload the three tons of explosive cargo. Worse, said Nellis, none of them would leave their trenches:

> This meant that we were left, too heavy for take-off in that confined space, and just had to sit there. After a while a couple of soldiers arrived and gave Fred and Mohammed a hand, but it was tense. Again, one of my greatest fears was, as always, that we'd be hit by an RPG. So I kept the rotors going and kept up churning the dust as we needed all the cover we could get.

Getting the ammunition away took longer than the crew might have liked and, once finished, Nellis again had to pass through a hail of small arms fire to get clear of Waterloo. Fred did well, he said. Immediately after lift-off he managed to kill a rebel, who was about fire an RPG, before he could launch the rocket. 'We were going through transition and moving relatively slowly and he slotted the guy as he was about to pull the trigger.' Both Nellis and Hassan were emphatic that were it not for Fred's skills with his GPMG, they'd most probably have been taken out.

CHAPTER FOURTEEN

THE WAR GATHERS MOMENTUM

The small town of Daru in the east of Sierra Leone had become quite notable as a strong government 'hold-out enclave' against rebel advances and Nellis and his crew, once again flying from Cockerill, were supplying the Nigerian Army there twice a week by air. Colonel Kholbe and his people insisted that the Air Wing stick to a strict routine. They left at the same time each Wednesday and Saturday and returned before dark.

For obvious reasons, I insisted on varying this. The rebels had become familiar with our routine and they would be waiting for us. If they were expecting us, when we'd get overhead they would let go with everything they had in their armoury in the hope of bringing us down.

The Nigerians thought otherwise. They insisted that they were paying Nellis and his crew enough to accept their orders. As he was flying an average of ten hours a day at $2,000 an hour, Nellis couldn't really argue. This meant that he had to stick to the routine.

One thing that Nellis was well aware of was that fighting in remote regions sometimes made for strange bedfellows. Just then, getting in and out of Daru was no exception.

There would sometimes be a journalist or two asking for a ride to the front, and although I would have liked to help—usually in the interests of creating what I reckoned was 'a more realistic image of what we're doing'—it often wasn't possible. Other times we would need to use what help was available, particularly in the early days, and curiously, there was always some willing hand hanging around the base who hoped that he could get involved with us.

One of those who came along was George Yazid, a gangling, confidant young man with long-boned walker's shanks. Although born in Sierra Leone, he had grown up with one foot in Ireland and the other in Africa. Jesuit-educated in Canada and trained in electronics, he was a useful addition to the crew, especially when some of the pernickety things that could go wrong with a helicopter, did.

As Nellis tells it, Yazid apparently had something of a military background, but what he and the boys were doing was all new to him. 'Anyway, as he told us all one night at Paddy's, he thought he could learn something if he could attach himself to us.'

Yazid had mentioned to Nellis that if he were stuck for help then he'd fly with him. As it happened, round about that time Nellis was suddenly

The only armour available in Sierra Leone through the war was a handful of battered old Soviet BMP-2 armoured personnel carriers that Executive Outcomes mercenaries had to try to keep operational if they were to be of any use. *Photographed in Angola while with EO by the author*

seriously short-handed. After recovering from his last bout of malaria, Juba had gone off to Europe, ostensibly to buy another helicopter, so Nellis was flying the Mi-17 on his own.

On their first sortie together, Nellis and Yazid flew to Daru, which, as luck would have it, lay at the far end of the helicopter's fuel limitation envelope. As Nellis recalls, the place was close enough to the Liberian border to mean trouble and the only people there were some Nigerian soldiers and a squad or two of Sierra Leonean Army troops who were so doped that they didn't know day from night.

'We'd barely got down and joined some of the guys on the ground, who were busy preparing their daily ration of rice, when the shooting started . . . there was incoming coming from all over the place.' The situation was extremely hazardous so Nellis urged his crew to get going, and waited impatiently for everybody to board.

Yazid, meanwhile, had occupied the co-pilot seat and seemed to view the process with the kind of detached equanimity that might have been better suited to a Sunday drive back home. Surprised, Nellis leant across: 'You're aware of course that we're being shot at?' he asked, his faced creased with a smile.

'Yeh, reckon so,' the youngster replied, 'but what's there to do about it?' Point taken. His laid-back approach both impressed and pleased Nellis. Yazid might be useful in a tight spot, he thought

Just then, eager as hell to get the hell out of there, Nellis upped the revs. Indicating with his hands, he told the others that he was about to lift off. It was the only way to settle everybody. With that, a Sierra Leonean Army sergeant major moved forward and brusquely ordered a Nigerian corporal out of the engineer's seat. 'Get up. I'm sitting there!' he barked and promptly sat down between Yazid and Nellis. He was a big guy, Nellis recalled and, anyway, it was no time to argue.

The NCO had barely strapped in when an AK round came though the fuselage and went straight into his leg. The exit wound it made was the size of a man's fist and, although it would have been worse had he taken a gut wound, the crew had a job on their hands trying to stop the man bleeding to death.

'Fucker had it coming', exclaimed Yazid when he told the story afterwards. 'Better him than me. But that bullet did come right between Nellis and me and hit him square on, so it must have been sooo close!' He said, laughing.

George Yazid flew regularly with Nellis and the boys after that. In the end, he proved to be a useful acquisition, although the group never had any money to pay him. However, he saw good action and used his new-found experiences to eventually get a job with PAE.

By mid-February, 1999, Juba Joubert had returned to Sierra Leone with a pair of Mi-24 helicopter gunships, which were crated in an Ilyushin transport aircraft. There were also great piles of ammunition on board, along with several Russian technicians, who were there to put the package together, and a Moscow-based test pilot. Nellis recalls:

> We didn't really need the man but, what the hell, he was there. About the third afternoon, I was tasked to fly to Lungi with a load of rations, and asked our illustrious test pilot friend if he'd like to come along for the ride. Trouble was, he spoke no English and I knew no Russian. He settled straight into my right-hand seat in the Mi-17 and I didn't argue. If he wanted to fly the chopper, I'd let him. It was probably the worst decision of my life.
>
> For a start, he'd been drinking vodka, by then probably half a bottle of the stuff. I could also see that, being accustomed to the cold climate of Eastern Europe, he'd underestimated the effect heat would have on the chopper lifting off. He started rolling forward and when he got to transition, he just lifted the collective to take-off, which meant that the helicopter dropped away at the end of our all-too-short runway. I would have liked to think that he was also aware that at 88 per cent power, everything cuts out, including autopilot and the machine's electrical system.
>
> I saw what was coming and grabbed the controls, but the Russian wouldn't let go: he simply froze. Sindaba, sharp guy that he is, quickly turned round and slapped the man across the face with a powerful backhand. Only then did the Russian yield, allowing me to control once more.
>
> Just then, the helicopter was over the swamps and water that surrounded the base on two sides out of three, and my only option

While Nellis fought the air war in West Africa, former Executive Outcomes members waged a maritime struggle against infiltrators and smugglers coming into the country from the sea. *Author's photo*

was to come down on power and allow the engines to build up revs. Several observers at the base said that they could see that our wheels actually touched the water several times. Had we gone into the drink that day, it would have been my third crash.

By the time the chopper got to Lungi, the Russian was severely shaken. His face was white and his hands trembled. Repeatedly, he said sorry. Nellis thought the best thing to do to get the man's confidence back was to ask him to handle the return flight to Cockerill Barracks, but he refused.

Only weeks later, the two Hinds had been tested and were ready to fly. Juba, despite his drinking, had effectively handled Nellis' conversion so that he was almost as confident at the controls of the Mi-24 as he was at those of the Hip. He'd quickly mastered the 12.7mm four-barrelled Gatling as well as the gunship's 57mm rockets. Nellis recalls:

We celebrated the event by taking President Kabbah and Brigadier-General Kholbe on a formation fly-past over Freetown. We did it, not only to show the populace and the enemy that we were serviceable and working, but to boost our own confidence as well.

By now, our beloved 'Bokkie' was very tired indeed. In theory, we could still get an all-up weight of 14 tons out of her but, once in the air, we'd be well below the accepted cruising speed. Also, the Hip was over-vibrating, which was worrying. It told us that she needed a serious overhaul. In reality, she actually needed a new set of engines, but there was no money for that.

Then the old girl's tanks started to crack and sometimes the floor at the back would be covered in kerosene when we got back to base. However, as we were being paid the stipulated two grand an hour, we kept on pushing 'Bokkie' to the limit, even though we knew something would eventually have to give. We just hoped it wouldn't happen over Injun Country.

It was round about this time that Nellis and crew were called out on a mission to Magburaka. They were to deliver rations to Nigerian troops operating in the region. On the way there, Nellis spotted some burning villages and it was obvious to everybody on board that there was a lot of rebel activity. They circled the area for several minutes but found nothing.

After we'd offloaded our cargo and were heading back to base, we spotted even more burning villages and also came upon a group of the enemy digging deep trenches across the only road linking that region to Freetown. Some of the holes were already two metres deep, which meant that they intended ambushing the next ECO-MOG convoy heading that way.

Of course, Fred opened up and the rebels retaliated with their AKs and a lone 12.7mm heavy machine gun, after which they all bombshelled into the jungle. After getting back to Cockerill, Fred did his routine checks and came back to the ready room with the news—it was not good. There had been half a dozen hits in all and one of the rebel rounds, probably from a 12.7mm DShK, had gone through one of the rotor blades, almost severing it. It was an understatement to say that we were lucky to get back home: the rotor could have snapped off at any time.

Sindaba patched the old girl up and we flew her across the bay to Lungi, but even that trip was tentative because the helicopter vibrated throughout the flight. It was the last time we took 'Bokkie' up, but it was some consolation that we knew it was way past her time to be put out to pasture.

The almost derelict Hip was sold some years later to a Lebanese businessman who, Nellis reckons, ended up doing something with her, although he reckons that it must have cost quite a lot of money because 'Bokkie' needed an extensive overhaul.

The start of full operations with the Mi-24s was marred by Juba's drinking. Since he'd returned from Europe, his boozing had got worse. The consensus among the guys was that the Frenchman JJ was responsible and that the man had a seriously bad influence on Juba. However, as Nellis conceded, Juba was the master of his own destiny and there was nothing Nellis or anybody else could do about it.

Then Juba went down with malaria again and was evacuated to South Africa where it was diagnosed as cerebral. Fortunately, he took JJ with him and he eventually recovered, although nobody was ever sure whether it was quinine or the booze that pulled him through.

The situation was further exacerbated by money. Juba had appointed himself as our financial expert and it didn't help that we battled every month to get enough from him to keep the show on the road. Finally, he sent us a message, saying that all our cash had been spent. 'There is nothing left', he declared.

Only much later did we discover that Juba and JJ had squandered much of it on holidays in France, which involved a minor army of women, and on hiring canal barges which took them all over Europe. Naturally, I was furious, and so were our other partners, Fred and the Ethiopian engineer Sindaba. They felt they had been seriously screwed over.

Totally unexpectedly, it was the Sierra Leonean Government that came to the rescue. The authorities in Freetown owed the group a huge amount of money and suddenly there was cash in abundance. They deposited their first tranche into a Freetown bank account and put Hassan in charge of all their finances.

> It was a relationship that was outstanding and it went on for years. Hassan was not only cautious with our finances but he was also meticulous and transparent. It was a major step forward for us all, especially now that Juba was out of the picture.
>
> At that point we decided to formalise our partnership with the government and created a commercial entity that we called Jesa Air West Africa Pty Ltd (Jesaair).

The name was basically an anagram, Nellis explained: the 'J' stood for Juba (Nellis kept him in the loop, although both Fred and Sindaba weren't happy), with the 'E' for Ellis, 'S' for Sindaba, and the 'A' for Alfonso, who was actually Fred Marafono. Interestingly, the name 'Fred Alfonso' was a legacy of the days when Fred Marafono worked for an anti-poaching unit in Southern Africa. He even burned off the 'Who Dares Wins' SAS tattoo on his forearm because, in the apartheid era, he could then pass for a 'darkie'.[1]

Juba eventually returned to Freetown but this made the atmosphere within the newly founded company very strained.

> Juba was totally out of control and I was actually worried that somebody might take out a contract on the man, which is not unheard of in an environment where a man with a $10 bill in his pocket is considered rich.
>
> Then Juba went down again, and his illness was more serious than before because he had contracted a form of tropical hepatitis that affected his liver. Give Juba his dues: he immediately stopped smoking and drinking and decided to return permanently to South Africa.

Meanwhile, with peace talks in the air, the war had also wound down significantly. That meant that Jesaair's contract with the government was scaled down. The enemy was supposed to have laid down its arms since members of the opposing junta had been taken into a coalition government. However, in reality, little had changed, even though Foday Sankoh had been given the role of Minister of Energy and Mines in the Freetown government.

As soon as the peace talks were mooted, a group of former RUF rebels started taking hostages and the Air Wing was again tasked to continue with operations against dissident groups.

We were called out to the Kenema area to do some reconnaissance work on rebel positions at Segbwema. We were returning late that afternoon to Cockerill, to refuel and rearm with ammunition for the Gatling, when JJ, who had been observing events in an adjacent area in the fixed wing, picked up a large force of rebel vehicles heading our way. He reckoned the force was about 1,000-plus strong and after spotting his aircraft, the rebels started using civilians as human shields.

Obviously, this was a job for the Hind, so I went across and saw the column, but I didn't know what to do. If I fired indiscriminately I reckoned that I'd kill civilians. Finally, I decided to fire my rockets about a third the way down the line, but as I started my run-in, I knew that my rockets weren't synchronised.

Then, quite suddenly, fate took a hand. The rebels all bombshelled into the jungle on either side of the road and their civilian hostages remained on the road, almost all of them paralysed with fear. I'd meanwhile readjusted my aim, put the pipper directly onto the civilians and fired, knowing full well that the rockets wouldn't hit what I was aiming at.

Every single one of the 64 rockets that I'd fired in that monumental salvo diverted from its original trajectory and veered off track. They exploded in a massive cluster where the rebels had taken cover in the jungle. Meanwhile, the civilians were all still huddled in the middle of the road.

With that, the rebels abandoned their hostages and turned around. Subsequent radio messages indicated that I'd killed about 70 enemy soldiers, without a single civilian casualty.

CHAPTER FIFTEEN

THE WAR GOES ON . . . AND ON . . .

Diamonds made the world go round in Sierra Leone, said Nellis when speaking about the lure of the precious stones in many African countries, 'and many of my detractors, people who deprecated my actions, insisted that I was only there to make my fortune'. He continued:

> To these people, it mattered little whether the rebels were cutting the hands and feet off children, or roasting their enemies alive and eating them. Instead, they concentrated their efforts on trying to dislodge this 'foreign mercenary' who was making a living by flying helicopter gunships in the war. That I was killing these barbarians was of no consequence to this pretty vocal bunch.
>
> Unfortunately, while being involved in this internecine struggle, I'd become a media figure. One of the reasons for this was that the word had gone out that I was working hand-in-glove with the British to try to bring hostilities to a close. A number of my Freetown 'enemies' worked for NGOs and many of them actually sympathised, and sometimes clandestinely associated, with the brutal murderers in the RUF. These people sought a means of terminating what they termed, my 'dreadful mercenary actions'.

They were an odd bunch, Nellis admitted. He would say that if you met them at a party in Hounslow or Clapham, they'd be like anybody else. However, he reckoned that they could be lethal.

I was tipped off at one stage, beforehand fortunately, that they even considered pouring cups of sugar into the fuel tank of my helicopter so that the Hind's engines would seize while we were out on ops. It never happened, of course, because they'd have had to get into Cockerill Barracks first. However, I know that had they been able to, they would have done so.

Then somebody put the word out that Nellis wasn't actually a military man at all, but a diamond smuggler. 'You can't win with some of these people', he flatly declared.

I was actually investigated several times by a United Nations Special Investigative Committee. They wouldn't be overly specific about what they were investigating but, soon enough, the diamond issue would surface. The first time was towards the end of 1999 when our entire crew was accused of smuggling diamonds. I was fingered as the principal culprit, although nobody was able to produce any evidence because there wasn't any. I was as broke then as I am today, which wouldn't have been the case had I been dealing in the stuff.

One of the 'Golden Rules' laid out by Nellis and Juba early on was that nobody on the team would get involved with either gold or diamonds. If they did, he said, even legally, they would be dismissed. It was what was termed a 'zero tolerance' issue. The same restrictions applied to drugs.

There was very good reason for us taking what some might have regarded as an uncompromising stance. We all knew that the Nigerians were smuggling diamonds. Not only that, they were doing so on an enormous scale . . . you couldn't miss it because the same people who sidled up and offered us parcels of diamonds, would later be seen doing deals with the Nigerian soldiers. Worse, they weren't even discreet about it.

Some Nigerians tried to load suspicious cargoes onto the choppers. A number of times Fred stopped them loading bags of what they said was 'gravel' onto both 'Bokkie' and the Hind. A Nigerian officer would arrive at a pick-up point in the interior with what he would say was rice—ten or 12 large bags of it. However, a closer examination would show that the bags were all filled with diamondiferous gravel.

We had some serious confrontations with these people. They told us that they had been deprived of their rights by our lack of cooperation and we left it to Fred to read them their so-called 'rights'. More than once we were threatened that the matter wouldn't be laid to rest.

So be it! We had Foday Sankoh's jungle bunnies on one side and the Nigerian Army on the other, but we won in the end, which just about says it all.

It was interesting, he commented, that none of the people working for NGOs, or even the diplomats at local embassies, would ever confront members of the helicopter crew face-to-face. However, they would later hear accusations of smuggling and, as Nellis commented, it rankled.

These people didn't have the balls to accost either me or any of the members of the crew directly. Once or twice I had to stop Fred from flattering the nose of some particularly obnoxious little shit who believed he could voice off and that we wouldn't dare react.

In any war, repeated success in the field invariably leads to charges of human rights abuses, particularly where innocent civilians are involved. As well as being denounced as a diamond smuggler, Neall Ellis was also routinely accused of using his Mi-24 helicopter gunship indiscriminately, especially when he targeted RUF vehicles parked in or near villages or marketplaces. As he declared to one critic, 'this was a regular ploy, used in the same way that the rebels would paint big red crosses on the roofs of buildings they used for military headquarters or operations centres'.

It was also pointed out that there was no International Committee of the Red Cross (ICRC) activity in the field either in Sierra Leone or Liberia, although that organisation was very well represented in the capitals of both countries. The truth was that the situation was just too dangerous in the jungle, where the fighting was at its most intense, for any kind of effective aid work. Anyway, the average pubescent rebel had no respect for the ICRC, the media, or the UN, for that matter. Most of these youngsters, high on liquor and drugs for 18 hours of the day, wouldn't have known the difference between a UN official and the postman anyway.

One of the more dedicated people to emerge in West Africa during this time was a young woman by the name of Corinne Dufka. Formerly a journalist, she had covered the war in the Balkans and was so badly wounded by a land mine in Bosnia that she had almost died. Corinne had been living in West Africa for many years, mostly in Dakar.

Nellis' Mi-24 coming into land at Cockerill Barracks. *Author's photo*

As the regional representative of Human Rights Watch, it was her job to check on all reports that emerged as a result of the war, and she was particularly scathing about some of the Liberian and Nigerian excesses. While organisations like Human Rights Watch are usually circumspect about their comments, Corinne Dufka was not afraid to call a spade a spade. Nellis comments about her:

I would return from a mission and if I spotted something unusual . . . [I would] get on the phone and tell her immediately, particularly once the RUF moved into its destructive second phase and started destroying villages and killing their inhabitants. You really couldn't miss it from the air because there would invariably be bodies strewn about all over the place.

Corinne was one of those rare individuals who would listen carefully to everything that emerged. Then she'd record the detail in her files and later, when a village was reported destroyed or possibly torched (the rebels would quite often claim I'd shot the place up), she'd refer back. A sharp lady, she always made up her own mind about these things and wasn't shy to ask questions that could make you squirm if you weren't being direct.

It didn't take Ms Dufka long to accept that Neall Ellis, for all his other faults, was meticulous about the way he waged his war. By his own admission, he never targeted a village unless he had prior information that the rebels were using the place to their own advantage or he saw evidence of unauthorised military activity. If he did unexpectedly come upon a group of men in the field, he would first check them out carefully for the kind of uniforms they wore and whether they carried weapons. Nellis recalls:

Most of the time, the rebels would hear the Hind approach and they would quickly scoot into the jungle . . . then, I knew I was onto something. One incident happened when we were returning from a sortie north of Makeni, the biggest town in the central region. I happened to fly over an RUF stronghold . . . I'd do so quite regularly just to wind them up. This didn't exactly go down well with the local UN command because they claimed I was antagonising the bastards, and of course they were spot on. That's what this was all about.

It was also one of the reasons why the UN was so fucking useless in Sierra Leone. They were terrified of the rebels and would back down every time they encountered them in the interior. More than once the RUF would surround groups of UN soldiers and demand that they hand over their firearms, which they would do without argument.[1]

I didn't listen to the UN, in fact nobody did. So I went about my business and the next time I flew over Makeni, I spotted four brand new vehicles parked next to the market, two with 12.7mm heavy machine guns mounted on the back. The other two were crowded with RUF troops and they had a 14.5mm gun there as well. We subsequently understood from a capture that they had originally come from Liberia and had either just returned from a raid or were in the process of going out on one. The bottom line here was that I caught them totally by surprise.

Of course, with all that firepower, they immediately opened up on us and the game was on, good and proper. They had suddenly presented us with some of their moveable assets, which were just too valuable to ignore. I wasted no time, and in my first pass I let rip with a clutch of rockets. This completely destroyed two of the trucks and, from what I gathered afterwards, killed quite a few of their occupants.

A few days later, a complaint was lodged by the rebel command through their unofficial representative in Freetown. It was claimed that I had bombed a market and killed dozens of unarmed civilians. Fortunately, I had detailed the attack in a dispatch to Corinne after I got back to the office and I had told her exactly what had taken place. She called me back some days later and repeated the same story, but obviously from the rebel perspective. Then a special court was convened in Freetown and I was told by UN officials that my name had been put forward for human rights abuses.

Nothing came of it in the end because Ms Dufka was called to testify and she obviously mentioned Nellis' earlier report. Another independent source had said she had seen the vehicles that the gunship had destroyed, together with the heavy weapons. 'I still keep in e-mail contact with Corinne. She is an all-round lovely person', says Nellis.

Much of this adverse publicity, some of it clearly linked to enemy misinformation that could be tied to people with rebel connections, came at a time when the Kamajors were at their best as a counter-insurgency force.

Officially termed Civil Defence Forces, these resilient fighters gave as good as they got, and then some, according to Nellis. It helped, of course, that they were extremely professional when it came to handling firearms, which was one of the reasons why the Nigerians included them within the ranks of ECOMOG. 'Though why Kholbe and his people subsequently subverted all Kamajor efforts remains a mystery', comments Nellis cynically. He believes that it was all part of the ongoing West African imbroglio that included Nigerian efforts to prolong the war, remain in Sierra Leone as long as possible and get a grip on the diamond industry.

The single biggest issue that faced the Kamajors, a Mende tribal people from the south and the east of the country, was that they were not militarily trained. For that reason, regular troops tended to look down on them and consider them the African version of country bumpkins. At the same time, although they were largely illiterate, they consistently outfought and outperformed both Fodah Sankoh's rebel forces and the RSLAF.

Another rumour that did the rounds, which was also fallacious, was that the Kamajors were ill-disciplined. They obviously had some bad apples, as do most military units, commented Nellis, but he recalls working with them during the second invasion of Freetown by Foday Sankoh's irregulars. While 'Bokkie' was still in use, he'd drop small groups of Kamajors and Nigerian soldiers, usually with his partner Hassan in the lead, and they would deploy against fairly substantial groups of RUF rebels who sometimes outnumbered them by 20 to one.

'It was rare that our guys came up short. The Kamajors weren't only good fighters, they were utterly fearless and they didn't take an awful lot of casualties either', said Nellis. They also took no prisoners, he told me much later. Nellis put the Kamajors way up there with the Gurkhas when it came to rating their efficiency in battle.

Earlier in the war the term 'Sobels'—soldiers by day, rebels by night—had been coined. Many critics of Kamajor prowess maintained that these tribal fighters were among the worst offenders, a claim Nellis dismissed out of hand.

'Sure,' says Nellis, 'there was the occasional Kamajor among the very irregular "Sobels", but almost all of these renegades were government troops on the plunder . . . I saw them myself, and there was no question about who were the apprentice turncoats', he declared. He added that when Chief Hinga Norman—the Kamajor spokesman, protector and mentor—

unexpectedly died in a Dakar hospital after surgery (the family maintains, with some justification, that he was poisoned) there was nobody powerful enough in Sierra Leone to take up their case. 'That was when the Kamajors were quite openly accused of "pillaging, terrorizing and killing".' They were also accused of recruiting youngsters under the age of 15, in contravention of the Geneva Convention. The truth is that the majority of the rebel forces were under age and almost nobody was brought to book on that issue after the fighting had ended.

Many stories about the Kamajors emerged during the war, some based on fact, others apocryphal. Shortly after the Makeni incident, Nellis and his crew were tasked to go to Moyamba to uplift as many of the Kamajor bush fighters as possible and fly them to Freetown. The rebels were marching towards Freetown and the intention was to deploy the tough and aggressive Kamajors in the defence of the approaches to the city. Nellis recounts:

> We'd earlier lost our one rear door and I had the other removed as well. The result was that we were flying with the back of the aircraft wide open, which was not a good idea. We would have no control over people who might have been trying to get on board in a chaotic situation. Also, we were aware that EO had lost one of their helicopters due to ill-disciplined soldiers running away from battle. When we finally did land at Moyamba, however, we had the Kamajors storming us for a different reason. They were all eager to go into battle against the rebels and we had been sent by their jungle gods to take them there.'

Ellis said that it felt as if an entire company of Kamajors had squeezed on board. Worse, not one of them would get off although the crew begged, pleaded and even tried bribery. In fact, they did a count afterwards and found that there were 91 of them in the helicopter. As these men were considered by one and all as a bunch of mean bastards if they believed that you were opposed to them, the crew were in something of a Catch-22 situation.

> They refused to budge and there was no way I could take off . . . we had reached stalemate. Basically, the LZ was a small football

One of the Hind's side-gunners takes aim at ground targets on a strike. *Author's photo*

field surrounded by dozens of tall trees, some more than 100ft high. Also, the outside air temperature was about 38 degrees Centigrade. While 'Bokkie' wasn't underpowered, the Mi-17 definitely didn't have enough engine power to get itself out of a relatively confined area with so many people on board, the total weight was roughly three times over factory limitations.

The crew kept trying, but even threats didn't work, Nellis recalled. They couldn't even get one of them to remain behind. Also, these guys were completely spaced out. Nellis explained that as fighters the Kamajors weren't into the kind of drugs that most of us in the western world are familiar with. However, before each battle, they'd go through a ritual of their own, which often involved gulping down an extremely potent concoction that tended to liven things up a little.

Just then at the back of the helicopter, these guys really were on cloud nine and making a healthy din as well. They could probably be heard singing and shouting from a mile away, which was when I realized that the only way to get them out of my machine was to switch off the engines and try to talk some sense into the heads of their leaders. We went through all those motions but that didn't work either.

The heat was steadily becoming more intense, as it does in the after-noons in the tropics. By late afternoon, Nellis knew it was like an oven in the back of his Hip with all those soldiers confined to a relatively tiny, air-less area. In fact, he recalls, they were propped up, standing against each other, and if ever the analogy about being jammed into a sardine can was appropriate, he reckoned this was it!

> After about an hour or so, the noise and chanting began to abate. Some of the Kamajors, soaked from top to toe with sweat, climbed out and went looking for something to drink. Obviously, there were quite a few who had become dehydrated, which probably helped in the end.
>
> After that it wasn't long before we managed to get some order out of the situation. I promised their leader that we would take as many as we could in the first run and return later to uplift the rest. That way we were able to select who was actually going to war. When we finally landed at Freetown, 54 of these Kamajor fighters disembarked from the helicopter, which was not bad for a 24-seater!
>
> Although they were skilled fighters, the Kamajors were up against an extremely aggressive enemy who had become accus-tomed to meeting little, if any, resistance, from government forces. When the war flared up again in late 1999, Foday Sankoh's RUF quickly demonstrated that it was better trained and more than ad-equately equipped than it had been in the past, in large part be-cause of the support it got from Liberia's Charles Taylor.

'Because of earlier results,' commented Nellis, 'we knew that Sankoh's rebel army was powerfully motivated to achieve its single objective: the control of the entire country by force. Moreover, their combat ability was obvious and they succeeded just about every time they set out to capture a position held by government forces.' Within a month of going back to war in 1999, Sankoh's revolutionaries could go just about anywhere they wanted, except in the capital of Freetown.

Foday Sankoh's twisted path to power as the head of the RUF spanned decades and meandered through several countries in Europe and Africa.

This radicalized 1970s student leader worked for a while as a television cameraman in Freetown before he joined the Sierra Leonean Army. He did part of his military training in Nigeria and the United Kingdom.

In 1971, Corporal Sankoh was cashiered from the army's signal corps and imprisoned for seven years at the Pademba Road Prison in Freetown for taking part in a mutiny. On his release, he worked as an itinerant photographer in the south and east of Sierra Leone, eventually making contact with a group of young anti-government radicals.

His anti-establishment stance always fringed on the criminal and he ended up in jail several more times. When he was freed the final time in the 1980s, Sankoh fled with fellow Sierra Leonean exiles to Libya, where President Muammar Gaddafi was stirring up West African dissidents like Sankoh.

Powerfully opposed to those with wealth and anxious to lead his own rebellion, it was at Sabha, a remote and isolated terrorist training base deep in the Libyan Sahara, that Sankoh crafted a convenient alliance with Liberia's Charles Taylor who was planning his own internal coup. Taylor's bloody uprising ended with him seizing the presidency in neighbouring Monrovia in 1998 and it took him eight hard years of fighting to get there. Meanwhile, Sankoh and confederates, Rashid Mansaray and Abu Kanu, solicited support from Gaddafi for an armed uprising to oust the Sierra Leonean APC government.

With the support of Taylor, Sankoh spent much of the two years following a ceasefire to totally revamp his revolutionary army. Gaddafi

Nellis fires a rocket salvo at an enemy heavy machine-gun mounted on the back of a Land Rover. It took a couple of passes, but the weapon and the vehicle were finally destroyed. *Author's photo*

provided material and financial support, while other countries linked to the rebels were Burkina Faso and, to a lesser extent, Sudan.

Another, more ominous, factor only emerged later, after the rebel threat had been effectively countered, which may have a bearing on why Britain took such drastic steps to defeat the rebels. Islamic cadres linked to Osama bin Laden were also involved in the war. The al-Qaeda leader's money funded a portion of the rebel diamond operations in Sierra Leone, and some of it was spent arming the RUF.

We now know that the RUF employed Russian, Ukrainian, South African, and other African mercenaries. Deployed operationally, many of these people were responsible for combat command and control as well as logistics and communications. For their part, the South Africans concentrated their efforts on imparting many of the principles they had used to good effect in their own wars in Namibia and Angola, which was one of the reasons the rebels initially gained as much ground as they did.

These 'hired guns' did not come cheap. Virtually every mercenary wielding a rifle or piloting a craft wanted diamonds, which was basically what the fighting was about. President Taylor's cut was about a half of the gemstones carried, driven, flown or shipped across his border. His take was so large that it explains why, within a comparatively short three or four years, Liberia emerged in London, Johannesburg, Antwerp, and Tel Aviv as a diamond exporting country of significance.

Meanwhile, the war dragged on. On two occasions the rebels fought their way to within spitting distance of the gates of Freetown. Both times RUF forces were beaten back by a single helicopter gunship flown by Nellis, the government's lone South African mercenary pilot. Distanced from their own supply lines, which ran out of Liberia, the rebels did not have the proper weaponry to counter the Nellis' airborne firepower. His gunship had a 57mm rocket pod mounted under each of its winglets and a four-barrelled 12.7mm Gatling mounted in the nose which could fire nearly 4,000 rounds a minute.

Once the war was over, Sankoh was handed to the British and, under jurisdiction of a UN-backed court, he was indicted on 17 counts for war crimes, including the use of child soldiers as well as crimes against humanity that included charges of ethnic cleansing, extermination, enslavement, rape and sexual slavery.

CHAPTER SIXTEEN

THE Mi-24 HELICOPTER GUNSHIP GOES TO WAR

There was also a lot of intrigue in Sierra Leone in June 2000. Neall recalls that:

> As the conflict gathered momentum, you never really spoke your mind to somebody you didn't know really well . . . and even then you could make a mistake. There were times when the war deteriorated into a kind of limbo and neither side was making headway. Then RUF supporters would quickly put the word out that the government was losing and that Sankoh's people had taken the initiative. In truth, neither side was actually winning, but it was difficult to prove otherwise because that's the way these insurgencies go. One of the immediate consequences was that many people hedged their bets. Like the Sobels, they would be government supporters one moment and powerfully pro-rebel the next. It was almost a kind of life insurance.

Neall says that those who acted this way included 'people who we believed we could trust and work with'. Among the worst culprits were some senior members of the Nigerian Army, in particular the unpredictable second-in-command of the United Nations Mission in Sierra Leone (UN-AMSIL) forces, Major General Mohammed A. Garba. Eventually, the UN Force Commander in Sierra Leone, Indian Major General Vijay Jetley, accused a group of Nigerian political and military officials at the top of the international military mission in Freetown 'of working hard to sabotage the peace process . . . and the Nigerian Army command of looting diamonds in league with the rebel leader, Foday Sankoh'.

This was nothing new, said Nellis:

The media had been aware for a while that the Nigerians were playing silly buggers with the rebels because they wanted their grubby paws on the diamonds, which was really what it was all about. Then, about halfway through my stay in Sierra Leone, things took another turn, following the interception of a signal at army headquarters which caused me to ambush a rebel convoy on the road between Lunsar and Makeni. That strike killed and wounded some of the key players in the rebel command.

Ironically, though Nigerian staff officer Garba was implicated in an anti-government plot, General Vijay Jetley, the Indian officer in charge of UN operations in Sierra Leone, ended up losing his job.

Nellis went on to say:

What Garba's subterfuge did for me was to indirectly offer the Freetown government the opportunity of a risky but daring raid against RUF command elements. It was an ambush that relied more on gut instinct than military intelligence and that it came off at all was remarkable . . . obviously we had our share of luck.

Here, Nellis outlines the events that led up to this attack and sets the scene for what followed:

A few days before 19 June 2000, we intercepted a radio message from the regional rebel headquarters in Makeni. Everything we heard suggested that the RUF command had been in contact with

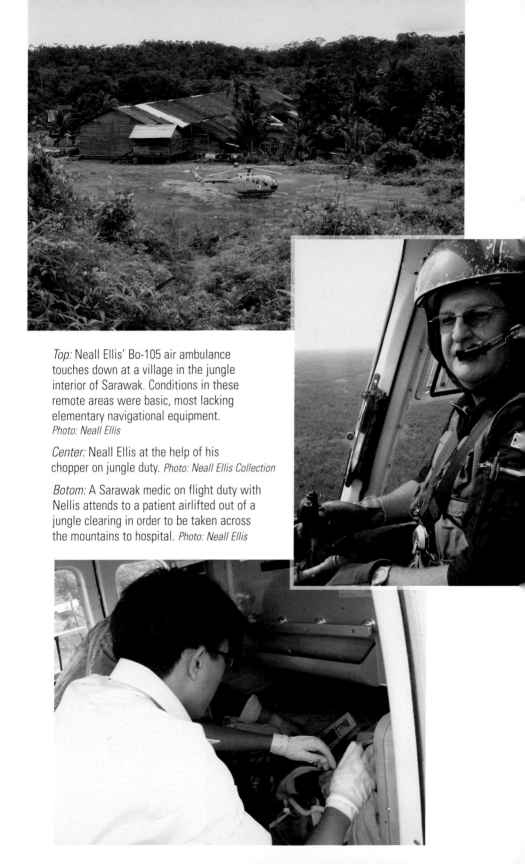

Top: Neall Ellis' Bo-105 air ambulance touches down at a village in the jungle interior of Sarawak. Conditions in these remote areas were basic, most lacking elementary navigational equipment. *Photo: Neall Ellis*

Center: Neall Ellis at the help of his chopper on jungle duty. *Photo: Neall Ellis Collection*

Botom: A Sarawak medic on flight duty with Nellis attends to a patient airlifted out of a jungle clearing in order to be taken across the mountains to hospital. *Photo: Neall Ellis*

Tropical downpours coupled with high winds when traversing mountainous or jungle regions in the Sarawak interior could make for treacherous flying conditions. *Photo: Neall Ellis*

Fighting fires in remote parts of the Eastern Cape in South Africa provided Nellis with an interesting learning curve after a career that was mainly military-orientated. *Photo: Neall Ellis*

The choppers were fitted with water scoops, such as this one, customarily suspended below the helicopter. This addition saved time when pilots needed large volumes of water to douse forest fires. *Photo: Neall Ellis Collection*

Helicopters in Africa attract a great deal of attention throughout Africa: As Nellis recalls, he would hardly have put down before the crowds came running and his crew had their hands full in trying to prevent some people from rushing headlong into the still-spinning tail rotors, especially in a nose-up condition prior to touching down. *Photo: Neall Ellis*

The Tanzanian presidential entourage that Nellis helicoptered about the country for several months: the incumbent president (green shirt), was sitting front right.
Photo: Neall Ellis

Typical African condition 'brown-out,' bringing the chopper down in remote areas where there are no paved landing pads. This could make landings hazardous, extremely so if there is no wind to dissipate the dust.
Photo: Neall Ellis

The three-month Tanzanian deployment took Nellis across the length and breadth of this vast East African country, sometimes over some of the most beautiful tropical coastlines, lagoons and beaches on any continent.
Photo: Neall Ellis

Repairs and maintenance while 'on the road' were cursory and most times improvised. Trucks with fuel and spares would be despatched from Dar es Salaam sometimes days ahead to await the arrival of the chopper at its scheduled destination. *Photo: Neall Ellis*

Below: The presidential pilot is thanked by Tanzanian President Kikwete himself at the end of the months-long electioneering campaign across vast swathes of Africa. *Photo: Tanzania News Agency*

Above: Neall Ellis was flying helicopter support missions in Afghanistan when this book went to print, seen here at his Mi-8 with pilots Peter Minnaar (middle) and Louis Venter (right). *Photo: Neall Ellis Collection.*

Below: On the way back to Kabul after a day's operational duties, co-pilot Mike Foster takes the Mi-8 over a partially snow-covered Afghanistan: the Hindu Kush can be seen in the background. *Photo: Neall Ellis*

Above: Taliban ambush scene along one of the arterial highways in the Afghan interior: it stretched for several hundred metres and must have been masterfully planned by the guerrillas. *Photo: Neall Ellis*

Below: American military helicopters are found in almost every location in which the civilian-owned support helicopters operate, such as this Chinook (with its side-gunner almost protruding) taking from a base in the distant interior. *Photo: Neall Ellis*

Above: Armed personnel are an essential component of every flight into the Afghan interior: if the helicopter is brought down either by enemy fire or mechanical fire, it is their job to protect everybody on board from a possible Taliban attack. *Photo: Neall Ellis*

Below: Isolated American military bases such as this one codenamed Pride Rock are integral to the ongoing war. It was the job of Nellis and his pilots to provide helicopter support for some of them. *Photo: US Army Captain Ryker Sentgeorge, taken while on active service at the base*

Above: A pilot's-eye-view of the Afghan panoply with the snow-covered Himalaya Mountains providing the backdrop.
Photo: Neall Ellis

Left: Marijuana is grown quite openly throughout Afghanistan (as are other drugs-producing crops such as poppies) in this case right up to the defences of this American base.
Photo: Captain Ryker Sentgeorge

Above: Kandahar air base, one of the busiest in Central Asia. Nellis was told by one of the ground operations commanders that this facility dispenses one and a quarter million litres of fuel a day, the average for a medium-sized American airport. *Photo: Neall Ellis*

Below: Picturesque view of one of the isolated regions in the Afghan interior. Every available patch of arable ground is cultivated in serried paddy-style because of steep inclines. *Photo: Neall Ellis*

Above: Retaliatory fire with a man-portable FGM-148 Javelin anti-tank missile, aimed at attacking Taliban positions in the mountains—the rocket can be clearly seen after leaving the tube.
Photo Captain Ryker Sentgeorge

Below: An aerial view of the ancient Afghan city of Qalat, said to be used as a headquarters base by Alexander the Great when he campaigned in this region almost 2,400 years ago. *Photo Neall Ellis.*

Above: A pair of Russian-built Mi-8s in the process of being prepared for the day's flight operations.
Photo: Neall Ellis

Below: Captain Ryker Sentgeorge with one of his Afghan soldier alongside an armoured vehicle
that had taken a battering when his base came under Taliban mortar attack.
Photo: Captain Ryker Sentgeorge

Above: A pair of German Air Force helicopters—part of the Coalition effort in Afghanistan—leave the security of their base for the interior. *Photo: Neall Ellis*

Below: One of the 'Shooters' attached to Nellis' wing waits to board prior to take-off from Kabul. *Photo: Neall Ellis*

Above: Dawn breaks over a relatively rare unpolluted Kabul. *Photo: Neall Ellis*

Below: A graphic shot of the Afghan desert creeping inexorably towards settlements in the mountainous interior. It is in the valleys that most the action takes place—and where the poppies are grown. *Photo: Neall Ellis*

Above: Nellis' Mi-8 helicopter parked on the LZ at Torkham PRT in the extreme south-east of the country. This Coatlion 'Frontline Base' is only a short hop from the city Peshawar in Pakistan from where the Taliban get most of their weapons and supplies and consequently comes under regular rebel attack. 'Shooters' are in attendance should there be problems. *Photo: Neall Ellis*

Below: American military choppers in an active role at one of the larger Coalition bases. *Photo: Neall Ellis*

Above: A group of private military personnel (Shooters) head towards Nellis' helicopter prior to departure from Kabul. *Photo: Neall Ellis*

Below: The reason why Neall Ellis and colleagues fly chopper support missions in Afghanistan: an American military vehicle totally destroyed by a Taliban Improvised Explosive Device (IED) on the road to the Koregal Valley. Without air support from private security companies like Nellis' Balmoral—the aviators of all nationalities fly hundreds of missions a day to the remotest corners of the country—this war would quickly come to a halt because of lack of supplies. *(Photo: Captain Ryker Sentgeorge)*

Though Neall Ellis never flew combat in Iraq, he spent time there with the mercenary group formed by former Executive Outcomes and 32 Battalion operative Mauritz le Roux who eventually created one of the largest private military companies in the region with several thousand employees under his control, many of them South African. The original idea was that Le Roux's company would acquire helicopters which would fall under Nellis' command. That did eventually take place, but by then this freebooter aviator had moved on. This selection of photos shows a variety of Baghdadi scenes including the house where he and his colleagues stayed, chaotic and polluted road traffic, and wreckage from the 2003 US invasion. *Photos: Neall Ellis*

Nigeria's General Garba. Sankoh's people couldn't have been aware that we were monitoring his calls, nor was Garba for that matter, and everything that subsequently took place only happened because we had good intelligence that he was already dealing directly with the rebels.

The message we'd intercepted said that the rebels had been given Garba's satellite phone number and that a meeting was scheduled for the following week. The nub of it was that Garba had apparently told the rebels that the UN wanted to deal which, of course, was nonsense. He told them that it was his job to explore the possibility of all the parties involved in the war making peace.

What he didn't tell the RUF was that the Freetown government had absolutely nothing to do with any of it. In fact, they didn't even know he was talking to Foday Sankoh's people, never mind that he had arranged a meeting. Essentially, he was committing treason.

There were no specifics about time or place, but Garba suggested in one of his secret calls that the conference take place in Makeni. He suggested that it should be with the rebel command and there would be representatives of several African countries present (again, under supposed UN auspices which, of course, was not the case).

We got the impression fairly early on that Garba was determined to be present, if only for the diamond rewards he imagined would be his if this tidy bit of sedition succeeded. At the time, only a handful of people were aware of what he was up to because details were restricted to a few of the senior people at the top, including the president. This was one time they didn't want any leaks.

On Saturday, 17 June, Army Intelligence had determined a tentative date for Garba's ploy. It was to take place on the following Monday, just two days away. At that stage, everything pointed to it happening not at Makeni, but at Lunsar, a small town between Freetown and Makeni, though we couldn't be certain. It made good sense though, as the town was close enough for both sides to get to without too many problems and Garba could reach it easily

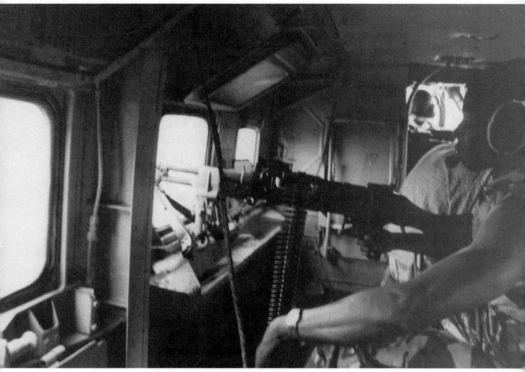

Side-gunner on board the Hind waiting for opportunities. Nellis' helmeted head can just be seen in the cockpit up front. *Author's photo*

enough in one of the UN choppers. Also, Lunsar was relatively isolated so whatever took place there wouldn't draw attention, especially from the government or the media. The probable time was set at about 10h00 hours.

On the face of it, it seemed that Garba had brokered an arrangement convenient to both himself and the rebels.

With this information in hand, Nellis spoke to Colonel Tom Carew, the Sierra Leonean Chief of Defence Staff, about the matter. Carew confirmed that the government was definitely not a party to any meetings between the UN and the rebels. The reply inferred that if the meeting were to happen at all, the (bogus) UN delegation would most probably get there by UN helicopter.

Being second-in-command of UNAMSIL, Garba could commandeer a helicopter at will, without questions being asked. The chopper could then be flown to a disused airfield near the RUF headquarters, adjacent to

Lunsar's old iron ore mine. Nellis' intention was to get airborne about 15 or 20 minutes before Garba's entourage lifted off and, he said, hope to hell that the rebels on the ground waiting for the delegation would believe that his rotors were those bringing in the Nigerian and his entourage. Nellis commented: 'Obviously, I was also counting on them all being gathered together in one area. I'd surprise them in the open, though I'd have to get in and out before the UN contingent arrived.' The intention was that the UN helicopter would be greeted by a lot of very freshly dead rebel bodies.

Nellis armed the Hind's Gatling and two pods of 57mm rockets, 'courtesy of the United Nations'. Ironically, these were munitions returned to Cockerill Barracks at General Jetley's behest only days earlier and it was Garba who had signed the release.

Rather than use the other Mi-24, with its larger 80mm rocket pods (which made for a bigger kill radius), Nellis reckoned that the smaller projectiles would be the more feasible option as he would be coming in low and fast. That way, he'd be able to launch the attack at the last moment and ensure sharper accuracy. It wasn't always possible to do that with 80mm projectiles, he explained, as he'd have had to stand off a bit. If the 80mm rockets aren't fired from a reasonable distance, there is a chance that the chopper can take hits from its own shrapnel if coming in on a very low profile, which, under the circumstances, was essential.

On the day of the planned ambush, Nellis met for an early breakfast with Chief Hinga Norman. Nellis was aware that almost nothing affecting the course of the war or those involved in it escaped Norman's notice and the chief had already been given the backdrop.

Nellis outlined his plan of attack. He wanted his boss' opinion on the political implications if he were to take out an RUF convoy on its way to supposed 'peace talks'. If he was successful, he knew, there would be some very loud noises made afterward in the world media. Also, he would most likely end up killing some senior RUF men including front-line commanders.

Chief Norman smiled at the news, sat back in his chair, and told Nellis not to worry himself about such things. That was his bailiwick and, as he said, 'you do what you have to do'. What Nellis actually wanted Chief Norman to do was officially sanction the strike. It was one thing to act on innuendo, but something else to receive a direct order. A wily old battler, the chief understood military procedures quite well, largely because he had served in the British Army when he was young.

As the issue was so sensitive, before Nellis left the chief's office, Norman phoned UN Commander General Jetley and asked Jetley whether he was aware of any UN operation in the Lunsar area that day. The chief explained that he wanted to task the Hind with a recce in that sector and was not able to guarantee the safety of anybody else who might be there.

'No', Jetley answered, his tone indicating annoyance. There was nothing happening and of that he was certain, he declared. Chief Norman warned the Indian General that the Air Wing would be conducting an armed reconnaissance around Lunsar and that his government couldn't be held responsible for any attacks on unauthorized UN patrols operating there. Jetley accepted that position and didn't argue any of its finer details.

The conversation was enlightening, said Nellis. If the Indian had been a party to this conspiracy, he would almost surely have asked more questions or possibly even have acted differently. There was nothing defensive about his responses. Instead recalls Nellis, he seemed straight up and down. 'Jetley's immediate reaction told us pretty conclusively that he'd nothing to hide', explained Nellis. It was significant too that Norman had not bothered to call General Garba. Everybody who mattered at Cockerill already knew of the Nigerian's involvement in the plot. 'Based on Jetley's response, Chief Norman gave me the clearance I sought', Nellis said.

> I was to carry out an armed patrol of the road between Lunsar and Makeni. Being the wily politician, he never instructed me to deliberately seek and destroy any rebel convoy, but instead, stated that he had been given assurances by Jetley that nothing untoward was expected, so I should go ahead and do my job, which I did.

Norman added one more thing in this tentative briefing. He told Nellis to use his discretion if any target presented itself. 'Those were his last words before I left his office', said Nellis.

Nellis' plan had a second phase to it. If nothing was happening at Lunsar by the time he got there, he would follow a route along the Makeni road and see if there was anything or anybody moving along it. Cockerill was aware that if Garba got cold feet and decided to cancel, he would not be able to get a message through to the RUF command in time to stop the convoy.

As far as Nellis was concerned, it was a great day for war. The visibility was perfect, as it was one of those bright, sunny West African days where a target can be seen for miles. Unfortunately, the clear weather cut both ways and the rebels would be able to spot his chopper from a long distance away. The Air Wing delayed their take-off by a little because time means nothing in Africa. Pitching up for an appointment an hour late is normal, Nellis explained.

Once over Lunsar, Nellis saw nothing. There were no vehicles in the area and no groups of people either in the town or in the surrounding area. It didn't make sense. What was immediately clear was that the RUF delegation was late. So, taking the second option, the Mi-24 went down the road, clipping along at less than 15 metres above the ground. The intention was to stay low because if there were any rebels ahead, Nellis wanted to surprise them. He knew, too, that the rebel vehicles would have anti-aircraft guns mounted on them.

Nellis liked the odds. As he says, he was pretty certain he would have

Two Royal Air Force Chinook helicopters parked together with a Royal Navy Lynx (in the rear) at Lungi International Airport outside Freetown. *Author's photo*

the advantage of surprise because the last thing the rebels would have been expecting was a gunship hitting them from the air. After all, they were meeting the second most powerful military man in the country, so the rebel command must have been confident that he would ensure that nothing untoward would be allowed to happen. In their minds, it was probably a given that he would ensure their safe passage. The meeting was believed to have been the UN's idea and that must have been a guarantee of sorts, believed Nellis.

Shortly after passing over the village of Macut, about 15 clicks from the town of Makeni, the gunship breasted a low hill. At that point Nellis spotted a four-vehicle convoy heading his way. In the lead was a Toyota land cruiser escorted by a pair of motorcycles. A pick-up with a DShK heavy machine gun mounted on the back followed a couple of hundred metres behind the three lead vehicles with a five- or six-man gun crew crowded around it.

Nellis' immediate instinct was to go straight in. With the first motor-cycle in his sights, he delivered a burst from his Gatling. The target disintegrated and hurled what was left of the driver and the bike into the bush, in a heap. The second bike wobbled perilously for a moment and then ran headlong into a ditch. Nellis locked the land cruiser in his sights and shattered its windscreen. A split-second later its fuel tank exploded.

The driver of the rear pick-up jumped on his brakes, but Nellis was able to get in a short burst, most of which went wide. By then the attack had lasted only seconds. Throwing the Hind hard to port, Nellis banked and came in again. Hassan shouted through the mike that the rebels were bombshelling from the last three vehicles which, as Nellis anticipated, probably carried the main delegation. As he recalled later, cover in the foliage was the only option left to them. With another whoop from Hassan, the two side gunners joined in. Both he and Lieutenant Schenks set about picking off targets with their GPMGs.

The next time Nellis brought the helicopter around, he decided to bring his rockets into play. A couple of rebels who were still with the pick-up were trying to swing the gun around, but they were struggling with a jam. A salvo of 16 rockets went into the pick-up, eight from each pod.

'Thus were a few more gooks sacrificed for the cause', was how Nellis later put it. Another low altitude turn and more rockets raked thickets where Hassan had spotted some of the rebels taking cover. After that strike, as he explained to his bosses at Cockerill Barracks that evening, there was no more resistance. The gunship was able to concentrate on eliminating the remaining vehicles as well as the individual members of the delegation still trying to escape.

Because the bush in that immediate area wasn't as thick as elsewhere, Hassan spotted some of them trying to crawl along a gulley. He asked Nellis to bank to starboard and then set about doing the necessary. Nellis explained that he knew they would never be able to account for every single member of the party, but it was not for want of trying. Anyway, as he declared afterwards, he had had a stoppage on the Gatling and that ended the exercise. Also, they were out of rockets, so he decided to call it a day.

The flow of radio intercepts at Cockerill didn't stop. They poured in from all over Sierra Leone—Makeni, Kono, everywhere. Some originated from Liberia, inquiring about the whereabouts of a General Sesay, the senior RUF officer in the delegation. The rebel command was definitely rattled.

Still more intercepts the following day confirmed that Nellis had knocked out the convoy's communications on his first pass, removing the radio operator's hand in the process. As a result, nobody at either Lunsar or Makeni had any idea of what had taken place, or even that there had been an attack. Only after dark, and then tentatively for fear of a night strike, did another convoy set off from Makeni. Their orders were to find out what had happened to the RUF interim leader.

With Foday Sankoh in jail by this time, Sesay had only recently been appointed head of the rebel junta. He'd been lucky because he had only been slightly hurt in the attack. Ten other senior rebel commanders had been killed outright, including several regional heads. Early reports suggested that Brigadier General Maurice Kallon, head of the northern axis of the RUF war effort, was dead, but this later proved false.

Another battlefield commander, Dennis Mingo, alias 'Superman', was wounded in the attack. In fact, just about everybody in the convoy took some kind of hit, with several badly hurt.

Much more damaging, especially to future United Nations/RUF relations, was that Garba and his entourage never showed up at Lunsar. Had the Nigerian commander at least made the attempt to do so, he might have

Executive Outcomes made good use of former Soviet Mi-17s in their Angolan and Sierra Leone campaigns: as did Neall Ellis, in various theatres of military activity, including the Balkans. *Author's photo*

had a case to argue. Even worse, nobody told the rebels that at very short notice that the meeting had been cancelled. Garba and several others with him could have easily used their satellite phones to call it off, but they did not. Consequently, the rebels had good reason to believe they had been betrayed and, of course, they had been. In their own words: 'The Nigerian betrayed us!'

The consensus at Cockerill Barracks was that Garba had probably been intimidated by Chief Hinga's questions to his boss. Nellis surmised that Jetley had spoken to his Nigerian deputy about the call and that Garba had probably sensed that a catastrophe was about to erupt.

Once the strike was announced, Garba resorted to invective. He immediately launched a campaign of words against several British officers seconded to the Sierra Leonean Army, accusing them of bugging his satellite phone and intercepting his messages. He followed that up with a bitter attack on Whitehall and Britain in general claiming that the African cause had been betrayed. 'They tried to undermine my command!' he told his deputy, spitting out the words in an already familiar display of fury.

Several choice comments were reserved for Colonel Mike Dent, the

CDS's opposite number with the British military advisory contingent. Sitting across the table from him at the next staff meeting, Garba traded more insults. Undeterred, Dent apparently told the man to go fuck himself.

In fact, Garba's troubles had only just begun. The rebels condemned him in the strongest language in their propaganda broadcasts. He was playing a double game, was the inference. They cried that they had been led into a trap and that he would 'pay for the murders'.

At Cockerill the mood was upbeat, even though nobody was fully aware of the details about how the rebel itinerary and dates had been leaked, or why the gunship was on the Makeni road at just right moment. Gradually, aspects of the ambush filtered into town and the event was portrayed as significant, with one daily calling it 'A great victory for President Kabbah.'

Looking back, Nellis is not certain his mission on the Makeni road was as successful as some made it out to be. The strike had indeed boosted the sagging morale of both the government and the army. The newspapers could not get enough of the story, though without the behind-the-scenes details. As more details emerged about the UN's—and, in particular, Garba's—duplicity, a visible rift appeared between the Nigerian and Indian factions in West Africa.

Ultimately, this divide led to New Delhi pulling its troops out of the UN force altogether, followed shortly afterward by UN Supremo Kofi Annan's declaration that the Jordanian contingent would leave as well. The moves depleted the UN 'peacekeeping' strength in Sierra Leone by about a quarter, and obliged Britain to take on a more obtrusive security role. Also, the Nigerian Army in Sierra Leone was forced to temper its dealings with the RUF. Had they been allowed to continue, Kabbah's government would have been pushed further into isolation.

There were several results that troubled Nellis. Both Jetley and Garba were aware that they had been duped. After the attack, both men refused to provide the Air Wing with help. Until the strike, the Hinds had been able to refuel at UN depots, both at Lungi and Hastings Airports. Jetley saw to it that those facilities were put off-limits to the Air Wing. Ammunition was also not forthcoming, which led to some serious shortages a month or so later. Whitehall had to schedule several emergency arms deliveries by air and these were questioned in Westminster.

In the past, a grudging pact had existed between the Air Wing and the UN forces, but relations hadn't been good since the first phase of the UN operation. There had been several fractious encounters in past months, and a deep suspicion between the two parties developed as a consequence. Jetley, who usually played the role of the panderer, treated Nellis and his crowd as adversaries. The consequence of Jetley's actions became more apparent about a fortnight after the Makeni raid. Nellis' Mi-24 was ordered to attack a rebel target and he was accompanied by Colonel Carew to Garba's office with requests for ammunition and spare parts in order to complete the mission. The moment the two men stepped inside the door the Nigerian became belligerent.

'He refused us anything we'd asked for, saying that he wasn't prepared to give us any assistance whatsoever', recalled Nellis. He also accused the Air Wing of destroying his efforts in trying to secure a peace process. Apparently, even with the CDS present, Garba was his usual obstreperous self. As Nellis said afterwards, he wasn't in a position to say anything and thought that perhaps he should have congratulated the Nigerian for being candid. As he commented at the time, at least everybody knew where they stood with each other.

It took the British military aid contingent and the Sierra Leonean Army several months of fence-building before anything resembling a working relationship was again in place. Although the situation improved with time, the relationship never reverted to what it had been before the 'Makeni Road Strike', as the newspapers called it.

The ongoing war and its daily rebel atrocities did not allow the impasse to go on indefinitely. Nellis' ambush might have scored points, but the rebels retaliated and intensified their barbarism in all towns and villages under their control. Fortunately, most of the civilian population had already fled.

Six weeks after the incident, the UN asked Nellis to take the Hind and attack a village in the eastern part of the country. Under Operation *Khukri*, the area had come under strong Indian Air Force Mi-24 fire during the rescue of a batch of UN soldiers held hostage by the rebels. Indian gunships had seriously razed the place and Nellis was told that there were still some rebel targets intact, including a radio centre.

The idea was that I should hit the village the day after Operation *Khukri*. Out of nowhere, Garba—all charm and snake oil—gives me a clearance to eliminate any infrastructures that were still intact and, as he said, I was to kill anyone found there. He was even willing to give me ammo. It started to smell bad.

Nellis had a reputation for being able to detect anything devious, and to him this operation had the hallmarks of a typical underhanded Nigerian move. Moreover, by now even the UN higher-ups in New York were aware that Garba was up to no good. The motive became clear soon enough. Garba's intent was to transfer blame for the destruction wrought by the Indian Air Force gunships onto Nellis and the Sierra Leonean Air Wing. This, in turn, would invite UN censure and allow the Nigerian general to tell the rebels that his people had never been involved in any attack.

'I wasn't prepared to become Garba's scapegoat for any UN whitewash', Nellis declared because, as he said, 'we had a fairly good measure of these people by then.'

Stretching the limits of his own credibility, Nellis reported to the UN office at the Mammy Yoko Hotel later that same day that neither of his aircraft was serviceable. He added that it would be impossible to carry out any strikes for a day or two. He was convinced that had he gone ahead and made the attack as Garba had suggested, pressure would have been placed on Kabbah's government to restrict all operational flights involving the Hinds. He and the rest of the crew might even have been expelled from Sierra Leone.

As Nellis says, looking back, the Makeni raid affair dripped with duplicity. Moreover, it had a direct effect on the ultimate course of the war and it surprised nobody to learn afterwards that once the people involved in this double-cross were identified, the British started to play a more pronounced role in the struggle. The man directly responsible for the turnabout, says Nellis, was the future British Chief of the Defence Staff, General Sir David Richards, a 'lowly' brigadier at the time.

CHAPTER SEVENTEEN

HOW THE WAR IN SIERRA LEONE WAS FOUGHT

With the benefit of hindsight, it is now known that there was an enormous amount of intrigue and double-play on the part of the British Government during the civil war in Sierra Leone. In an edition of the satirical magazine *Punch*, published in October 2000, about a year before it was all over, Pete Sawyer declared that 'whoever wins the bloodbath of Sierra Leone, a group of British businesses can't lose'.

In fact, Sawyer maintained that duplicitous dealings in British companies might actually 'have exacerbated the conflict in the relentless drive to control Sierra Leone's diamond resources'. It was, in Sawyer's words, 'a really ugly scramble for mineral wealth with international mining conglomerates pulling all the strings despite the pious words about Britain's "ethical" foreign policy'. Harsh words, but true. Although he doesn't say as much, all these backroom machinations were the reason there was such a brouhaha about Sandline and the so-called involvement with a mercenary pilot. It was all intended to deflect attention from the real issue, and precious stones lay at the heart of it.

When the British decided to become fully involved in the war, 200 men from 1st Battalion, the Parachute Regiment (who seized Lungi International Airport) were sent, followed soon afterwards by a contingent of

Royal Marines in May 2000, and the war went into overdrive. They were soon joined by the carrier HMS *Illustrious* and the helicopter carrier HMS *Ocean*. Meanwhile, four Chinook helicopters were flown directly to West Africa from the United Kingdom, making it the longest operational delivery sortie yet achieved by these bulky craft.

Lieutenant Colonel Rob Symonds was the Military Liaison Officer, British High Commission, Freetown at the time. His comments about what was going on are instructive:

> When the war in Sierra Leone started again on May 6, 2000, Neall Ellis was among the first to go into action. He was sometimes averaging three or four combat missions a day in the government Hind helicopter gunship. Twice, he went up six times in a 24-hour period, the last sortie having taken place after dark using night vision goggles to spot rebel concentrations. His logbook shows that in eight weeks he clocked more than 130 combat missions. Pilots in the majority of the world's air forces—unless they are in a major war—rarely see that much action during the course of their careers.

This is a significant tribute to Nellis from one of the men who was at the heart of much of the war, and the two men remain firm friends—there are few people who, once having been embraced by this remarkable aviator, fall out with him.

Just about everything that happened in Sierra Leone's air war during 2000 revolved about the Air Wing operations room at Cockerill Barracks. More properly known as the Corps Operations Centre, it was a kind of home from home for Nellis and his guys. An untidy place, which had a certain disordered charm about it, it was a combination of office, social club, intelligence clearing house, food store, telephone answering service, map room and conference centre.

Situated well away from the main block at Army Headquarters, the expansive, sparsely furnished ground floor office was entered through a pair of steel doors. Once inside, squarely in the middle of the room, was the desk of Sindaba Meri, the head of the Air Wing's four-man Ethiopian technical squad who kept the gunships flying. Stashed against one of the far walls was a pile of automatic weapons, mostly AKs. Of necessity, while the assets were airborne, the steel doors remained locked.

Cardboard boxes, some of them half open, lay clustered about. They held propaganda leaflets which were to be dropped on enemy positions. However, that usually happened only during an operational flight once all the ammo had gone, and then with reluctance. Nellis made it clear that he didn't like the idea of dropping pieces of paper in areas where the rebels were active. He argued that, while justifiable if it saved lives, the exercise exposed him and the crew unnecessarily to ground fire. Also, it put the helicopter at risk. 'The gooks know that when I'm dropping that shit . . . I'm not going to be using my weapons', he remonstrated with one of the British officers.

Still, he went along with it because he had to, and the gunship made several pamphlet drops that urged the rebels to come in under a UN-brokered amnesty. They were told that all they had to do was hand in their guns at any UN post and they would receive cash for them. Curiously, quite a few did as the war progressed.

A little more rotund than earlier in his career, his hair close-cropped so that it's difficult to see whether it's thinning or not, Neall Ellis has never been regarded as the archetypal soldier of fortune. In Sierra Leone, when he talked about his 'office' he was referring not to the barracks but to the helicopter he flew every day. Soft-spoken, articulate and well read, very few people ever saw him angry, although like everybody else on Freetown's roads, he could be pretty cantankerous behind the wheel. Those who got to know him well were aware that there was a darkness in his eyes that was sometimes indefinable. His language could also be explicit, especially when he missed a target. In contrast, he was never critical of his crew, even though they all made mistakes at times.

On Nellis' desk, which was on the left as you entered the office, were papers, more maps, his battered old laptop, electricity bills, cardboard plates from the previous day's snack and several heavily bound catalogues offering the latest killing machines from the former Soviet Union. Most had the Rosvoorouzhenie imprint, which was formerly Moscow's State Corporation for Export and Import of Armaments and Military Equipment. Other catalogues were from its successor, Rosoboronexport. Tucked away, almost unobtrusively in a pile of its own, was a letter from a British weapons supply company. Addressed to Nellis, it offered the Air Wing a reconditioned Mi-24 engine for $545,000 cash.

In another corner lay the remains of a pile of British Army ration packs. A small refrigerator held the day's supply of butter, pita bread, sausage spread or whatever else Hassan had managed to scrounge from the Lebanese supermarket down the road in Wilkinson Street. The room was air-conditioned, but because there were so many power cuts, refrigeration was essential. For that reason, anyone who wanted to smoke went outside and stood alongside the pad where the unit's second gunship was parked.

That second Hind was also fully equipped with a Gatling and under-wing rocket pods, although these were 80mm, as opposed to the 57mm pods with which the other Hind was equipped. This second helicopter saw little action, the main reason being that the larger projectiles were in short supply and nobody was ever certain when more would be ordered. Also, it wasn't air-conditioned. Nellis would go out and come back drenched in sweat; it would sometimes take him an hour or two to recover.

For much of the time that he worked out of Cockerill Barracks, Nellis' domain at Army Headquarters kind of ran itself. Two or three times a day he would liaise with his bosses and then things would just happen. At one point, shortly after the Royal Marines had stabilised the situation in and around Freetown, Whitehall appointed an RAF squadron leader to 'supervise' Nellis' team under the guise of what they termed their 'Sierra Leone military training program'. It was a shrewd move.

The new RAF arrival, Nellis said, was technically an advisor and he was basically running the show. He added that 'these guys also see that the money that the government owes us keeps on coming, which is good, because then we eat again'. Shortly after the arrival, a report appeared in the British press that claimed that the Royal Air Force was supporting mercenaries and it suggested a repeat of the Sandline debacle. It was expected that Whitehall would backtrack, but then the unexpected happened.

Days later, a London newspaper report written by Caroline Davies, said that the Ministry of Defence had stated that the RAF officer (based at Cockerill Barracks) was advising Sierra Leone on how to build up 'a proper structured air wing' and that the gunship 'belonged to the government, not mercenaries'. The story went on: 'If the Sierra Leoneans haven't got anybody who can fly these helicopters and if they want to get South African nationals who can, then that's up to them. The RAF does not advise them on their role on a day-to-day basis'.

It was the first time that a modern British government had actually acknowledged that it was in any way involved with irregular military forces such as a private military company (PMC), which was quite shocking in an age when hired guns were an anathema throughout the civilized world. One commentator suggested that this was the shape of things to come in an Africa that was in the process of unravelling. In fact, since then there has been a flurry of articles advocating the use of PMCs in some of the more isolated conflicts where any kind of regular intervention wouldn't make good political or economic sense.

Nellis' ops centre was run very differently from everything else that went on at Cockerill. It had a very distinctive atmosphere and for part of the day, the wails and squeaks from communications equipment in the radio shack next door would saturate everything. The technicians, even when they weren't trying, would create noises that could invoke demons. It was at its worst if they had had to revert to batteries, which happened every time there was a power outage, which was often.

Basically, the technicians monitored enemy radio transmissions around the clock. As it was sensitive work, the ops centre was also the most heavily guarded area of the complex and there was an armed sentry on permanent duty outside the entrance. Most of the intercepts could be seen by anyone in the office as they came in, which almost certainly diminished the level of military security. However, that was the problem with the war from the start: secrets just didn't keep in Freetown.

The majority of messages that came in weren't coded and those that were in code took a bit longer to filter down to the ops centre. It was instructive that the rebels used a Slidex code in their more important messages. As Nellis noted, that, in itself, was unusual because the system was cumbersome. He felt it possibly reflected a South African presence among enemy ranks. The old SADF, he explained, was one of the last of the more sophisticated establishments still using Slidex and it might have been former SADF personnel who had passed it on to the Liberians.

To Nellis, it was unacceptable for former SADF personnel to go across to the enemy. He felt it was a betrayal and he took it personally. In Ondangua during Namibia's border war days, and at Swartkops near Pretoria and elsewhere, they had all been good buddies. In a sense, being military, they were all part of one big family. The wives and children knew one another because they were often thrust together for months at a stretch in remote postings such as at the air force base at Ondangua.

It was no secret that some old EO hands were also fighting for, or training, rebel forces. The money was good and since opportunities for this kind of work were limited, many grabbed the opportunity when it came about.

There were many reasons why senior Sierra Leonean staff officers would sidle down to Nellis' ops centre for a chat. For a start, because of his role, he was the best source of intelligence in the region. While flying, he missed very little that was going on below. Further, what he had to offer was always an accurate, reasonable and balanced assessment of enemy ground force activities, based mostly on the kind of subliminal instinct that comes with good experience. Years of flying in primal environments added a distinctive edge to his reports.

Invariably, he was spot on. For instance, while in the air, he could judge simply by a man's actions on the ground—how he walked, what he was carrying and whether he was being evasive—whether he was the enemy or not. He could 'read' the bush and, having identified a target and gone in 'hot', it was often only at the last moment that anyone else would see what he was aiming at. Most of the time it was a cunningly camouflaged vehicle or building.

His actions could certainly galvanize the mind, especially when under fire. On one occasion he strafed a position, targeting something in the kind of primitive forest that most of the handbooks would classify as impenetrable. Only on his third pass did the fuel-carrying vehicle and its 12.7mm HMG explode in a fireball. Until then, it had been seemingly invisible. With time, Hassan also honed these skills.

On another occasion, he passed a fairly large boat heading down the Little Scarcies River, not far from the Guinea border. It wasn't unlike several other partially enclosed motor craft plying the hundreds of kilometres of inland waterways that sometimes made Sierra Leone's coastal plain remarkably like the Mekong Delta during the wet season. This one, a bit bigger than a Pam Pam, but not large enough to be ocean going, stopped in midstream as soon as his helicopter came into view.

On his second pass, Nellis said he was going in. The boat blew up when its cargo of fuel ignited. When asked about it later he admitted that there was no real reason for the strike, except that the first time round he could see that the crew was ready to swim for it.

'They don't normally do that, so what else to conclude but that there was something in that boat's hold that could hurt. Also, the men on board were armed and jumpy', he stated blandly. In Sierra Leone, he explained, that just about said it all. Since the entire region through which the Little Scarcies flowed was in rebel hands, he surmised that whatever those crewmen had on board was almost certainly destined for the RUF. A rebel radio intercept later proved him right, although Nellis is the first to admit that he sometimes made mistakes.

'You must remember that this is a very real war. It's not an exercise. Here, it's us or them and many people are getting killed', he told a visitor to Cockerill who had made an issue about innocents being targeted.

Nellis scoffs at the suggestion that being a mercenary is reprehensible, although there are those who use much stronger language when his name surfaces. One of his favourite comments was that 'diagnosis of the problem was one thing, prescription quite another'. That, he believed, applied specifically to Sierra Leone. 'We're performing a service', he would say whenever there was a discussion about the role of what was euphemistically termed 'contract pilots'.

He would go on: 'We're the guys who are saving lives, killing the bad guys. You don't think that doesn't make me feel good? *Think again!*' he'd erupt. He had a few premises of his own about war and one of them went something like this: 'In conflict, all else being equal, raw aggression wins, most times anyway.' To one of his colleagues he once said that war was the greatest game available to mankind: 'either you kill or, if you are not good at your job, you end up dead.'

Anyway, he declared, it worked for him, and he'd explain that he'd seen the consequences of such aggression often enough. Whenever the gunship approached, the rebels would drop everything. They would discard their weapons, vehicles, supply packs, whatever and dash frantically for cover. Being Africa, the word gets about!

Avionics had an altogether different dimension when flying combat with Neall Ellis. The first consideration, he would say early on, was that if something happened, there would be no back up: 'If we are forced down, either because of engine problems or incoming fire, we're going to be on our own in the jungle', were his words.

Nellis admitted that he might have been able to talk to one of the control towers before he swung the Hind into a bit of open ground, but in the jungle, he said, you never knew. There were places where the forest went on forever and sometimes there were no breaks anywhere. Also, taking the machine down in water would be the end for us in front. There was no easy way of exiting from either of the cockpit bubbles, he warned, although it had been done.

If he had time, he could possibly have given those listening on the same frequency a bearing. However, what they would do with that info was problematic. Perhaps a UN chopper team would be put on the alert, but even that wasn't assured. The UN command structure—from Turtle Bay down, all the way to West Africa—was about as enthusiastic for what Nellis was doing, as was he for their shambolic 'peacekeeping' efforts. Nellis reckoned:

> Every man on board was aware that, as with all helicopters, if we took a serious hit our survival would depend on finding a place to put the bird down safely. So, bottom line is that we'd then have to face the probability that if we crashed, there would be no rescue attempt.

'To start with, we'd need a soft landing, which would be difficult in a 12-ton heavyweight.' He would explain that once on the ground, the crew's only real hope would be that one of the British helicopters from the carriers might react. However, even that would need authority all the way from the top, especially if an extensive search were to be launched. In the nether world of 'contract' flying, Nellis and his crew knew that such issues were borderline.[1] Also, much would depend on who was on duty at the time as Nellis wasn't everybody's favourite person.

The way Nellis moved about in a land where there were no navigational or flying aids was amazing. There were two modest air traffic controls systems in operation in the Freetown area: one for civilian helicopter as well as Air Wing activity centred at Lungi and the other, a mobile unit operated by the UN, was at the chopper pad at the Mammy Yoko Hotel. The mobile unit should have been deployed at Cockerill where there was a high-rise concrete tower built specially for the purpose. On arrival, however, the UN thought better of it as they preferred something a little closer to their headquarters. The government helicopter gunships across the narrow, mosquito-ridden swamp that separated them from the UN base probably had something to do with it. Whatever happened, if Nellis did crash, he'd have to talk to at least one of those stations, and even then, radio contact would almost certainly be erratic.

One of the problems relating to flying in Sierra Leone was that while there are some fine natural landmarks, especially among the mountains in the north and to the east of the country, a good deal of the south and central regions are desk-top flat; elsewhere the terrain is undulating. Although there was always something in sight on the horizon, flying 30ft above the jungle wasn't conducive to good navigation unless you'd been doing it for a while. Also, with no co-pilot, Nellis was in absolute control. The crew might have helped with spotting and the occasional ancillary task such as tripping circuit breakers or activating the IR jamming system, but the rest was up to him.

He not only flew the helicopter, but he also picked out the targets and manually activated the weapons systems. Then, without any apparent reference to a marker, he would move across some of the wildest bush country in the world to the next target and do it all over again.

Getting directly to and from an objective over this green pea soup of a terrain must have taxed his skills. He constantly had to calculate fuel, distance, speed, reserves and much more. Also, there were no convenient army bases or towns where he could top up if he needed to. He always flew with a map on his lap. When something came into view, he'd first log it onto his portable GPS so that he could get back to the place later. Only then would he turn his attention to establishing whether the target was worth a strike.

Back at base afterwards, as the Chief of Defence Staff and British Army intelligence came and went, he would relay his findings. These would include grid and map references as well as an interpretation of events, enemy strengths, weaknesses and deployment. Most of what he had to say came from memory, which was remarkable, although he did have the occasional lapse, such as forgetting where he'd put his keys. He'd joke that he was suffering from what he termed 'Tropical Halfheimers'. It was a regular crack that he could remember only half of everything that had happened the previous night.

Operational mishaps were nothing new, especially in Africa's ongoing wars. There had been numerous incidents involving South African gunship crews in Angola and Sierra Leone having been shot down or come down unexpectedly for a myriad of reasons. In most cases, the crews survived. Obviously, much would be in store for a crew if they ended up in rebel hands, which was one of the reasons why Hassan was furious when somebody stole his Colt .45 pistol out of his desk. It was his 'last resort', he fumed. Not altogether tongue-in-cheek, he begged Allah for reparations.

Everyone knew that if they crashed, it would be difficult to outrun the rebels on their own turf, even if no-one was injured. As long as the crew had a few hours start, they could perhaps keep ahead of the pack and use the heavier automatic weapons such as the GPMG for the occasional ambush, but the odds certainly wouldn't be in their favour. Nellis never flew anywhere without his issue AK-47 as well as his personal 9mm pistol for back-up. To that he would add his GPS, as well as a tiny portable VHF radio that he might use to speak to aircraft if somebody came looking.

It was marginally reassuring that, weeks before, three British officers— Major Phil Ashby, Lieutenant-Commander Paul Rowland and Major Andy Samsonoff—and a New Zealand Army signals officer David Lingard, trudged across some of the most difficult country in Africa after having escaped from a camp that had been surrounded by an RUF rebel group armed with heavy weapons. Much of the country they traversed was jungle and, in places, barely penetrable. It took them four days to cover 80km to the nearest UN position, having left Magburaka, just south of Makeni, in the middle of the night. They moved only in the dark and spent daylight hours in thick undergrowth because rebel squads were out looking for them. Afterwards, they recounted their ordeal, which included having no food, and nothing but swamp water to drink (in which floated putrescent things) as well as being seriously devoured by mosquitoes, showing the amazing hardships the human body can endure.[2]

Birds were also a big problem facing flying crews while they moved about West Africa. In this tropical haven there were some really big species and bird strikes were a niggling fear. One moment Nellis would be ambling along, and the next he would slam the stick to the left or right and the chopper would shoot off tangentially. It could be very unnerving, when heading in low at 160 knots, to suddenly find vultures or a fish eagle directly in the flight path. It says much for Nellis' ability that he avoided contact so many times.

In Sierra Leone, Nellis possessed a rather disjointed philosophy about conflict. He would taunt the enemy, rather as one would rag a pit bull. What he said he always hoped for was some sort of reaction that would expose what he liked to refer to as the 'enemy's underbelly'. He relished pushing his Hind forward into a vulnerable position in the hope that the rebels would use some of their bigger guns against him, perhaps their four-barrelled ZSU-23 quads. Talking to him afterwards, he'd light up, sit back and say: 'Of course they shoot at us, but then they haven't had my experience.' After a slight pause he'd go on: 'Anyway, I know how to retaliate and those mothers don't!'

Nellis wasn't a braggadocio because, simply put, he wasn't that sort of person. Instead, most of his off-the-cuff statements about what he did for a living were rarely more than a succession of statements of fact. British pilots who flew with him and spent time in his company would tell you that Nellis was among the most self-effacing of individuals they'd met. As one of them commented, 'he's very atypically the war hero'. Someone else was heard to say that this was a man who had long ago learnt to sublimate his fears to the extent that some of his colleagues considered him reckless. Coping with the unknown, obviously, had to be part of it, but he was also relentless in the face of fire. Certainly, some of the things that he did were terrifying.

Naturally, there have been questions about the way that Nellis operated, especially as he repeatedly went in on a variety of targets, at Makeni and elsewhere, without regard for the SAMs with which the rebels were equipped. With this in mind, it didn't help that he'd sometimes hover interminably over clusters of rebels, some of whom must have had him in their sights.

While the way he fought his war wasn't everybody's recipe for survival, his actions in the end gave him the targets he sought. In some of the engagements he knew that the enemy had heavy weaponry, even if they didn't use it to their best advantage. There was always a surfeit of DShK and gas-operated NSV 12.7mm heavy support weapons in rebel hands because dozens were taken from UN units that capitulated early on in their deployment. They also had quite a few wheeled, twin-barrelled 14.5mm KPVs, which is a most effective anti-aircraft weapon. Nellis would hover over likely rebel concentrations in the hope that they would use said weapons. Occasionally they did, exposing their positions, which Nellis would then destroy. This rather frightening tactic was actually safer than it seemed as the people handling the weapons inevitably had dreadful aim.

Eventually, the Hind was causing so much damage that the rebel command upped the price on Nellis' head to US$2 million. Australian broadcaster Mark Corcoran reported that he saw a message addressed to the merc pilot saying that 'if we ever catch you, we'll cut your heart out and eat it'. Of course, that sort of thing appealed to Nellis. He was actually a little flattered and would quietly chuckle to himself. Then he'd say something about anybody who knew Africa would be aware that the chances of collecting any money at all ranked somewhere between zero and nil. It was all hearsay, he'd argue, and he might actually have been right, because most of the time even he got it third, or even fifth hand. However, the rebels did eventually give his gunship a name. One of the rebels taken captive near Lunsar said that it had been dubbed, in Mende one of the local African languages, '*Wor Wor* Boy', which means 'Ugly Boy'.

It was interesting that there were pilots from a host of nations who were eager to fly with Nellis. He was constantly getting calls from friends or 'friends of friends' abroad. Most would have liked to join him 'just for the experience'. Quite a few were willing to fly for nothing. However, these were short-term options and Nellis was wary of taking on anybody who lacked commitment. He had discovered to his cost that under the brittle crust of some fliers' camaraderie, there lay paranoia, particularly with some of the Americans who wafted through the region.

Sierra Leone was so far off the beaten tourist track that he had to question the motives of anyone who willingly bought an air ticket to a country enmeshed in civil war simply for the sake of seeing what it was like. It didn't make sense, he reckoned, especially when those involved were throwing dollars about as if they owned the place, while everyone else was counting their pennies.

Some of the Americans worried Nellis. He felt they were different from the average Europeans. Nellis confided once that he never really knew where he stood with many of them. Most would view the world loftily, with the kind of detached amusement that didn't warrant close attention. He said that he often had to ask himself what their real agenda was.

He was aware that in Africa quite a few of these Americans were involved with Washington's multi-tiered intelligence services—CIA, DIA, State Department and so on. Nellis didn't have to be told to be wary, because that came with the job. Naturally, there was the occasional American flier who was willing to sully his reputation with no questions asked. However, once Nellis started to explain how things worked and that the locals would kill for the Swatch on your arm or your Nikes, most were appalled that he worked in such terrible conditions. To some, they were conditions that were practically primordial. It didn't take these newcomers long to discover that the Sierra Leonean Government had no support system for the Air Wing if things came unstuck.

'Support system?' Nellis would query cynically. 'Shit, we don't even have the flares we need for our missile dispensers!' There wasn't the money and, anyway, the crew had long ago learnt to live with the way it was, he'd explain. Consequently, few American pilots hung about Freetown for long. Even some of the NGOs in Freetown such as ICI of Oregon, who had their own helicopters, got former Soviet pilots to handle their machines for them.

CHAPTER EIGHTEEN

OPERATION *BARRAS*—THE FINAL PHASE IN SIERRA LEONE

As Tim Butcher recalls in an article he did for the London *Daily Mail*, 'It was a famous military *coup de théâtre*—the spectacular SAS rescue of British troops held by vicious Sierra Leone guerrillas.' The real story, he maintained, 'was 200 rebels killed, their corpses hidden, and the truth buried by Tony Blair'.[1]

Neall Ellis is more forthright because he was there. He was a participant in the one of the most successful rescue efforts in recent times, which, he reckons, was as good as it got because of the incredible level of planning that went into getting the British hostages back.

The main problem facing Whitehall was that Operation *Palliser*, the British Armed forces operation in Sierra Leone, was over and Foday Sankoh's rebels were all but vanquished, with Sankoh himself having been taken prisoner. Therefore, almost all British forces and their air assets, including helicopters, had been withdrawn.

Then came disaster, as a small contingent of British troops were taken hostage by a rebel group. Almost overnight, the Ministry of Defence had to set in motion a major West African rescue operation. Nellis remembers:

Apart from two Lynx helicopters, which arrived on HMS *Ocean*

One of many villages occupied by the rebels that became a target of the mercenary aviator. Smoke can be observed emerging from a grass-roofed hit, centre, following a strike by the Hind. *Author's photo*

and HMS *Illustrious*, the British had to fly in three Chinook HC2 heavy-lift, transport helicopters from Britain. It had been done before. The first time that British forces went in, four Chinooks were flown out to Africa, and at the time the effort was regarded as the longest single transit by Chinooks ever attempted.

Nellis, with a senior SAS operator on board his Sierra Leonean Air Wing Mi-24, was to play a significant role in the drama that subsequently unfolded. As he recalls, 'we gave the rebels enough of a thumping for them never to be able to reorganise into an effective force in that area again . . . I reckon our Hind must have been responsible for scores of them, all armed dissidents . . . never mind the enemy killed by the ground forces or the Lynxes'.

Neall Ellis was told by the British commander at Cockerill Barracks that after British forces had done what they had been tasked to achieve, the area around the former rebel base was his to dominate.

I was told that the entire area had been frozen and was my responsibility. I was also instructed to do what was needed to clear out the rebels from the region . . . the West Side Boys needed to be taught a proper lesson, was the consensus.

I was operational for two days after Operation *Barras* and, cumulatively, we must have been in the air over the disputed zone for at least 12 hours. Then, I went back there a few days after it was all over and it was amazing to see how soon the original inhabitants had returned. The rebels were history and those poor people who had been persecuted by the West Side Boys for months, were able to get on with their normal lives once more.

What took place on that momentous September day in 2000 started with 11 members of the British Army's Royal Irish Regiment being kidnapped. They were moving about in the Occra Hills to the east of Freetown in their Land Rovers more than two weeks previously, on 25 August 2000. They were on their way back from visiting an element of the Jordanian UN contingent, although there is some dispute about that.

The British soldiers were making their way down the main road that linked the town of Yonibana to Freetown. Why they were there at all remains open to question as that part of Sierra Leone's Northern province had seen much bloodshed during the course of the civil war and it was known that it was an area where there was still an undefined rebel presence: not large numbers as in the earlier period, but potent enough to make the area dangerous..

Following a casual meeting along the way with what seemed to be a fairly amicable group of young men, Major Alan Marshall, the leader of the patrol, was persuaded, ostensibly on a friendly basis, to get talking to a group who called themselves West Side Boys. The British soldiers, accompanied by Lieutenant Musa Bangura, their Sierra Leonean Army liaison officer, were then held up by two or three young kids carrying AKs. The leaders were called and, once disarmed, the Brits were forced to follow them to their base.

Their captors declared themselves to be members of a military group called the West Side Boys which, under the circumstances, was hardly notable because there were scores of similar groups of young men operating throughout the country. In fact, hardly anybody had ever heard of them before, or of their brutally unstable and psychotic boss, the 24-year-old Foday Kallay.

Once in custody, all the hostages were taken to an area adjacent to the Rokel River, where Kallay's main base had been established in the village of Gberi Bana. The Land Rovers remained on the opposite bank where two more villages, Magbeni and Forodugu, were situated.

London was immediately advised of the abduction and within 48 hours the first of several preliminary reconnaissance missions were launched by both the SAS and SBS. They found the area to be difficult to traverse as the Rokel River was on one side and on the other there were swamps and rice paddies, features of many of the tiny settlements in the area.

Although efforts were made to communicate with Kallay, he warned that any sudden action would result in the deaths of all 12 men. As Nellis commented at the time:

> It didn't take a great stretch of the imagination to realise that the only way the Brits were going to get their people back would be to rescue them . . . Kallay might have been an idiot, but he was also an exceptionally dangerous idiot, known for executing his own men for disobeying orders. Also, because of the difficult, water-logged terrain the rescuers would have to come in by air, probably by chopper.

At that stage, already having been given the go ahead to launch a rescue mission by Prime Minister Tony Blair, the three Chinook helicopters were despatched to West Africa from the UK. The 5,600-ton *Sir Percivale*, a Royal Fleet Auxiliary (Landing Ship Logistics) that had taken part in the Falklands invasion, and was the first British ship to re-enter Stanley Harbour after the Argentineans had been overwhelmed, was diverted from operations in the Mediterranean to Freetown.

By now, Brigadier John Holmes had been appointed overall chief of the rescue mission and had already flown out to Freetown to coordinate arrangements. While negotiations continued throughout this period, with the aim of bringing the matter to a non-violent end, it soon became clear that the West Side Boys were both belligerent and uncooperative. Because they had hostages, they would argue, they were 'untouchable'.

Meanwhile, small squads of British Special Forces clandestinely surveyed the immediate area around where the British soldiers were being held and made preparations for the rescue. They meticulously laid out a flat-plan of the hostage house and within days were rehearsing for a full assault. According to Tim Butcher, 'when Barras was launched, the troops were given free rein to engage the enemy'.

Surprisingly, the West Side Boys released five of their prisoners, all of them British. They kept the other six British soldiers and Lieutenant Bungara, who was treated particularly viciously. Imprisoned in typical RUF-style in a pit in the ground, they beat him regularly with their rifle butts and would also defecate onto him from above.

Butcher tells us that the Special Forces observation team used high-tech listening equipment and vision-enhancers to assemble the clearest possible intelligence picture of where the six prisoners were being held and the exact defensive capabilities of their captors. A British Special Forces source told him:

> What the hidden troopers heard and saw from the secret observation post changed everything. West Side Boys gunmen were inflicting a violent sexual assault on at least one of the British prisoners. That was the point when the decision was taken to go in and get them out.

Cockpit on one of the British helicopters that took part in the Barras raid to free a dozen hostages held by the RUF rebels. *Author's photo*

From the start of Operation *Palliser*, Neall Ellis had worked closely with some of the SAS operators deployed to Sierra Leone. In fact, in the *Barras* raid their captain and team leader was a South African.

Nellis would routinely take one or more of their operators up in the Hind on scouting missions into the interior, in large part because there was nobody else in the West African state who had spent so much time flying over Sierra Leone. Essentially, he had intimate knowledge of the people, the towns and the deployment of the RUF rebels. He had effectively become a valued reconnaissance asset for the British and could also inflict serious damage on the rebels with the Mi-24's rockets and Gatling whenever contact was made with the rebels.

It was no secret that Whitehall had given instructions that the South African and his mercenary team were to be kept at a distance. While the British Ministry of Defence accepted that the Air Wing was integral to the Sierra Leonean defence establishment, that association was not to extend to British military interests, London emphatically declared.

However, as one SAS observer told Nellis, what the bosses back home didn't know, wouldn't hurt, so the liaison went on right to the end. It became even more pronounced during Operation *Barras*. Nellis recalls:

> Although we only came into the picture immediately prior to the raid on Gberi Bana and other villages in the vicinity, we got word from the senior SAS officer a couple of days before that action would be taken and that we were to be on standby when it happened. He wasn't overly specific, except to say that it would be a major effort and that everybody involved would be playing a role, including us.

It made good sense, of course, Nellis commented afterwards. All other British offensive capabilities had left the country after Operation *Palliser* was over. Fairly early on he was also told that the entire region around the Rokel Creek where the West Side Boys had their camps had been declared a no-fly area.

> They didn't want me nosing in there with the Hind and shooting the shit out of anything and possibly causing Kallay to do something stupid . . . it made good sense.

British ground troops vigorously patrolled all approach roads in the vicinity of Freetown following their arrival in the country under then Brigadier David Richards, early 2000. *Author's photo*

Apart from that we didn't have much to do with either the SAS or SBS guys. They very much kept to themselves, although a couple of them did come to the house one evening to talk business, but it was the only time. They didn't socialise much either . . . in fact, I don't think I ever saw any of their lads in Paddy's Bar . . . they were a very private bunch of guys.

On a business level, Nellis reckons his relations with the British Special Forces personnel were excellent:

We spoke the same kind of language. Then, a few days before the op, one of their electronic boffins fitted a UHF radio aerial to the Hind and I was told that one of the SAS people, somebody from headquarters, would be going up with us to coordinate things on the ground. We were quite chuffed at the responsibility.

Nellis remembers the day of the attack well:

Then, the day before it all happened, I got a message late afternoon telling me that they were going in at first light the next morning and that we all had to be at the base at 04h00 hours for our briefing. I was aware that there had already been a lot of meetings and briefings among British military personnel, but we were never a part of them.

We were there on time and were shown the plan, which basically involved the SAS guys fast roping from the choppers directly onto the heads of Foday Kallay and his men at Gberi Bana.

British serviceman prepares his heavy machine-gun mounted on the cab of an army Land Rover. *Author's photo*

The Paras, he was told, would be dropped in a green field across the river. Their area of operations would be the area around Magbeni and Forodugu where they would suppress any threat of a counterattack from rebels based there.

I interjected and said that it wasn't a field that the Paras were going into, but a rice paddy. I also told them that in parts of the adjoining areas the water, which was interspersed with sections of swamp and mud, was quite deep. That stopped the briefing officer for a few moments, but he replied that it was too late to do anything about it: the men were about to go in.

Bad mistake, I warned, and so it was. Some of the Paras were dropped in water up to their shoulders and with them laden down with weapons, ammo and other kit, they were lucky that nobody drowned . . . it could very easily have happened.

As planned, the raid took place at dawn, shortly before 06h00 hours on 10 September. It was an incredibly efficient effort, recalls Nellis, with all the hostages quickly released and most of the serious fighting over within half an hour. 'There was still a lot of mopping up to do and that's when the choppers, us included, came into our element.'

The Hind's role was largely secondary, but Neall Ellis and his team were given an area towards the south and south-east of the river, opposite the Gberi Bana complex where he would perform stopper group duties.

There was no shortage of targets either . . . those West Side Boys who survived the initial attack had scattered as soon as they were able to, many of them running right into our guns.

Strictly speaking, I suppose our role could have been equated to close air support because we would send off our rockets as and when needed, firing in volleys of four or eight at a time. It was the same with the Gatling. We only left the scene of the action to return to base to refuel and gun up again before heading back to Rokel Creek.

Questioned about numbers, Nellis reckons that about 40 rebels were probably killed by the British gunships and the main attack force in the initial onslaught. It would have been more but for the fact that one of the Lynxes had to pull out because of an engine problem. He estimates that by the time he returned to Cockerill in the afternoon, he had probably killed another 50 or 60.

British forces lost one man, Brad Tinnion from the SAS, who was hit by a round from an AK-47 although there were several others lightly wounded.

The war in Sierra Leone officially ended in January 2002 and, once it was over, there were few people in Freetown who did not acknowledge the sterling role played by Nellis and his little band of brothers in their helicopter gunship. Even today, more than a decade later, Neall Ellis is warmly welcomed in the homes of just about everybody in this great city, including those of people who probably didn't even know him. Everybody is aware of what he did and what his role ultimately meant to the country. He is a white hero in a staunchly black African country.

This was also one of the reasons why, in a personal letter to the author dated 14th June, 2010, General Sir David Richards KCB CBE DSO ADC Gen, Chief of the General Staff in the United Kingdom (and soon to become Chief of the Defence Staff), acknowledged an informal greeting from the South African aviator from Afghanistan.

General Sir David wrote: '. . . I hugely appreciate Neall Ellis sending me his best wishes. He is a great man; I and everyone in Sierra Leone owe him much.'

CHAPTER NINETEEN

IRAQ—GOING NOWHERE

In September 2004, while I was still in Sierra Leone, Mauritz Le Roux approached me and said that he had set up a private security company in Iraq. It was called OSSI-Safenet and he was in partnership with John Walbrige, an American. He intimated that things were moving ahead at a steady pace and they already had contracts with large companies involved with reconstruction work in what the media was calling 'a war-ravaged country'.

Basically, the job in Iraq was to get the contractors in and out of their work places each day and to provide on-site protection while they were there. It was pretty straightforward. However, as was the case with other companies doing this kind of work, such as Haliburton, KBR, and Triple Canopy, they were targeted from time to time and, more often than not, had to slug it out in close-quarter combat. Convoy ambushes were a favourite ploy of the dissidents, who included a good sprinkling of al-Qaeda.

To begin with, Mauritz suggested that I should travel with him to Saddam Hussein's old fief. The idea was to look at some helicopters and engines he was contemplating buying. He thought he needed some kind of air capability to move his staff around Iraq and it sounded promising.

Getting into Baghdad from Dubai wasn't all that easy at the

263

time. Mauritz met me in Dubai and we spent a couple of days looking for scheduled flights to Iraq. We had no luck, as everything with wings heading to Baghdad was full. Finally, he suggested that we just go down to the airport and see if we could 'hitch a ride'. I thought he was joking but, as usual, the man has no inhibitions and we started walking around Dubai's airport apron, looking for an aircraft that might be heading east.

Finally, we approached an Il-76 captain, a Russian who said he was going to Baghdad. He wasn't interested in taking any passengers, he said gruffly. Mauritz discreetly handed him $500 in crisp American bills and suddenly we had a deal.

After about two hours in the air our plane dropped into a steep spiral-descent as we headed into Baghdad. It was a bit like those long-ago days in Ondangua when Angola and the South-West African borders were hot, but I didn't complain. Better a quick entry than the alternative; only a short while before a DHL freighter had taken a SAM missile up its tailpipe.

My first impressions of Iraq were mixed. For what had been a war zone only a short time before, the place was humming. There were huge numbers of military personnel about and, in spite of the apparent confusion, things seemed to work. The terminal itself was packed with private military contractors, mostly American, swaggering, gung-ho types. We arrived without visas, but *baksheesh* quickly took care of that. Mauritz's people were waiting for us in the main terminal and the drive into the city was yet another kind of experience.

OSSI-Safenet had a policy of preferring to blend in with the locals. That meant that Mauritz rarely used new or upmarket vehicles, such as the Hummer or American-built Suburbans that most of the American PMCs preferred. Rather, the company stuck to older, more ordinary sedans such as battered Mercedes sedans or Japanese mini-buses. These vehicles sat quite low and I thought that the suspensions might have been shot. However, I soon realised that they were armour-plated and, obviously, the additional weight made a significant difference. As somebody said, 'better slower and safer than sorry'.

Within the Mauritz organisation, I immediately recognized several former South African Special Forces and Army vets from my SADF and EO days. In fact, wherever you went there were South Africans involved in security in Iraq. At the peak, there were about 30,000 private security contractors in the country, of whom more than half were from South Africa. What was certainly comforting with OSSI-Safenet was that just about all its members of staff were professionals. There were hardly any who had not seen solid action while in uniform.

Before leaving the airport, I was issued with a ballistic jacket and an AK-47. A briefing on the kind of procedures we were expected to stick to followed, with the emphasis on drills to be observed should we be attacked. We were then told to hop into one of the cars and we left the airport in a convoy of three vehicles.

One aspect of the briefing was puzzling. We were told never to purposely peer into cars using the same highway, even if they pulled up right alongside us. Essentially, it was stressed, the company liked to mind its own business. I wasn't sure that I agreed as I thought that if someone was intending to attack us, it would be better to keep a wary eye out for belligerents with weapons. How, otherwise, would we know if we were going to be at the receiving end of a 'drive-by' killing?

Although nothing happened on that journey, it was an exhilarating experience. I was thinking that while I had survived more hairy situations than I cared to recall at the controls of combat, and other, helicopters, I was now going to die because of some maniac driver hurtling down Route Irish. It really was scary. Just about everybody in Baghdad seemed to drive like a lunatic. Speeds of 120kph were slow and, moreover, basic road courtesy simply did not exist and it was every man for himself. However, our drivers had obviously driven the route often enough before and they knew the ropes. I found the coordination of the vehicles moving about the narrow streets impressive. There was constant radio chatter keeping the whole group in the picture about the situation ahead. Delays would be reported as soon as they happened to prevent one or more of the cars being cut off or hedged-in by trucks, which was invariably the prelude to an ambush.

It didn't bother any of the guys that there was a constant sound of gunfire with a never-ending series of explosions, automatic fire, single fire, shotgun fire, and more. There was also the constant scream of fighter jets and choppers overhead: there were British Pumas, American Apaches, Chinooks and quite a few others. Anywhere else in the world, it would have made for a pretty impressive air show.

After a few routine stops, Mauritz headed to a hotel where he had a suite and where I would be staying. On that leg of the journey our security detachment was even more impressive. Each of the vehicles in our convoy had a shooter sitting alongside the driver with another in the back seat. We were told that if there was any serious trouble, we'd find heavier stuff like PKMs and RPGs in the trunks, and everybody was carrying a pistol.

An outstanding organiser and tactician, Mauritz had geared the routine so that we could immediately adapt to new circumstances. Thus if any of the vehicles were attacked, the men in the others would be able to react and give fire support. Essentially, it is the South African way that comes with experience and it worked very well.

As we approached the hotel, the street was cordoned off by massive three-metre-high cement blocks, acting as blast walls for suicide car bombers and positioned so that we had to weave in between them at a snail's pace. At the entrance there was a longish contraption that had spikes on it. The guards were ready to haul it across the road and puncture tyres if they thought there were insurgents trying to force their way in. All the security personnel at the hotel were Iraqi but it turned out they were also working for Mauritz.

Once through the door, everybody suddenly relaxed and the banter was infectious. It was a marked change from when we were on the road, when nobody said a word unless they had to and the drivers were constantly checking their rear view mirrors for any vehicle getting too close. The only chatter then came from the radio.

I sat around the hotel for the next couple of days while Mauritz had meetings, and coordinated our visit to where the engines and spares were stored. It was then that I was able to compare his set-up with that of some of the American PMCs working in Iraq.

By and large, Americans working security in Iraq, with some notable exceptions, of course, could hardly have been described as unobtrusive. The former Special Forces operatives, veterans from the various Seal Teams or even Delta Force, were a zealous bunch who liked to publicly display their prowess. They would wear their battle jackets, side arms, usually a bandana or two and dark glasses, and they used a variety of camouflage kit with aplomb. If they were fit and strong, and most of them were, they'd often wear the skimpiest T-shirts and strut about to show off their physiques, which went very much against the grain of the average British or Commonwealth operative who, in contrast, were always low key. Get talking to an American at the bar and he would invariably tell you his life story in the first 20 minutes, which could be embarrassing as he'd invariably boast about himself and his achievements. It was very much in contrast to the British attitude. You'd have difficulty getting somebody who had spent time in the SAS or SBS to answer even a few fundamental questions about his old regiment.

It was the same with Mauritz's crowd, who eventually numbered several thousand including a preponderance of Iraqis. OSSI-Safenet operatives were encouraged to adopt local dress, which would sometimes include the traditional Arab headdress, the *keffiyeh* or *shemagh*, and to grow beards. Others in the group would don long robes, which were ideal for concealing side arms, and since most spent a lot of time in the sun, they all sported good tans, which made them look partly Arab anyway. Basically, this was an unobtrusive bunch of fighters and they never went looking for trouble. After the third or fourth ambush on one of the roads out of Baghdad to a construction site at Fallujah, they retaliated so strongly that they ended up killing quite a few of their attackers without loss. After that they were left alone

A few mornings after I arrived we were off again. We travelled in a three-vehicle convoy into a part of Baghdad where none of the guys had been before. The warehouse—the object of our interest and where our contact said the goods were stored—was tucked away in an unusually quiet part of the town. Even local drivers used the area sparingly. They went in, did what they had to and left again, always in a hurry.

From our perspective, it was worrying that there were few people around and no Coalition Military forces. There was no question that our shooters were extra vigilant. We waited in the street outside the warehouse while Mauritz and the man who had initiated the visit negotiated an entrance to the premises. We could see security was tight and that the place was protected. Once inside, we found an expansive shed packed with about 30 wooden crates which I immediately recognized as the kind of boxes the Soviets had once used to deliver aircraft spares—all were painted grey.

Having started the inspection and found the engines in reasonable shape, it was also apparent that there were no 'passports', which are Moscow's equivalent for component logbooks. That straightaway rendered the engines and other spares useless because to get replacement documents would take time and cost good money.

There were supposed to be some helicopters, type unknown, included in the deal, but storage space was limited and there was certainly not enough room left for choppers, even if they were still in their original crates. However, interestingly, there was a South African Mamba armoured vehicle for sale. An ideal armoured personnel carrier that could carry ten passengers plus the drivers, it offers good protection against small arms fire and landmines. It had obviously either been stolen or illegally sold because it was in almost mint condition.

As Mauritz commented, that Mamba would have been ideal for his purposes but, under the circumstances, it was a very definite no-no. Anyone buying it would immediately be fingered as there were not too many South African-built APCs on Baghdad's streets in those days.

The visit was a disappointment: no choppers, no deal. However, as we left, a particularly surly individual, who was in charge, said that if we drove to Kirkuk, in Northern Iraq, the next day, he'd show us the helicopters. It was a long shot, but Mauritz seemed quite happy with the idea, if only to visit some of his employees who were based in Kirkuk.

Early the next day we were on the road again, once more in a three-vehicle convoy, this time destined for Kirkuk. We travelled to Kirkuk at great speed, on a road that was quite narrow and packed with traffic. Parts of the trip were terrifying, especially when Iraqi drivers, quite fearlessly, overtook on the wrong side of the double white lines in the middle of the road.

We were almost halfway there when our driver shouted something out loud and started to take evasive action. When I looked up, there was a huge cloud of dust ahead with large chunks of a vehicle blocking the road. There were bodies everywhere and, on one side, a bloodied woman was trying to crawl out of a wreck. Our driver managed to negotiate a path clear of the obstacles and one of our shooters got out to clear the road. Our driver slowed to walking pace, but did not stop. When I queried this, he said that the insurgents sometimes liked to simulate accidents in a bid to kidnap Westerners. He added that there wasn't much we could do because locals would stop and help. It seemed a bit harsh but Iraq, as the media liked to say, was 'both difficult and dangerous' in those faraway days. It was not really a place for us foreigners to wander about in anyway.

We arrived in Kirkuk late in the afternoon and met our contact. The helicopters were buried in an underground bunker, he said, which immediately raised flags. However, he assured us we'd be taken there the following morning.

We met Mohammed early the next day. Our source had indicated that he was local and had family ties with Saddam Hussein. Although he confirmed that the choppers were buried, he had no idea what kind they were. More flags went up. Although Coalition Forces were aware that the Iraqi Air Force had buried some of its larger military aircraft in the desert, which were found years later, there was never any mention of the same being done to secrete helicopters.

Then our new-found friend Mohammed said that the choppers weren't in Kirkuk after all, but in Tikrit, Saddam Hussein's home town. He also stipulated that in order to view and inspect them, I'd have to go with him, alone and unarmed. We insisted on providing an escort but Mohammed was firm. No, he said, that would create problems.

By then I thought the only thing likely to emerge from that lot would be a hole in my head, after I'd been held hostage for who knows how long. I'm a pilot, not some kind of super hero, so the next day we climbed back into our vehicles and had another nightmare drive back to Baghdad.

Meanwhile, life in Baghdad went on as usual. The OSSI-Safenet houses in Baghdad were comfortable, we had good food and Mauritz looked after his people very well. The houses were strictly 'dry' and anybody caught drinking alcohol was sent home. Being a teetotaller himself, Mauritz was quite happy to enforce the rule. Another rule was that there would be no fraternization with local woman or even Western females who were working with the various organizations operating in Iraq. This rule was occasionally broken and a few of the crew were sent home for illegally 'dipping their wick'.

One of the guys latched onto a very attractive lady who was linked to a client. He would sneak out of the house late at night and get back to base before the others were up. Unfortunately, he got caught returning from one of his nocturnal forays and was on a flight out of Baghdad, heading back to South Africa, that same afternoon. Basically, we were all fine as long as we abided by the basic rules, which were in place to protect us, as you simply did not wander about Baghdad on your own after dark.

The one problem that worried senior management was the presence of Iraqi female cleaners in the house. They would arrive in their black hijabs or burkas but, once they'd entered the confines of the base, that all came off and the pilots were left with some very fetching young things in tight jeans and sometimes even closer-fitting T-shirts. There was no doubt that some of these girls were in search of the original white knight in his shining armour to whisk them away from the horror and poverty of everyday Baghdad, with its shootings and suicide bombers, to a secure home in the West.

Some of these nubile young girls were quite beautiful, and sexy too. If anyone showed interest, they would zoom in, fluttering their eyelids and making very provocative displays of swinging their sexy derrieres about in front of the pilots, some of whom hadn't been laid in months. Under the circumstances, it could be difficult not to be fazed. Very occasionally, much to the surprise of everyone, a match was made and a new life would beckon for the young lady in question.

Part of the reason for my staying on in Baghdad was to write an operations manual for our air operator's certificate (AOC) application. However, it wasn't long before the close confines of four walls and sexy cleaners started to get to me and I would look for opportunities to get out. I'd noticed that certain days, when there was a changeover of personnel, there was normally a shortage of the armed escorts, or 'shooters', needed to protect clients or convoys travelling Route Irish to the airport. I regularly volunteered to fill in as a shooter, and I came to enjoy it because it got me out and about and gave me a change of scenery. I also liked the prospect of a bit of action.

The other 'sport of the day' was to stand on the roof of our house and watch 'incoming' going into the Green Zone. Our place was nearby and situated in what was classified as the Red Zone. Consequently, you could hardly miss rocket fire overhead and the guys would rush to the roof and watch the fireworks, usually with accompanying U.S. helicopters circling the zones from where it was suspected the rockets had been fired. It was a fairly regular event and we'd hear the ambulance sirens afterwards.

The best displays were at night when the USAF Spectre, the gunship variant of the C-130, would react to a contact. We'd watch as it spewed great streams of tracers into target areas.

For all his foibles, most of which made good common sense, Mauritz was a good boss, a good leader and a fair arbitrator. When he visited Iraq, he would spend a lot of time with the boys and was always a good listener. Our management staff were top drawer as well. The in-country manager, and Mauritz's right-hand man, was Gerhard Nel, a former South African Army commandant, or half-colonel.

Gerhard ran a tight ship and I reckon that much of the success of Safenet-OSSI was because he was at the helm. His rapport with the men was excellent and he was also popular, which was unusual under the circumstances.

While I was in Iraq, I made contact with Iraqi Government authorities about OSSI-Safenet acquiring an AOC to operate within its borders. It was no easy task. We also had talks with the U.S. Military about using one of their bases as an air wing headquarters for the company.

We had meetings with the Iraq Civil Aviation Authority as well but, curiously, nobody could tell us what procedures we should follow. The Iraqi Government was opposed to allowing civilian aviation companies to work there. One of their reasons, they said, was that if we were shot down, we'd become a liability. While the Iraqi director in charge was helpful enough and said that he could 'arrange' something, he also asked for US$10,000 up-front. Of course, the money would have gone into his pocket, but by then we were frustrated and I approached Mauritz about paying the man, which he did.

I also had meetings with various U.S. Army officials and finally ended up talking to an officer who commanded a unit in Camp Victory, which would be an ideal base because all the facilities for the crews were present. Things started badly with this half-colonel. He was rude and antagonistic and ended up telling me that there was no way that he would he allow what he termed 'a bunch of civilian cowboy helicopter pilots' to launch an operation from his base. It was a pity because, apart from security and being able to live in secure quarters, we would have had access to their DFACs, together with the quality food they customarily provided.

Shortly afterwards, I returned to Sierra Leone, from where I started looking about for a helicopter to buy for the operation in Iraq. My thoughts initially centred on the Eurocopter AS350 Ecureuil, or 'Squirrel', which is fast, simple to maintain and operate, and would perform quite well in a high-temperature environment like Iraq. Mauritz thought that the initial cost was too high and that I should look for a less costly airframe.

Then I spoke to Grant Williams, an old friend, who proposed Alouette III choppers. That was fine with me, but I would have to accept that it was very slow and did not have the range of the Ecureuil. However, the price was good and Mauritz told me he had sourced the 319 version of the Alouette III helicopter, which could carry a couple of hundred kilograms more. It was also slightly faster and had the same ruggedness as the Alouette 316 version that I flew in the SAAF.

We eventually found a pair of them through an American contact initiated by Mauritz. It all seemed pretty much above board and I took Mauritz's word for it that I was dealing with someone who was well established in the business. He was but, as we found out too late, the man had a rap sheet that went back years and had several times involved the FBI. Although I'd flight tested both the Alouettes that we acquired—and carefully checked their engines and the rest—the machines I tested were not the same machines we ended up with. That Yank ended up screwing Mauritz out of half a million dollars and me out of a job.

CHAPTER TWENTY

AIR AMBULANCE IN SARAWAK

Take strong winds and heavy rain, add the mist rising up out of the jungle of the Borneo highlands, and there's the potential for some 'interesting' flying conditions. Neall Ellis found exactly that as a lone pilot at the controls of a relatively unfamiliar Bo-105 helicopter. The situation was further complicated by air traffic controllers, whose Malaysian-accented English was not always easily comprehensible, and the knowledge that civilian lives were at risk.

Martin Steynberg, chief executive of the South African-based Titan Aviation, and his partner, Seton Kendrick, had negotiated a contract to supply helicopter-based emergency medical services (EMS) in Sarawak. Before they could fulfil the contract, however, a local AOC was needed. That's where Sarawak's Layang Layang Aerospace came into the picture. The work would be undertaken in the name of that company, using its AOC. Likewise, Layang Layang would make available its established facilities at Miri, Sarawak's second city, in the north-east of the state and the centre of Malaysia's oil industry.

Nellis flew out to Miri in December 2007 to start up the operation. Altogether, Titan had bought four ex-German Bo-105s earlier in April. Two went to Sarawak and two to South Africa. The intention was to base one of the Bo-105s at Miri and the other inland at Sibu, in the far west of Sarawak.

Ground teams during anti-forest fire operations while with Langeni in
South Africa's Eastern Cape. *Photo: James Mitchell*

Because of a shortage of experienced South African pilots and technical
staff, Titan had not found it easy to sign up crews willing to go to Malaysia,
says Nellis. 'Those who wanted to go either didn't have the experience, or
were greedy. One pilot wanted US$500 per day, which did not make me
too happy because I was earning, after daily allowance, the equivalent of
around $200 per day. However, in the end he decided not to come and I
think everyone was relieved because his demands were too high for the
job.'

The insurers have demands of their own with this kind of work. They
require that pilots have a minimum of 1,500 hours' command time on
twin-engine helicopters before they fly EMS aircraft. This may not seem a
lot of hours, but with the high cost of helicopter flying, it can be difficult
to attain that many hours. There are a lot of young pilots who have 'Robbie
time' (time on the small, piston-engine Robinson R-22 often used for
training), but they do not have the twin-turbine time needed.

Nellis' own acquaintance with the aircraft they would be using was
also pretty limited. 'My training on the Bo-105 consisted of a single ferry

flight from Durban's Virginia Airport to East London, south along the coast, as effective co-pilot.' On top of that he had something like 40 minutes of running through emergency procedures at Grand Central Airport, halfway between Johannesburg and Pretoria. Nellis had never so much as got a Bo-105 going on his own. 'It was a pretty new experience for everything', he reckons. 'My total training time added up to just two-and-a-half hours. I even had to teach myself how to start the machine!'

Once out in Sarawak, Nellis soon found that the Malaysian airborne emergency medical services were considerably different from the paradigm that is commonly used in the United States and South Africa. In both these countries, such services, whether public-funded or private, include emergency medical technicians, paramedics and sometimes even doctors, to resuscitate and give first aid, stabilise patients and care for them en route to a suitable hospital facility.

In Sarawak, in contrast, a more limited air ambulance service was expected. It was one that merely transported patients from, say, countryside clinics to city hospitals, or provided hospital-to-hospital transfers. That 'countryside', however, posed its own problems. Nellis comments:

> I was expected to take family members on board to accompany the patient. This was a problem, because legally we are not allowed to carry persons aboard during flight unless they are strapped to an aviation-approved seat equipped with seatbelts. My lack of knowledge of the Malay language was also a problem in these situations, because I was not able to explain why we could not take everyone. In the end we had to get a letter from the Health Department circulated to all the clinics explaining why it was not always possible to take family members on board.

Another problem was that Nellis felt that Seton Kendrick was not always ready to listen to advice.

> As much as I find him a great guy with an incredible sense of humour, he is a typical upper-class Brit, at times very arrogant and not prepared to believe that there are other people in the world who may have a better idea of how things should be. Sometimes

he and I would clash about the 'right' way of doing things. Furthermore, there seemed to be a sense of professional jealousy between him and Martin Steynberg, in that each was trying to prove to the other that he was capable of doing the job better. This applied especially to Seton, who at times became very sensitive and took criticism in a negative way, although it was not meant to be taken that way.

The biggest problem I perceived was that the management in South Africa wanted to dictate how the operation would work and, although most of these inputs were positive, some would not work in the circumstances we experienced in Sarawak. At times there were some pretty overheated phone discussions between the two countries and it was difficult to stay neutral.

I had to try to maintain the balance between the South African Civil Aviation Authority rules and business requirements . . . without breaking any CAA regulations. Initially, we were operating on the fringe of local CAA legality, although once the *klein politiek* between the two bosses had been sorted out, the modus operandi became more comfortable. After all, it was not only the emergency medical services operation on the line, but my credibility and my pilot's licence as well.

The company managed to find a stand-in pilot for two months, as two pilots were needed to handle the workload. They employed Rory Halse, an old friend from the South African Air Force. Rory had been around in the flying game for some time and wasn't partial to the politics involved. In fact, he is a straight-down-the-middle sort of guy. His relationship with Seton deteriorated rapidly because he was not prepared to push the envelope as much as I did. I was very keen to see the operation continue, particularly as the contract at that time was a temporary six-month one, with a tender for a four-year period being put out by the Sarawak Government later that year.

However, Rory had nothing to lose as he was off to a very lucrative contract once his eight weeks with Titan had expired. It was difficult trying to maintain the peace and also balance the legal aspects. In the end, against his wishes, Martin was forced to agree with Seton that if South African crews could not be recruited, the company would have to look at finding pilots from the region. This, obviously, suited Seton quite well because, in his opinion, pilots are overpaid for what they do and are not much better than truck drivers.

He was forever looking for the cheapest option, even though it might not be the most economical solution . . . [he was] very tight when it came to money. There were no local Sarawak helicopter pilots looking for employment, so Seton was forced to look at Filipino pilots, and managed to find two aviators who were suitably qualified for the job. Speaking selfishly, I was not too happy that other pilots had been recruited because I was experiencing a very comfortable lifestyle in Sarawak, and would have been quite happy to live there on a permanent basis. It's far from both the United Kingdom and South Africa, and all my responsibilities seemed to melt away, leaving me at peace with the world and myself. Even relatives in the UK found it difficult to contact me.

The first few flights proved to be 'a bit hazardous', Nellis admits. It was a long time since he had flown as a single pilot, handling all the navigation and radio work in addition to the flying. Plus, as mentioned, he was flying a new and unfamiliar aircraft in a country totally new to him, which had a different operating environment from any he had worked in before and which included those difficult-to-understand air traffic controllers.

If all this were not enough, in this remote corner of the world the north-east monsoons run from late November until March, bringing steady north-east winds and heavy rainfall, so that between December and January the weather can make flying conditions marginal, at best.

On one occasion Nellis had to fly the Bo-105 from Miri, on the northern Sarawak coast, some 285km south-west through the inland mountains to Kapit, pick up a patient and head west to Sibu, around 130km further on. However, just 20 minutes out of Miri the weather deteriorated so badly, recalled Nellis, 'that I was flying at 50ft above the jungle looking for a route to get to Kapit. The visibility was no more than about 200 metres in the rain and when it starts to rain in these monsoon conditions, the mist seems to rise up from below to meet it.'

The intervening highlands and the Dulit mountain range didn't help either. Nellis subsequently discovered that he was the only pilot flying in that area at that time and recalls: 'Sometimes I was flying just above transition, at 40 knots, weaving the helicopter in and out between trees, all the while trying to keep contact with the ground. There was actually no place where I could put the helicopter down . . . the jungle just stretched on'.

Kapit, lying on the south bank of the muddy Rajang River, features some modern administrative buildings. However, the traditional Iban, or Sea Dayak, 'longhouses' on stilts, peering out of the jungle towards the river banks and housing a whole community of families at a time, remain a feature in this part of the world. Their only concession to modernity is that longhouse roofs are now generally rusty, corrugated iron rather than the palm thatch of the past. Once in Kapit, picking up the patient and accompanying medical staff was no problem. The flight to Sibu Hospital then followed.

Initially, it seemed logical to continue flying along the west-flowing Rajang River. It was about 200 metres across at this stage but widened to around 500 metres closer to the inland river port of Sibu. However, this proved not such a good idea as there were sometimes wires straddling the waterway. Nellis made the decision to go somewhat inland, and almost inevitably, the weather started to deteriorate badly once more.

'I thought if I could find Sibu Airfield I'd be OK, and that should have been relatively simple. However, there were still plenty of high-tension power wires and microwave towers, and all the time I was flying, peering ahead, looking for obstacles.' Finally, he found himself over the airfield, some 15km to the east of the town.

> There I was, flying down the airfield, and I said to the tower: 'Requesting permission to cross the airfield.' The woman in the tower asked my position, saying she didn't have a visual on me because of the visibility . . . it was so bad that she couldn't even see the runway from where she was.
>
> I said: 'Look down in front of the tower and you will see me.' But the only answer I got was a nervous giggle.

Eventually, Nellis acquired the hospital, offloaded his patient and accompanying medics, and then decided he'd had enough. He left the aircraft where he had landed, 'booked into a hotel and had a beer . . . and got my heart rate down as well'.

Monsoons and mountains apart, he found Sarawak 'a great experience'. The lifestyle was laid-back and the people, he thought, were generally among the most honest to be found anywhere. Furthermore Nellis, who likes his food, found he liked the local cuisine. He recalls:

> I also managed to get quite fit; I'd wake up in the morning and go down to the public swimming pool. Eventually, I worked up to 2,000 metres a day. Sometimes I was the only person in that massive pool . . . it was almost a case of living the high life with one's own private Olympic-sized pool!

As is his wont, Nellis also sealed some friendships during the course of this tour. Among those he got to know was an Australian, Peter Salkowski, who had served with 8 Battalion, Royal Australian Regiment (RAR), in Vietnam. Nellis also had the impression that Salkowski had been involved in Special Forces at some time, presumably the Australian Special Air Service. 'He was an interesting guy, and we clicked well. He didn't drink, but he'd once been quite a hell-raiser. Even so, without booze he carried on pretty well.'

In fact, Nellis' new friend had quite a reputation. During the Vietnam War, in late 1970, Corporal Peter Salkowski and two privates had been drinking in their company canteen until it closed. The logical next step seemed to be to break into the adjacent Australian Reinforcement Unit (ARU) canteen. Inside, and in the dark, they were about to pass some cartons of beer out of the window when the lights were switched on and an ARU sergeant was seen to have his 9mm pistol pointing at the head of one of the errant troops—the other had meanwhile jumped out of the window.

Salkowski, who had been behind the bar uplifting the beers, then apparently came running out between the sergeant and the private, who by then had his hands up, and yelled: 'Don't shoot him; he's one of my men!' Although they spent the rest of the night locked up, they were lucky not to be charged, the apparent explanation for this leniency being official reluctance to initiate disciplinary proceedings as these would inevitably have been publicised in Australia at a time when involvement in the war was becoming increasingly unpopular.

Now long out of the Australian Army, 'on the wagon' and in his early sixties, Peter Salkowski had built his own catamaran yacht, a Grainger 38, which he christened *Zosha*. As Nellis remembers him, Salkowski was 'a short, stocky, well-tanned man with a great turn of phrase, and a wicked sense of humour'.

He was 'living his life as he liked', adds Nellis—somewhat wistfully. 'He'd sail from place to place, tie up alongside and stay as long as he felt comfortable and then move on. If things got too hot with social contacts, he'd set sail again.' Nellis continued:

> Pete has the ability to talk to anyone and wherever we went . . . there was always someone who would greet him and we would have a temporary halt while they chatted. I think he had been to just about every bar in Miri, and there would always be a flock of girls seeking his attention, more often because they knew he would buy them a drink so they could fulfil their quota for the night. Life with Peter was never dull!

The trouble is, unwanted 'social contacts' cannot always be escaped as easily as Peter managed it. When Nellis was working later in South Africa, one such contact made in Sarawak—who had possibly read more into their brief friendship than he intended—kept on sending him one SMS after the other with ever-more insistent suggestions that he convert to Islam and wed her. The was nothing necessarily wrong with that, but if your counter-intelligence skills are getting a bit rusty and you keep leaving your cell-phone around for your current partner to check out the competition, things can get a tad fraught!

The way Nellis puts it is:

> I formed a friendship with a masseuse who was managing a hotel spa adjacent to the Ship Café. She was one of three Indonesian girls there. It was the first time I'd ever had a professional massage. It was not a 'happy-ending massage' and when I brought that up they were quite offended.

Heliborne medic attends to a patient after he was pulled out of a remote jungle village by Nellis in Sarawak. *Photo Neall Ellis*

The Ship Café is one of the finest bars I have ever been to. The music was solely Country and Western, piped during the week, and on weekend nights, a live band played. It was a bit incongruous to walk into a bar in the middle of Borneo and be surrounded by cowboys and cowgirls all wearing clothing straight out of a Western movie . . . without the hardware of course. However, it was a fun place and the locals were incredibly friendly. I never once saw or felt any sign of aggression, and whenever I walked into the bar I felt quite welcome. The best part about the bar was that few expatriates would frequent the place so it was a great place to get to know the local native population. Likewise, there would be very few Chinese. It was also a place where a single woman could have a drink and ask a man to dance, without fear of harassment or expectations. It was a dark, smoky bar, with a great atmosphere. The clientele was mainly 30-plus, so you did not have to sit around and watch the silly adolescent antics of the hip-hop crowd.

One thing Nellis quickly learned about Malaysian women was that they are not free with their sexual favours.

> In fact, because of the Muslim influence, there is a very high moral standard. According to information explained to me, if you end up in bed with a Malaysian woman, it means she is in love with you and is expecting a marriage commitment. If you get into bed with a woman on a casual basis, don't accept an invitation to visit the family . . . unless of course you want to marry her!
>
> In Sarawak itself, apart from the 'ladyboys' on the streets, I saw very little evidence of female prostitution. If one needed sexual release, there were spas that dealt in sex for payment, but I never went to one so I had no experience of the underground night life.

Nellis found the people of Sarawak to be very tolerant, particularly the Iban who live along the rivers and waterways, and the Bidayuh, or inland Land Dayaks, who prefer the fertile highlands.

> Seton's business partner in Sarawak is Patricia Simbit, a very beautiful Bidayuh woman in her early forties, who looks not much older than thirty. She has a passion for life and one of the most effervescent personalities I have ever known. At her age she is still running the weekly Kuching HASH (social harriers) and in her spare time takes friends out on the river for kayaking trips. She's an amazing woman and, often, when on night stops in Kuching, we'd go out for dinner and spend the evening chatting over a bottle of red wine.

Nellis observed that Indonesian contract workers appeared to be treated as cheap, unskilled labour with few rights. Referring to one he got to know socially, he said:

> Laila's boss would take her passport, and only return it on the completion of her contract. However, unlike some other foreign employees she had relative freedom, but she never had a day off. They paid her a pitiful salary of 500 ringgit a month, plus 15 per

cent commission, so if she was lucky she might end up with 1,000 ringgit [approximately US$300] a month.

It says a lot that Laila did not work in a bar. She was the masseuse and, as Nellis recounts, he got to know her very well. 'She was definitely not into offering any sexual favours.

While in Miri, Nellis used to frequent the Globe Bar, where he learned something about the harsh economics of the bar hostess business.

There were two Filipina girls, one of them fluent in English. She had a bubbly character . . . aged about twenty-one or twenty-two . . . beautiful. [She was] on a five-month contract. They were on duty from seven in the evening until the last customer left at, say, four in the morning. Then they were imprisoned in their rooms and the gate was only unlocked at four that afternoon to let them out to do whatever shopping they needed. They weren't allowed to have any relationships with men.

With a basic salary of just 500 ringgit, their whole purpose was to encourage patrons at the Globe to buy them so-called 'ladies' drinks'. These were just watered-down orange cordial, costing 15 ringgit [a bit more than four U.S. dollars], but they had a target of, say, 3,000 ringgit-worth of 'ladies' drinks' sales a month. That works out at about three drinks an hour and so, every twenty minutes, the senior hostess would go around, tap on the bar, take a glass and indicate that a hostess must get the man she was with to buy another drink.

Inevitably, and despite the 'locked barracks' accommodation for these contract Indonesian hostesses, the rules occasionally got not merely bent, but busted wide open. 'One of the guys we knew had managed to form a relationship with a rather attractive woman', notes Nellis. 'She visited his lodgings, and then one afternoon her boss found out about it. She was physically abused, never received her salary, and for a month wasn't even allowed to leave the premises to buy toiletries and so on.' It was, he says, a case of 'semi-slavery', made worse by the fact that the mainly Chinese employers seemed to treat the Indonesian contract workers as a lower form of life.

Despite all this, if you were passing through like Peter Salkowski, or selling your skills in Sarawak like Neall Ellis, there was much to enjoy. Fuel, before the price shot up internationally, was a mere 1 ringgit 50 sen per litre (US$1,70/gallon).

'We never had to cook; every night we had food at one of the restaurants . . . Chinese or Malay-style', recalls Nellis. The cost of living was low, but for those trapped there by birth or by their lack of skills, it was a far less attractive place. That is perhaps why, said Nellis when he looked back on the experience afterwards, he could perfectly understand why some bar hostesses were desperate to forge links with foreigners who might be willing to help them escape.

From Sarawak, Nellis went on to do forest fire protection work in Transkei on South Africa's Eastern Cape. He had done such work for a couple of years and though the flying was different from that of a war zone, it was no less dangerous. Neall comments that 'it was almost as dangerous as flying combat in Sierra Leone.' He's referring to the dangers of flying high in the Eastern Cape, where at several thousand feet above sea level the air was less dense, carrying a full load of fuel. The fiery heat made the air, through which his machine's blades had to claw their way, even less dense and buoyant as he flew up dead-end, no-safe-exit valleys and on wooded mountain slopes running up to sheer cliff faces, all the while dangling two tons of water below, ready to drop onto a raging forest fire. Nellis adds: 'of course, without the danger of getting shot at.' Then he smiles wryly: 'though there was that too, I suppose. Farmers didn't always appreciate when you took their precious water to fight a runaway forest fire.'

The law permits the use of anyone's water to fight a fire threatening life and property, he explains. However, for a farmer whose livelihood is constructed around a delicately balanced equation of grass plus water equals livestock, such law doesn't always make sense, which is why a few potshots could sometimes be loosed off from a farmer's old hunting rifle. It was much less dangerous, of course, than a 12.7mm DShK anti-aircraft machine gun or a SAM. However, it was still capable of being deadly if a round hit the wrong part of a rotor assembly, or even one of the crew. In the United States, airborne firefighting is considered, outside of combat, to be the most dangerous flying there is. In California particularly, at the

time of writing, there is a strong debate about whether the extent of the
inherent dangers are sufficiently recognised. 'During the 2003 Southern
California infernos, for instance, pilots coped with smoke, wind shear and
debris such as kids' play pools and full sheets of plywood careening past
them at 1,500 feet.' reported the *Oakland Tribune* of 9 May 2005.

Although the Mi-8P Nellis was flying was originally designed to carry
up to 28 passengers, that was in cold, dense-air European conditions. 'For
every degree change in temperature above 20 degrees Centigrade, we for-
feited or gained 70 kilogrammes', Nellis explains:

> With a 2,000-litre Bambi Bucket, if the outside air heated up by
> 10 degrees, that meant the aircraft could lift 700 litres less. Also,
> we would start off with 1,000 litres of fuel on board, so burning
> off fuel meant we could carry more water to put out fires. The
> whole time, I had to be mentally aware of weight, air density and
> altitude parameters.
>
> We were flying continually at our limits, at the aircraft's max-
> imum all-up weight. Of course, generally fires happen in dry, hot,
> windy conditions, and we were called out when the ground crews
> couldn't put out the blaze. Some 95 per cent of the time we were
> working up on the slopes of the mountain that vehicles and people
> on the ground couldn't access. In gulleys, and on the sides of cliff
> faces, there were associated updrafts and downdrafts, plus extreme
> turbulence.

In one incident, when fire penetrated into the forest, the flames, says
Nellis, were intense. Sometimes such flames could shoot well above the
30-metre-tall trees, perhaps even another 15 metres up, even higher than
the aircraft was flying. Dense smoke could add to the difficulties. Then
there was the danger posed by the aptly-named 'widow-makers', the leafless
trunks left after a tree had died, possibly in an earlier fire, that were hard
to spot against the ground.

To fight that specific fire, Nellis and his crew had to empty their bucket
into a gulley, while flying up the overall slope of the land, but at the same
time going downwind. Normally, to disperse the water load properly, they
aim to drop at around 100kph. Nellis recalls:

But now we were trying to concentrate the load. We had to slow down, and it became very unsafe. Should we have lost an engine, we would have gone right into the side of the mountain. It felt as though the wind was picking us up and throwing us into the mountain. I remember thinking: If I don't do this right, I'll have to do it again.

With the revs of the two Klimov turboshaft engines unable to provide enough power to prevent the main rotor revolutions from drooping, Nellis was 'trying to mentally pull the controls up to get that little extra bit of height'. The Bambi Bucket hung 10 metres below the helicopter, meaning the aircraft needed to fly at 15 metres above ground level. It took fine judgment as the ideal was to drop water from some 5 metres above the fire and it had to be released along the line of the fire. If the aircraft was flying too fast, then the water would be too spread out and dissipate. If it was too slow, or low, then the rotor wash would fan the flames. At the same time the massive bucket posed a danger of its own to the aircraft. In a commercial forest, not only are there trees all around, but also power lines as well as the ever-present 'widow-makers'. 'Ideally speaking, we should have dropped and picked up another load within two minutes', says Nellis. 'But the water could easily be five to ten minutes' flying time away, adding to the difficulties.' He continues:

> We did some very strange aerobatic manoeuvres to get out of trouble that day. Altogether, we completed about 12 drops, with the fire spreading through the forest and threatening the sawmill itself. A Kamov Ka-32, normally based at Ugie, slinging a 4,000-litre bucket was brought in to assist. There was smoke. It was extremely dangerous flying. That's why we got paid a bonus for each hour of flying—people didn't like to say it was a danger allowance, but it was.

CHAPTER TWENTY-ONE

TANZANIA

*Neall Ellis tells his own story during his detachment to East Africa
to help with the three-month Presidential election campaign.*

For those of us who have spent most of their working lives in Africa, the appeal of the so-called 'Dark Continent' can be irresistible despite all its problems. To some, it's the call of the wild.

Therefore, when my tour of duty in Afghanistan finished in the summer of 2010 and I was asked by the Titan Operations Department to go to Tanzania, I jumped at the chance. I had never flown in East Africa before. In fact, Dar es Salaam was little more than a name to me, even though most of the insurgents I had fought against over years in Rhodesia, Namibia and Angola had been routed to their respective war fronts through the Tanzanian capital. The offer was an opportunity I simply could not miss. Consequently, at the end of August that year, I was on my way back to my beloved Africa.

The Tanzanian contract was for two months. We were to fly the incumbent Tanzanian leader, President Kikwete, together with a fairly hefty entourage, around the country on one of the biggest election campaigns the country had experienced. A vast, underdeveloped and mostly under-exploited region, Tanzania had its own set of problems, but after seeing those of Central Asia, they were minimal. At least there would be no Taliban aiming their guns at us.

For the duration, there were three helicopters set aside for the programme: an AS-350B3 French-built Squirrel; a Bell 205 from Aeronautical

Solutions, a South African-based helicopter company; and an Mi-8P from Titan Helicopters, which I would fly with Braam Wessels and Johnny O'Neil as crew. I was happy working with both men because we'd all worked together on firefighting deployments in South Africa. However, the choppers we'd been given to complete the task worried me, the Hip especially.

In a word, the machine was tired or, more aptly put, exhausted. The last time I'd flown this helicopter, its main rotor blades, as it is phrased in the lingo, were almost 'calendar life expired'. The engines weren't much better. I was concerned that Titan had never bothered to replace either the engines or the rotor blades after I'd first reported these shortcomings to their head office in Johannesburg two years earlier.

When I had last flown the helicopter on firefighting missions in South Africa two years earlier, its engines were not performing well. Since then, it had been on a contract in support of government elections in Mozambique, and who knows what else had happened in the interim? Moreover, the machine had no sand filtering for the engines, which meant that every landing in dusty zones was likely to cause compressor blade erosion and subsequent loss of power. From what I'd heard even before I arrived in Tanzania, there were very few paved runways or landing areas outside the country's main centres, which meant that a large proportion of our touchdowns and take-offs would create dust, probably in abundance.

Nellis' chopper stuck in the bush during his deployment in Tanzania. The pilots sometimes needed tractors to haul them out.
Photo: Neall Ellis

One needs to look at the background of this helicopter to understand what was at stake. The Mi-8P is the passenger version of the MI-8T, a first generation model of the Mi-8 helicopter. Their TB2-117 engines use relatively antiquated technology compared to those installed on today's choppers. They produce only 1,500SHP compared to the 2,200SHP produced by the TB3-117VM engines on the newer generation Mi-8MTV.

Put another way, the 'P' model has a MAUW of 12,000kg compared to the 13,000kg of the MTV. The MTV is quite capable of operating with a full load in 'hot and high' conditions, whereas the 'P' model is a bitch to fly in those conditions and even thinking of touching the collective causes the main rotor revs to drop. In other words, to use a phrase first used by one of my American aviator friends, it is a machine that any pilot has to have his arm out of his arsehole to fly without killing himself and crew.

I was also aware that the helicopter in which I'd be flying the president of Tanzania around is what some experienced airmen would regard as unforgiving. As the pilot at the controls, I wouldn't be able to relax for a moment if I wanted to stay alive. Even tail rotor effectiveness is far less than the MTV. The bottom line, then, is quite simple: in hot and high conditions, the 'P' model is challenging to fly. However, because I had quite a lot of experience flying the same helicopter while fighting fires in South Africa, I was not too concerned. What did surprise me, though, was that Titan should have chosen this decrepit old bird to fly the head of state of an African nation about on duties that would take him to some of the remotest places on the continent.

In late August 2010, I landed at the Julius Nyerere International Airport in Dar es Salaam in the late afternoon after a relatively short flight from Dubai. Despite the humidity and sweltering heat, I was pleased to be back in Africa. Almost immediately I could feel the excitement and the buzz of an African people going about their business and I felt as though I had arrived home.

After spending the night in the Movenpick Hotel, I was flown in a small, twin-engine Cessna to Kigoma, a medium-sized town on Lake Tanganyika in the far west of the country. It was here that Sir Henry Morton Stanley crossed the great lake on his epic journey down the Congo River to the west coast of Africa in the 19th century.

Because we took off late, we arrived at Kigoma well behind schedule. I was met by Louis Venter, the Titan chief pilot, who had ferried the helicopter from South Africa for the contract and had flown the first week in the south of Tanzania. He briefed me on some of the problems they were having with the helicopter, and his parting words to me were something like, 'good luck . . . you're a better man than I am to carry on flying this piece of shit'.

He added that he had found the dust on landings a real challenge and that he was happy to be leaving. Venter also mentioned that the helicopter had been grounded because engine oil was flowing through a seal into the gearbox. In a nutshell, that caused the low pressure oil light to illuminate and the oil in the gearbox to overheat. This was a problem the helicopter had experienced for the last couple of years that nobody had bothered to fix.

I was familiar with the old chopper and knew how to deal with such issues, so I wasn't too fazed. All that was required of me, apart from flying the beast, was to carefully monitor the oil in the engine and gearbox. This meant using a large metal syringe to suck out oil from the main rotor gearbox and then using the same oil to top up the engine oil. The engineers actually wanted to replace the engine, but I convinced them that we'd managed quite well for several years and that I knew what was needed. Replacing the engine would have taken time and put the electoral schedule out. The next day we ferried the Hip to Dar es Salaam and linked up with the rest of the team.

All three helicopters had been chartered by a South African mining company to fly the president and his electioneers around the country, obviously at a price. We gathered that the gesture was in return for mining or mineral concessions of some sort or another and that there was obviously a lot of cash involved. Contractually, we were allowed to fly 60 hours per month. If we exceeded that basic contractual allowance of 120 hours for the two month period, including ferrying the choppers to and from South Africa, the government would compensate. The contractor was thoroughly professional and we were well treated during our eight-week East African sojourn.

All our food, accommodation, transport to hotels and elsewhere, internet and the rest, was covered. All we needed to bring to the party was cash for beer.

Remote, lagoon-side village along the Tanzanian coast. The electoral campaign took in most of them. *Photo Neall Ellis*

While still in Dar es Salaam, Braam Wessels was replaced by another Titan co-pilot, Janneman Erasmus, who would stick out the contract to the end. In addition, Sacha, a Russian technician flew in, fresh from the Russian summer. Between the rest of us, we couldn't speak a word of Russian, and he didn't understand three consecutive words of English. It took a little while to figure out, but eventually communication was achieved by using a language translation programme on Janneman's computer. He would type in a phrase in English and then press the translate button. It would be passed to Sacha to read and the Russian would reply in the same manner. It was primitive, but it worked.

The start of the Tanzanian election campaign was a good distance north of Dar es Salaam at the port of Tanga, not that far from the Kenyan border.

Wherever we went, it was evident from the enthusiastic crowds who gathered for the president's address that he was a popular man. I could quickly see that the chances of him winning the election were good. We'd land and be swamped by crowds of his ululating, demonstrative followers, although there were moments when I wasn't sure whether it was him or the choppers that were the main attraction.

Using helicopters the way that President Kikwete did was a shrewd election ploy, especially in this African backwater. We'd always be tasked to land as close as possible to where he'd be giving his speech and, truth be told, the LZs were mostly far from ideal. It might be a small football field surrounded by trees that were 30 metres high, or a school with buildings nearby. Always, we'd be faced with our rotors stirring up a fine, powdery dust and there were quite a few 'brown-outs'.

The rallies were a spectacle. Loud music would invariably blare out from a succession of speakers positioned on vehicles parked around the fringes of all the venues. The masses added their own touches of Third World panache with dresses and kikois in bright yellow and green, the colours of the Chamu Cha Mapunduzi (CCM) political party. There was always plenty of food and drink available, which meant that the venues hummed because everybody turned out. Some of the people there would have walked for two or three days from some distant village because the occasions were very well publicised by government agents months beforehand.

Curiously, although we were part of the presidential group, we never experienced any attitude problems from Tanzania's political opposition, even though the rival political party would often hold its own rallies a couple of hundred metres away. With people wandering everywhere, the politicians would loudly proclaim their respective agendas, always to the kind of applause that can best be described as boisterous.

While our faithful old Hip performed well along the coast, the dust soon caused problems with the engines and main rotor gearbox cooling systems. We experienced more serious problems with power performance once we moved inland and operated in the rural areas.

Tanzania's inland elevation averaged around 5,500ft, and temperatures hovered around 30 degrees Centigrade, sometimes more. In effect, it was a classic 'hot and high' scenario. Obviously, the whole crew was aware that the Russian Mi-8P model had originally been designed to operate in the colder climes of Soviet Russia, particularly Siberia, and was not really suited for tropical work.

At temperatures below 20 degrees Centigrade, the helicopter was able to perform quite well, even at higher elevations. Once the temperature went beyond that though, there was a rather drastic reduction to our basic lifting capability for every degree increase in temperature. At a rough guess, this is a reduction of about 70kg for each degree of temperature increase. The result was that once we'd started working inland, I had to carefully calculate our load, based on the temperature and altitude graphs.

The owner of this helicopter had leased his machine as an 18-seater and, in theory, able to carry a full load of fuel anywhere and at any time. Under the circumstances just then in Tanzania, that was twaddle.

Figures from the Hip's performance graphs stated that five per cent of the time I could safely carry ten or 12 passengers, together with enough fuel for 90 minutes flying time—the usual endurance is just under three hours flying time with full fuel. It was left to us pilots on the ground to make the best of a bad job, and that meant walking an extremely fine line between the safety of everybody on board and working beyond the specified operational limits of this otherwise capable Russian machine.

The reduction in range and carrying capacity naturally upset the client who, obviously, was paying a lot of money for every hour we were in the air, so was not happy to have only half of the performance promised.

Then there was the fuel, which added another dimension to the imbroglio. Its provision at all our stopover points became a major problem. We were refuelling from drums trucked to remote villages where we'd arranged for the fuel stops. Often the vehicles loaded with our fuel would leave a distant depot the day before in order to rendezvous with our arrival in good time. If that did not happen, the resultant delays could create huge problems for the election rally. That meant that extra fuel stops soon became something of a logistical nightmare. To their credit, the Tanzanian support crews did their best. Most of the time they were in position as originally planned and there would be no delay to the campaign.

When I arrived at the first fuel stop, the crew was refuelling the helicopter with a hand-driven Macnaught pump. It took quarter of an hour to empty a 200-litre drum of fuel. Worse, to manually fuel the helicopter this way could take two hours of solid elbow grease. I immediately bought the company a petrol-driven pump, which made our lives that much easier. The bean counters who handled the money at Titan were not happy and they said so, but then they were not out there in a remote corner of Africa working the way we were. It was no joke labouring under the hot sun in 35 degree Centigrade temperatures, even if we did have the help of some of the locals.

To reduce the friction caused by some of the empty promises, I had to play the role of the ultimate conjuror and pull numerous rabbits out of the hat. Take-offs, consequently, were mostly rolling to pick up speed and lift. As the surfaces we sped across were usually unprepared for that kind of action, there was much bouncing and jerking around during some take-off runs.

In the end, it was the dust that created the most havoc and some of the implications were severe. For instance, it was not always possible to see the anthills or the potholes along our take-off paths, which was worrying because anthills in Africa are sometimes the size of small cars. Some of the landings were just as hairy, because just about every field in which we touched down became a dust bowl. At times, the murk was so thick, that when I wound up the engines to flight idle in preparation for take-off, I often had to reduce the main rotor revs to ground idle in order to let the dust settle, just to determine that there were no obstacles in our take-off path.

More than once, I had to revert to the 'bouncing-back-into-the-air' technique in order to leave the ground, and co-pilot Janneman learned very quickly to have good faith in me and the helicopter. Some of the passengers who regularly flew with us named the old helicopter *Makirikiri*, which, loosely translated from Swahili, means 'the one who shudders and shakes'.

Dust would also play serious havoc with our systems, making it a constant battle to keep the oil coolers clean. We ended up cleaning them almost every day. Filling the fuel tanks from drums was another hazard, as the fuel was invariably contaminated, either with dust or water. At times we were forced to clean our fuel and engine air filters twice a day to prevent engine failures, something that in the normal servicing schedule is only done every 100 hours of flight time. Add to all those problems the fact that the helicopter was already in a poor serviceable state when we took it over, and we had a real can of worms on our hands.

We rarely stayed at any location for more than a night, which meant that the contract could be fairly demanding on the crews. Once we started to operate in some of the more remote areas, food would become ethnic. We'd actually end up eating what the locals had and that was not always palatable to some of the younger members. At some of the so-called 'guest houses' in which we were billeted, there would be no electricity, no running water, lots of young girls banging on our doors at night and more often than not, our toilets were communal 'long drops' in the back garden.

Clean bedding sometimes became a luxury and I often wondered who had shared my sheets the night before, as the rank stench of filth and sweat from some departed guest fuelled the imagination for as long as it took to fall asleep. However, wherever we went, we were always able to find a cold beer or six after a full-day's flying, and, once we'd consumed a couple of 'sleeping pills', things weren't too bad.

We would often land at, or soon after, last light, and then be airborne very early the next day. There was no provision for any kind of rest or recreation time, as required by standard international aviation regulations. Any talk of allowing the crew to relax a little was met with either a stony silence or a totally uncompromising approach from the campaign organizers. In general, though, the officials appointed to act as our liaison officers were quite amenable and tried their best to make our lives as comfortable as possible.

At the end of the day, we were to discover that Tanzania is an amazing country. It is blessed with an abundance of natural wealth including open plains teeming with wild game and some of the finest game reserves in Africa. Take only one example, the Serengeti game park, an awesome stretch of natural wonderment that goes on for miles and miles. Its rolling, grassy plains are inhabited by herds of hundreds of thousands of wild animals and some of the herds we flew over seemed to stretch from one horizon to the other.

We spent a night at Ngorongoro's famous Wildlife Lodge, in the heart of what had once been a volcano, and it too was an incredible experience. The moon was full, and as I lay in my bed listening to the sounds of Africa—lions roaring, hyenas cackling and an impala buck barking a warning—I was enthralled. Jackals and the chirrups of the cicadas completed what I'd like to term the symphony of the African night. There is no question, Africa does have its remarkable moments.

Back on the election trail, we had more problems as the helicopter steadily lost performance. There was no letting up though, and we carried on working to complete the contract. However, there were moments when I wondered whether we would get the helicopter back to South Africa in one piece. More than once I considered walking away, but each time professional pride got the better of me and I stuck it out. Janneman was also not happy, and I think there were moments when he would rather have been at home than nursing a lame duck across the African veld. We were both aware that our engines were not up to some of the demands made of them.

I am pretty sure that President Kikwete and his staff weren't aware of some of the risks we took. Had they been, alternative arrangements to move him about the country would almost certainly have immediately come into effect.

The risks were real. One time, I was obliged to land in an extremely dusty LZ. During a turn, to position the aircraft into wind in preparation for take-off, I side-swiped a small tree on the edge of the LZ with our tail rotors. It was a catastrophe as, even though there were no injuries or lives lost, it made the helicopter inoperable. That also meant that we were on the ground for a week waiting for a spare set of tail rotor blades.

Apart from the embarrassment, we ended up staying in a very small town in the middle of nowhere with few luxuries to compensate. Of course, there were also recriminations from the owner of the helicopter, which was obviously losing him a lot of money. The fact that we had been on duty from first to last light for the previous couple of days, mostly in tropical conditions did not matter to him. It would not have concerned him that we were taking the old girl down onto dusty football fields with no proper rest facilities, or any decent shade cover or that we hadn't had a decent meal for days. Never mind the bugs, the mosquitoes, the filth and the dust, the owner had lost money and someone had to take the blame.

The highlight of the contract came at the very end, when we were invited by President Kikwete to a private dinner with his wife at the State House in Dar es Salaam. We were given the opportunity to relax and talk freely and it was one of the highlights of my career. I had discovered very early on that the President of Tanzania is a remarkable man.

CHAPTER TWENTY-TWO

NEALL ELLIS FLIES RUSSIAN HELICOPTERS IN AFGHANISTAN

The war in Afghanistan is unlike any other fought by the West in the past century and a half. It is a clash of cultures and ideologies that almost defies description. As one journalist who had been there recently stated, there are parts of the country still furiously galloping into the 14th century!

A youthful Winston Churchill once commented that Afghanistan was a land that almost invited conflict. However, once embroiled, he warned, it was a devilish task to disengage—a statement that is as pertinent today, in the second decade of the New Millennium, as it was when he made it.

Neall has been handling support missions in Afghanistan in Russian-built helicopters for the last few years. He is based at Kabul International Airport on the outskirts of the Afghan capital and at one stage there were more than 50 expatriate pilots flying for his employers in Afghanistan. He says that working in this troubled and hopelessly fragmented land has been different from anything else he has experienced. While he admits that it has not all been 'uphill', there have been moments when he would rather have been working elsewhere.

Ellis takes up the story:

Getting to Afghanistan the first time, in August 2009, was a memorable experience. While still in South Africa, I had been contracted to fly a Russian support helicopter, the Titan Mi-8 MTV, for an American-based company. We would be operating out of Kabul International Airport and tasked to fly missions in support of a government agency, USAID.

The Russians specially developed their Mi-8 MTV helicopters, fitted with TB3-117 VM engines, for operations in Afghanistan. Arguably, it is still the best helicopter in the world for its weight/ class for operations at altitude, often in unusually rugged conditions. Indeed, no Western helicopter in the same weight category can perform as well. With the Mi-8 MTV we could uplift 22 personnel plus crew.

Our helicopter had originally been loaded at Cape Town into an Ilyushin-76 aircraft for transport to Kabul. Prior to that, we'd looked at several other options, including actually flying the helicopter from South Africa to Afghanistan via Pakistan, a journey that would have taken ten days if there were no hold-ups. The decision was finally made to take her in by air, with a team of technicians in place by the time the helicopter arrived at Kabul. They would assemble it in time for my arrival. Therefore, my first view of the country, as the sun lifted above the horizon, was in a Pamir Airbus-320 from an altitude of 30,000ft.

On route to Kabul there were many aircraft passing below us, and the terrain was almost brutally mountainous. My initial impressions were that the terrain below looked dry and inhospitable and that there was no way that I would have liked to end up on the ground in those 'hills' and have to walk back to safety. Apart from the rivers in the foothills and snow in winter, there was very little water once you left the lowlands. Should an aircrew be unexpectedly brought down, either by enemy action or mechanical failure, escape and evasion from the enemy would be a serious matter. Finding water in the mountains, in the summer especially, would be hugely problematical.

Our final approach into Kabul was uneventful. From the air, the city presented a picture like nothing I had ever seen before, the proverbial dust bowl that stretched all the way to the horizon. As we descended, it seemed that that city was surrounded by a grim cauldron of grime. Visibility deteriorated the lower we descended and just about everything reflected an unending monochrome of dusty brown. I got the impression that there were very few trees and certainly no great green grass expanses such as can be found in other parts of the country. In fact, there was very little cultivation within sight of the city.

It was no different once we stepped off the aircraft. Even though it was still early morning, the dry heat all but sucked the air out of my lungs. I was immediately reminded of time spent in Iraq, where I had experienced the same sensation on leaving air-conditioned buildings and going outside.

Kabul Airport, lying at an altitude of 8,000ft is an international airport surrounded by dry, dust-swept mountains that reach up to altitudes of about 14,000ft above sea level. The international airport caters for both civilian and military aircraft of all makes, nationalities and types with different ramps for each arm. Those who observe goings-on at Kabul Airport for the first time will never have seen so many helicopters operating out of one hub at the same time. Most are civilian Mi-8s and all work for a vast range of support groups.

Once on the ground at Kabul, I was met by our local facilitator and, after money changed hands, we headed out to my new home at the compound at Qalah Fatullah. After settling into rudimentary, but clean and comfortable, accommodation I had a few moments to contemplate the next two months in the 'Stan'—two months was my basic period of contract. Crew rotations in Afghanistan can vary from 12 weeks in-country and a month out, to six weeks in-country and six out.

Pay scales for aircraft commanders range from US$300 per day for non-U.S. contract pilots up to $1,000 a day for those flying for the U.S. contracted companies. Co-pilots on multi-crewed helicopters earn anything between $300 and $500 a day, while flight engineers can sometimes demand $500. Russian crews tend to be

Four, sometimes five months of the year, the higher regions of Afghanistan are covered by snow and ice. While the images are graphic and often quite beautiful, conditions are tough for the air crews. *Photo: Neall Ellis*

paid less than their Western counterparts, in part because there is a surfeit of them looking for this kind of work.

Recently, I was talking to a Ukrainian pilot who had flown Mi-8 and Kamov-32 helicopters for Kabul Air, which enjoys a contract with Supreme, an American firm. Its role was to re-supply American and USAID Provincial Reconstruction Team (PRT) bases in the interior with water and food.

Kabul Air's pilots were being paid a basic $8,000 a month which was based on 70 hours flying time. If pilots exceeded 70 hours flying time, they got an extra hourly rate of $100. That meant that to earn additional cash, the aviators were likely to exceed 200 hours a month airtime.

It was illegal as, according to Afghanistan's civil aviation laws, the most a pilot is legally allowed to fly is between 100 and 120 hours a month. Consequently, there was a good deal of subterfuge going on, with many of the helicopters not even having legal documents. Also, their servicing was minimal, which meant more risk. The fact is that pilots as well as companies can lose their Air Operators Licences if they exceed established limits and since the people flying these helicopters get very little time off, one observer described conditions as tantamount to forced labour.

One company operational in Afghanistan has a preference for veteran Russian pilots who flew during the Soviet invasion. If they do not have the requisite civilian licence, it pays them $3,000 a month simply to 'fill the seat'. Moreover, not many people are even

aware that their licences are simply being rolled off from a computer in the company offices in Kabul, which underscores the
reality that there is actually very little control over some of the
Russian companies working in Central Asia, in part because American contractors are not familiar with the Russian system. Also,
these aviators are hungry and they come cheap.

There are a number of civilian operators on flying contracts
in Afghanistan. There is Presidential, a subsidiary of Zee (ex-
Blackwater) flying Puma S330s, the Department of State (DOS)
Air Wing which uses Huey 2 helicopters, Evergreen with their
S-61s and Puma helicopters and Molsom, a subsidiary of CHC,
flying Bell 212s.

We often worked with the DOS Air Wing as their Huey-2
helicopters would escort our helicopters while we transported important dignitaries into the interior. These ageing battle-craft were
customarily armed with 7.62mm machine guns, although some
were fitted with M134 six-barrelled Gatlings. These remarkable
automatic weapons are not only capable of laying down a tremen-
dous amount of firepower, but their gunners are among the most
professional in the business and, as I was to discover, a pretty good
bunch to mix with. All were former military, which means that
the majority perfectly understand the demands of Afghanistan's
formidable environment.

The DOS Air Wing falls under The U.S. State Department's
Bureau of International Narcotics and Law Enforcement, which
is basically Dyncorp, an American security company. In addition,
Dyncorp flew the same helicopters as we did, the Mi-8 MTV,
as part of a huge, ongoing and absolutely futile drug eradication
programme.

Various Eastern Bloc countries also have contributions to
make, with companies such as Panj, Burundaiavia and others,
again equipped with Mi-8s. Some local companies such as Kam
Air and Kabul Air lease Mi-8s on contract, where they are used on
such missions as supplying Supreme, a logistics company that ships
out food supplies to various military bases. There is also Vertical

Aviation, a South American Colombian company on contract to the U.S. Army Corps of Engineers and Abu Dhabi Aviation which was leasing two Bell 412 helicopters to USAID while I was there at the end of 2009.

Top of the pile in a shadowy mode is an extremely secretive unit that we know only as Pegasus. More paramilitary than civilian, they operated a number of Mi-171 and Mi-172 helicopters, which are a more advanced version of the Mi-8 MTV, and flew mostly night operations. Information sources suggested that Pegasus was tasked to support some of the 'Super Spy' units operating in remote areas along the ragged frontier with Pakistan and, who knows, perhaps beyond that as well.

Apart from the Russian crews, most of the helicopter pilots flying in Afghanistan are ex-military. In fact, some of the companies such as the DOS Air Wing stipulate that military training with an NVG qualification is essential.

It is difficult to estimate how many helicopters are operating in Afghanistan. If all military units are taken into account—and you add in civilian-registered planes—the numbers must easily be in excess of 500 airframes. This raises another issue: the monumental task of just keeping all these machines operational.

The logistics to provide fuel and ammunition requirements to the many and varied operators are formidable, especially since almost all supplies are brought into the country by road. Some civilian helicopters fly up to 90 hours per month, and once you do your sums, it becomes clear that getting enough fuel into the country to supply these thirsty machines must be a nightmare, particularly since many of the fuel tankers come from Pakistan and convoys are routinely attacked and often destroyed en route by Taliban factions, not only within Afghanistan's borders, but in Pakistan as well. The majority of these tankers are privately owned, and the owners clearly suffer significant losses as guerrillas like to target every resupply route within reach.

The day after my arrival merged into a haze of briefings, signing Red Tag notices, NOTAMs and other Special Operations Procedures related to flying operations in Afghanistan. These were

followed by briefings on the use of the various tracking devices
that we take with us in the aircraft. We were given standard clothing to wear for flying: khaki trousers and Task Force khaki shirts.
Because the operation was very low key in terms of military support, we did not even wear flying overalls.

Notably, we were issued with ballistic jackets, the idea being
to wear them while flying. I prefer not to use them, in part because
of a fellow pilot from the Rhodesian War who was forced down
by ground fire and who died because he was wearing one. He
wasn't killed by enemy fire, but by the ballistic jacket, which shattered his throat when his torso was thrown forward on impact. In
fact, throughout my operational flying, I have never donned a ballistic jacket and my reasoning is basic. Over many years of piloting
helicopters in combat, my machines have taken numerous hits.
Usually they would strike the helicopter from the sides or from
below and there is no protection on either side of a ballistic jacket.

It was also not lost on me that the helicopter we used in
Afghanistan did not have the protection of any ballistic panels.
Consequently, had we taken a hit, there would not have been
much that we could have done about it.

My personal philosophy about combat flying in choppers is
simple: the pilot should fly profiles that do not put him in danger.
Firstly, he needs to keep his speed high for as long as possible. If
he is shot at, he should avoid evasive manoeuvres. Such flying
tends to rapidly bleed off speed and it is unquestionable that a
slow-moving machine presents the enemy with an easier target
than a relatively fast one.

Also, while I don't wear a ballistic jacket, my survival vest is
an altogether different matter. As far as I am concerned, the vest
is one of the most important pieces of equipment any pilot working in a threat environment should wear. The reason is simple—
if the helicopter is forced down, either because of engine failure or
ground fire, the only equipment a pilot might be left with to aid
his survival is what he has on his body.

It is pointless to keep survival equipment stowed in the back
of the aircraft. Once the aircraft has hit the ground and started to

burn, or if you go down as a consequence of enemy ground fire, it may be impossible to try to recover anything from the back of the aircraft, especially when there are bullets flying. There have been many cases of downed aviators ending up on the ground in unwanted circumstances, with only the contents of their pockets to aid them.

I carry standard stuff such as a hand-held GPS and a VHF air-band radio, a signalling mirror, a whistle, a 'day-glo' panel or two, a torch, knives, a fold-up water bottle and a small medical pack. To me, an essential item in this kit is a supply of anti-inflammatory painkillers. Should I have to start running in the hills on an escape and evasion venture, pain killers would allow me to carry on well beyond my accepted physical limits.

It is common knowledge that the approach to landing and the brief period that follows lift-off are the two most dangerous phases of flight in Afghanistan. The Taliban often take up positions close to some of the military bases to shoot at helicopters as they come in to land. Their most favoured weapon for this purpose is still the tried and trusted RPG-7. With a range of 900 metres before self-destructing, it can do a lot of damage to a machine if it strikes in the right place. Small arms weapons such as the AK-47 and the PKM machine gun are also extensively used by the guerrillas.

I am a fierce critic of Russian flying techniques when it comes to take-off and landing in remote areas, of which there are a lot in Afghanistan. The most widely used Russian technique after take-off from an LZ is to select a relatively steep climbing angle at the best rate of climb of something like 120kph. Granted, the climb-rate is relatively high, but these pilots refuse to accept that in choosing this option, they become a slow-moving target for somebody with automatic weapons.

Similarly, their technique for landing is to approach an LZ with a steep descending angle at a low speed, barely a fraction above transition. The few times I have flown with the Russian crews, either as a co-pilot or as a passenger, I have become acutely aware that we made ourselves into an excellent target for anyone with an RPG, or even an assault rifle. There have been numerous civilian Russian helicopters shot down in Afghanistan, and most of them were downed either in the final stages of the approach to landing or, on a few occasions, just after take-off.

In SAAF operational flying training courses, we learned that speed was always the best way to counter incoming fire. The technique was to fly as low as possible after take-off in order to allow the speed to build up before initiating a climb if required. On any landing approach in a hostile area, it is essential to come in as fast as is safely possible before touchdown. The idea is to present a difficult flight path to anybody on the ground intent on causing damage: you need to prevent him from determining a tracking solution that will allow his rounds to enter the airspace at the same time as you do. This is not an easy option for the attacker if the helicopter is moving swiftly. However, if the speed of the aircraft is limited, or almost in the hover, the tracking solution becomes a simple matter and the machine will take a hit.

Our first flights after deployment in Afghanistan were carried out always with one of the experienced helicopter co-pilots accompanying us in the cockpit. These people are familiar with the area as well as the procedures for approaching and landing at the various USAID PRTs scattered around the country. Some of the PRTs are co-located with NATO Forward Operating Bases (FOBs) and because of heavy artillery in some of the locations, we needed to know the correct frequencies as well as approach paths so as not to enter one of the firing lanes while approaching an LZ. Several times we got frantic radio calls from operational personnel warning us off from our approach. When this happened we would orbit in a safe position away from the base until the artillery had completed their fire plan.

This was not an ideal situation: orbiting for any length of time in some of Afghanistan's hot spots often results in the Taliban firing on slow moving aircraft. Also, flying in circles over an area gives those hostile elements on the ground plenty of practice. You might miss an orbiting helicopter ten times in a row but, if it hangs around long enough, eventually you are going to score a hit.

In certain operational areas, there was sometimes the additional problem of badly coordinated, and often completely uncoordinated, communications between ground forces and aircraft. We'd come into a base and on short finals there would be a huge explosion from an adjacent artillery position as a round or two was fired.

Most of the areas where we land have cement landing pads, with large stones scattered around the LZ. The idea is to prevent dust from being scattered while the helicopter is operational, either coming in or going out, as the pilot losing visual contact with the ground is a hazard in itself.

Very few Afghan bases have runways along which wheeled helicopters might be able to make a rolling start to get airborne. This technique makes for the use of less power as we go through transition to get off the ground. Once through that initial transition, we are able to get airborne with larger or heavier loads and the helicopter can accelerate safely to cruise at speed.

We customarily had four armed 'shooters' on board our USAID-contracted Mi-8 helicopters. The job of these professionals was to provide protection should we end up on the ground as a result of a precautionary or forced landing. As pilots for an American government agency, we were not allowed to carry weapons. However, with those armed 'passengers' in the back, we were confident that we had adequate protection.

Our 'shooters' were mostly expatriate military-trained personnel and most had some form of Special Forces background. Generally, they were an efficient and capable bunch, just the type to have around if a serious situation arose, not only on the ground but also in the various bars scattered around Kabul that we liked to visit.

As part of a programme of Team Continuation Training, we regularly conducted the kind of drills we would have followed should we have had to make an emergency landing. The 'shooters' also arranged firearms training for the air crews at some of the bases we flew to and gave lectures on the various types of weapons that we might have encountered so that we could keep our weapons-handling abilities current. Throughout, they stressed that we should know exactly what to do in an emergency situation and what was expected of us. As one of them succinctly put it, 'when the shit starts to fly, that's not the time to learn a new bunch of drills'.

With Afghanistan in an escalating state of war, the Taliban will do what it can to bring down a helicopter, or even a fixed-wing plane. Despite this, more often than not, our Mi-8s tend to live up to the demands expected of them. However, as happens so often in wartime, one tactic is superseded by another. The rebels have recently started taking up positions in the foothills to the east of Kabul, where they just wait for the opportunity to shoot down an aircraft. As they like to say, we might have all the aircraft, but they have the time—lots of it.

In July 2010, several fusillades of RPGs, as well as small arms fire, were directed at a civilian aircraft heading for the runway. Fortunately, the shooting was poor and they missed, but the pilot admitted that he was lucky. Then, also in July 2010, a C-130 on final approach was hit by shrapnel from a self-detonating RPG-7. The plane was able to land safely and nobody on board was injured, but as somebody commented afterwards, it might have been a very different kind of ending. What has become apparent is that the Taliban is now much more focused on shooting down aircraft, especially in the vicinity of Kabul Airport.

As these rebels increase their strength—and there is no shortage of either new recruits or adequate war materiéls to stoke the ongoing conflict—they have become more daring. It has become more and more likely that an aircraft will be brought down. This immediately raises the spectre of what will happen once the rebels obtain MANPADS or SAMs. Should that occur, the game will drastically change and everyone will have to adapt their flying techniques to counter this radical development.

It is worth mentioning that news reports emanating from Central Asia during 2010 and 2011 suggested not only that the rebels had ground-to-air missiles, but that they have already been deployed against Coalition

Force aircraft. One report mentioned a heat-seeking missile that brought down a NATO transport helicopter in 2007 killing five American troops as well as a Briton and a Canadian.[1] The US-built Chinook was struck in its left engine shortly after taking off near the Helmand River. The report stated that the impact 'projected the aft-end of the helicopter upwards as it burst into flame, followed immediately by a nose dive into the ground that left no survivors'.

There has been little follow-up on that development and Nellis has his doubts that it was a MANPAD. Instead, he puts the loss down to a strike from a well-placed RPG-7. Still, he and his colleagues are concerned because the civilian version of Mi-8 is not equipped with exhaust suppressors or flare dispensing systems to counter missile lock-on. Once the SAMs do arrive, he reckons, pilots will have to revert to flying fast and low, which would then take them into the threat zone of small arms fire.

As he comments, the helicopter's exhaust is substantial and would obviously attract any infrared (IR) seeking missile, which makes it particularly vulnerable to ground-to-air missiles. Additionally, some of the new generation SAMs are contrast trackers, so even IR suppression equipment, such as exhaust protection or low infrared reflective paint, would not be all that helpful.

At the same time, this is not something new. It is on record that the Americans gave the mujahideen rebels their first hand-held Stinger missiles. They also taught the rebels how to use them, which they eventually did with aplomb, bringing down hundreds of helicopters and jets during the course of a war that ultimately contributed to the collapse of the Soviet Union.

During the Soviet invasion, the rebels employed every opportunity to fire at aircraft—both fixed-wing and helicopters—and almost always from well-located strategic positions on hills and mountaintops. These attacks are customarily referred to as 'Nomadic Ambushes'.[2]

What quickly becomes clear to those who are aware of Afghanistan's recent history and who visit the country regularly, is that many of the tactics originally employed by the mujahideen against Soviet forces in the 1980s have been adapted by today's Taliban guerrillas. There are numerous instances of rebels targeting civilian aircraft in remote areas. Recently, a helicopter belonging to one of the private security groups took a lot of fire while flying down a valley in the Khost area, a strongly contested region adjacent to Pakistan's northern frontier districts.

Because of the mountains, the pilot was not able to take a direct route to his destination. Ideally, he should have crossed a series of ridges, but as he admitted afterwards, these were too high for his machine. Consequently, he had to follow a circuitous route below the peaks—a flight path that took him through several valleys that had seen recent action.

One of the areas he traversed was just below a mountaintop peak, where he had to fly barely 300ft from the granite cliff face in order to break through into the valley below. Clearly, the Taliban had seen this happen before and they were waiting. The helicopter was not only holed several times by heavy machine gun fire, but one of its passengers was wounded.

The consensus among a number of pilots operating in Afghanistan today is that, given the opportunity, the Taliban has the ability to muster its forces in a short space of time, especially when aircraft are involved. As Nellis comments, that is exactly why he insists on flying the more direct routes over the hills but, obviously, he varies his track by a couple of miles whenever he uses the route. Most of the other pilots, the military included, he says, tend to use the same flight paths when they enter the region and it is to be expected that some of them end up being blasted. He recalls:

> So it wasn't all that surprising that shortly after first arriving in Central Asia, one of the pilots accused me of being reckless for avoiding established routes. A couple of days later he came back after a flight and said he had been shot at while following a route through the mountains that I'd always made a serious effort to avoid. What every pilot knows, or should be aware of, is that if a helicopter flies low over an area where there is an insurgent presence, the Taliban will attempt to destroy it.
>
> Just after I started flying in Afghanistan, while returning to Kabul from Sharana, we were flying about 1,000ft above the ground over a village when I heard the distinctive sounds of rounds passing pretty damn close—it was that same old 'rat-tat-tat typewriter noise' of old. The firing lasted only for a few seconds, but it certainly got the adrenalin pumping and was quite an experience after all these years. The shots missed and we suffered no damage,

but then it is not easy to hit a moving target, especially at any kind of altitude.

These experiences are among a slew of problems that our crowd recently experienced in Afghanistan and part of the problem is that there is precious little sharing of essential operational information within the aviation fraternity working there. The truth is that the military gives away absolutely nothing. If one of the civilian helicopters encounters a problem, there is no central organization that effectively disseminates details of the dangers that might be involved, even when they are of critical significance.

It is of little concern to those higher up that by withholding such intelligence, lives might be lost. It will obviously filter down eventually, but there is no hurry. For example, if a helicopter is shot at from a specific location, the other operators often hear nothing about the incident for a while. More often than not a helicopter from another company will fly to the same location, and because the pilot has had no prior warning of what he may encounter along the way, he is also targeted.

Another major problem in Afghanistan is the lack of communication between some foreign pilots and air traffic control. The truth is that some Eastern European pilots not only speak bad English, they barely understand the language. Most are either Russian or Ukrainian and the majority are coached to handle basic air traffic control language and not much else. In fact, there is nothing about Afghanistan—either in military or civilian contexts—that is 'average'. Pilots are often instructed to change course or hold over some area because of rebel activity or because the local circuit is busy, which they often are. Consequently, there can be confusion between foreign pilots and air traffic controllers. Total chaos has almost reigned on numerous occasions, with more near misses involving helicopter traffic than anybody is prepared to acknowledge. However, choppers are not high speed, so the pilots involved usually have ample warning and are able to break away from harm's way.

As Nellis admits, there can also be a problem, when operating in the vicinity of built-up areas such as Kabul, of heavy frequency jamming initiated by NATO Forces to prevent Improvised Explosive Devices (IEDs) being detonated by mobile phones or radio signals. As he explains:

> The result is a harsh, high-pitched, ear-shattering ruckus, something akin to the din from the microphone feedback of a heavy metal rock band. Sometimes, the jamming gets so intense that we are unable to hear instructions from the tower, which could develop into a serious flying hazard. It is particularly bad around the airport and adjacent diplomatic areas.
>
> There have been times when we've been unable to follow tower instructions . . . even worse, we couldn't visually acquire the tower. Had we been on a collision course in poor visibility, we probably wouldn't have been able to take evasive action in time.
>
> I remember returning from Bagram Air Base after a sortie in weather that can best be described as marginal. We'd been enveloped in rain and slight mist: something like 200ft AGL and had very poor forward visibility. Vectored to the approach for the runway by the tower—who was also keeping separation from other helicopters arriving at the airport more or less at the same time, there were some tense moments because we were aware that there was a formation of two other helicopters positioning the same approach. As it happened, we all landed safely. However, the most stressful moments I experienced flying over Afghanistan always occurred when I was returning to Kabul in conditions of that same poor visibility.
>
> Also, the weather in Afghanistan can be extremely demanding and often changes very rapidly and without warning, especially during winter. Every year aircraft are lost in bad weather, with many of them crashing into the mountains. One technique one pilot soon assimilated when flying in potentially bad weather was to continually visually check the route behind us and for good reason. Weather fronts often close in very quickly, cutting off what is occasionally the only route back to safety. Airframe icing is also a constant problem during the cold months. We would make a point of avoiding snow and rainstorms or any evident precipitation, particularly if the temperature fell below 5 degrees centigrade.
>
> Bad weather pilot stories in Afghanistan are legion. A couple

of years ago, one of the more experienced Bell-412 pilots was head-ing back to Kabul in relatively marginal weather conditions, when he observed a snowstorm ahead, which within minutes had completely enveloped his aircraft. He had to make an immediate precautionary landing as he was in total instrument meteorological conditions (IMC) and was on the verge of losing visual contact with the ground. Left with no other option, he was forced to land in a walled compound belonging to one of the local farmers who, fortunately for the crew, was not a Taliban sympathizer. The local family took the crew into their house and looked after them until a security force was able to reach their position, secure the heli-copter and take them back to Kabul. The helicopter was recovered untouched a couple of days later after the bad weather had suffi-ciently cleared. Apart from the poor visibility, we also avoid flying in IMC conditions because we are not issued with oxygen breath-ing equipment.

To be able to safely fly in cloud or in poor weather and to carry out effective instrument let-downs at Kabul, we need to get to at least 18,000ft to avoid the mountains that surround the airport, which is Afghanistan's main airfield. According to Civil Air Regu-lations, we are not allowed to fly higher than 12,000ft without oxygen, so our operations are strictly day VFR flying. Helicopters are allowed to fly at night in Afghanistan only if they are equipped with night vision goggles (NVGs) and the pilots are trained to use them.

Then comes summer, when temperatures can rise to more than 40 degrees Centigrade. These conditions require a totally new set of parameters and pilots have to be careful how they load and fly their aircraft. High temperatures make the air less dense at higher altitudes. This means that careful planning has to be carried out before each flight, as well as for take-off out of some of the confined LZs in which we are required to land. Some helicopters have crashed after take-off because there was not sufficient power available in hot and high conditions.

The same situation holds for Kabul, which is also hot and high in the summer months and where, at the best of times, visibility is

barely acceptable. The haze that results from dust combining with
the smoke from tens of thousands of wood fires, lit by local inhabitants to cook their food, is sometimes so bad in the mornings
that the airfield is declared IMC. Moreover, navigating your way
out of there to reporting points can be a nightmare experience as
not only is the visibility bad, but the air lanes are overcrowded.
Returning to Kabul can be even worse than leaving, as Russian pilots can seldom be found over the point where they have reported
themselves to be, which is a serious hazard facing all aviators
operating in the region.

Dust storms in the drier season are intermittent and often
appear without warning. On numerous occasions we would return
to Kabul to find the airport and the town completely obscured.
As a result, we would be forced to fly the approach paths from the
compulsory reporting area that surrounds the airfield at 100ft AGL
with forward visibility of less than 200 metres. When the numerous radio and telephone masts and towers in and around Kabul
are added into the equation, it means that bringing an aircraft in
to land needs a constant awareness of the pilot's position over the
ground in order to avoid flying into one of these obstacles.

Then follows the ultimate delight: the occasional Afghan

The world's
largest
transport
jet—this
one built
by the
Russians—
regularly
landed at
Kabul
Airport,
usually on
charter to
Coalition
Forces.
Photo:
Neall Ellis

citizen who simply has to test his AK-47 the moment a helicopter flies over his mud dwelling. Fortunately, the visibility is so bad under these conditions that the shooter usually has no time to take aim. The only thing that can be done is to keep the speed of the aircraft as high as possible and disappear into the gloom.

The reality is that the insurgents are extremely trigger-happy. They will use every opportunity to shoot down overflying helicopters. It doesn't help that many of the USAID military bases are situated in some of the most inaccessible parts of not only Afghanistan, but of the whole of Central Asia. Although there are roads linking these outlying bases to main roads, they are normally unsurfaced and most have been primed by the Taliban with IEDs. That makes road travel dangerous and the personnel based in these camps obviously prefer to travel by air because of the threat of ambush on the ground. Where there is no suitable runway for a fixed-wing craft to land, helicopters are extensively used.

When we were tasked to fly to Qalat in the Zabol Province south of Kabul, on one of our routine supply runs, we would off-load our passengers at the PRT base and then fly to Lagman FOB to refuel, which is a journey of perhaps two or three kilometres by road. The reasoning given by both military and civilian personnel at the two bases was that it was too dangerous for the passengers to have to travel by road from Lagman to the PRT, even though the two were less than a rifle shot from each other.

I argued often enough while in the country, that if NATO forces were actually serious about dominating the areas around their bases, pro-government personnel and troops should be able to walk the short distance without too much fear of attack or kidnapping.

However, as a South African with considerable experience in our bush wars in Angola, South-West Africa and Zambia during the 1970s and 1980s, I know that it was often not easy to comprehend the background to the politics behind some of the decision-making that takes place, usually behind closed doors. Even so, the question needs to be asked: why has the situation been allowed to deteriorate to this parlous state? Like the Soviets before them, the Coalition are fighting a counter-insurgency campaign that has escalated steadily in the past few years, yet, Coalition Forces on the ground in Afghanistan remain isolated behind their fortifications for the duration, instead of venturing out in a bid to dominate the countryside. Effectively, the powers that be have allowed the Taliban to take control. More to the point, the average Afghan knows it.

It is no longer a secret that the Taliban are in the process of not only dominating, but also consolidating their hold over, just about the whole of the country, particularly the rural areas. In some areas the Taliban command structure even dictates to NATO forces and government officials exactly when the local commercial mobile telephone transmission towers can be switched on or off. I am not the only outsider who finds it amazing that the guerrillas are in a position to dictate what happens in an area which was pretty well populated by NATO troops. Then again, some of the more obscure European partners in NATO forces deployed in Afghanistan are notoriously loathe to committing themselves to any kind of offensive action, never mind fight a war.

During the normal course of operations in Afghanistan, we flew with three separate GPS tracking devices fitted to our helicopter. All were for emergency purposes. The first was a Blue Force Tracker that was issued by the U.S. State Department. When its emergency buttons are activated, it is supposed to offer some kind of result within 15 minutes and this can be anything from a close air support, fixed-wing, strike aircraft or a heliborne ground support group.

Then comes the Fast Wave Tracker, which is monitored by our company operations room in Afghanistan and a third alarm system known as the SpiderTrack System, which is monitored by company operations personnel in South Africa. Essentially, the idea was that should we be fired upon during flight, obliged to make a forced landing in hostile terrain due to enemy ground fire, or even have an in-flight emergency such as an engine failure, we would activate our distress signal and, in theory, assistance should be forthcoming almost immediately.

However, there was never a guarantee that the cavalry would respond. We were operating civilian aircraft, which were regarded by some of the military as distinctly low priority, even if we were responsible for supplying outlying bases with most of their essential needs.

On one flight from FOB Kalagush in the Nuristan Province to Asadabad to the East, I had my one and only in-flight engine failure while flying in Southern Afghanistan. We had our first warning of impending problems just as we crossed a ridge at an altitude of about 10,000ft. As expected, the mountain sides were almost sheer and, from a quick look at the options, I realised that there was nothing that even vaguely resembled a suitable landing place as there were valleys and gorges just about everywhere with very little flat country in-between where we might have been able to put down in an emergency.

After the faulty engine had been shut down, we initiated our Blue Force Tracker system and broadcasted a series of Maydays. This was essential since we were flying over territory that was acknowledged as hostile. Obviously, had the remaining engine also given up the ghost, we would have preferred to have an armed escort to provide us with adequate top cover as we were unsure of the situation on the ground. This insecurity was most probably due to the fact that two days earlier we had witnessed a very substantial military operation against insurgent positions in the same valley as the one along which we were flying.

There was no immediate reaction to our Mayday calls. Instead of an escort arriving, we received a telephone call over the mobile network asking if we were okay. The operator queried whether we had perhaps pushed the wrong buttons by mistake! In the end, everything turned out well and we were able to reach Asadabad where a successful single engine approach was made and the helicopter landed without any damage.

Luckily for us, the Mi-8 MTV is a very powerful helicopter, and its single-engine performance proved phenomenal. Thus, even with all the weight on board, we were able to stabilize single-engine level flight at 8,000ft, all the while maintaining a healthy clearance between us and the mountains all around.

We established afterwards that the cause of our engine mal-
function was the failure of certain moving parts in the fuel control
unit (FCU). With time, these parts had disintegrated into small
particles, which basically became iron filings. These, in turn, ended
up blocking the helicopter's fuel filters and caused fuel starvation.
Had it affected both engines at the same time, we'd have gone
down.

By the time we realised what was going on, we'd lost power to
the point where the malfunctioning engine suddenly became
totally useless. As we were unsure of the cause, we decided to shut
it down and use only the remaining good engine. That way we
prevented further damage to the faulty one.

Once we touched down at Asadabad, we requested a new FCU
by radio. When the replacement had arrived and been installed by
our flight engineer, we were able to fly back to Kabul.

In moving about vast swathes of Afghanistan we must have visited
scores of different bases over time and generally got a very good
reception from the military personnel there. Lower ranking military personnel were always helpful and often went out of their way
to assist with minor problems, or with refuelling.

In contrast, some the officers we encountered in our daily me-
anderings among the mountains were nothing short of arrogant.
Many seemed to believe that because we were not military we
could be treated with disdain. There were those who even resented
our presence on their little stretch of turf, even though they
couldn't have managed without the cargo we unloaded from our
Mi-8s and our role in Afghanistan was to assist them in their war
effort.

Towards the end of 2009, a particularly strong weather front
moved over the country and flying conditions suddenly became
hazardous. A Russian-crewed helicopter landed at an American
base late one afternoon, and the Russian flight captain made it
clear to the base commander that not only was he not happy about
flying any further that day, but that it would be precarious to take

off again so close to nightfall. He'd already been warned by radio that the weather between the base and his final destination, Kabul, was worsening.

The base commander, a colonel, was quite blunt about refusing the Russian's request to stay overnight at his base. In fact, he instructed the helicopter crew to depart as soon as they had offloaded their cargo. Although the pilot explained that flying would be dangerous, he was told in no uncertain terms to get himself and his chopper out of there. Obviously intimidated, the pilot and his crew lifted off for Kabul and flew straight into a snowstorm. They were all killed when their 'blinded' helicopter crashed into a mountain.

Because the weather stayed bad for several days, the missing helicopter with its distinctive white livery was only discovered in the snow after a search and rescue effort that lasted almost a week. One can only speculate whether the colonel who was directly responsible for those deaths was ever brought to book because he refused to let a helicopter crew sleep over.

There is another problem that appears to be unique to Afghanistan. The kite flying season in Afghanistan—it is a national sport—presents aviators, especially the uninitiated, with potential dangers. Pilots operating around some of the larger towns continually have to take evasive action to avoid kites because the cords used can easily get tangled in the controls. Often, while carrying out our usual after-flight inspections, we'd discover what is best described as 'birds' nests' from kites tangled in our rotor controls. Fortunately, the Mi-8 is a powerful helicopter and this twine does not seem to affect the moving controls.

We're uncertain about whether the kite-flying is a deliberate ploy by the Taliban to push these obstacles into our flight paths in the hope of doing damage. However, what does quickly become apparent is that there are usually many more kites in the air on the approach and take-off routes in and out of Kabul Airport than anywhere else in the country.

During one flight into the Kandahar PRT, some locals

launched kites directly into our flight path during our final approach, which caused us to take hasty evasive action. It happened all the time and it has become clear, with time, that it was intentional. Obviously, we couldn't help thinking that there was something devious going on and that it could eventually become a serious problem. We have complained about it and we are all aware that it would be a simple matter to ban kite flying anywhere within a mile or so of all airports in the country. However, this not likely to happen anytime soon.

Arguably, the most disturbing development for companies running supply missions into the Afghan interior—including some bitterly contested areas—is that in late 2011 some of their helicopters were suddenly targeted by the Taliban. Formerly, the enemy seemed to regard these 'freighters' (together with their requisite complements of 'shooters') as of secondary importance to the war effort; military targets were always given preference in any attacks carried out by the mujahideen.

However, in September 2011, two civilian-operated helicopters came under RPG fire. American pilot Terry Shay explained afterwards that in the second attack he had been on finals to land at the helicopter LZ at the military base at Baraki Barak, a few hundred kilometres south of Kabul, when he noticed that the children playing football on the football field next to the base were acting strangely. 'They moved to one side of the field and didn't throw stones or show abusive signals at landing helicopters as they usually do', he wrote in his report.

Thinking this behaviour was rather strange, he changed his landing profile and while preparing to hover for landing, he heard a loud explosion to the rear of his helicopter and initiated a go-around. The 'shooter' in the back of the helicopter looked back and saw a plume of dust next to a house outside the military perimeter, about 150 metres away. Presuming that they were being attacked, Shay continued his flight without attempting to land. Military personnel at the base later confirmed that an RPG had been fired at the helicopter, but missed.

At a meeting at Kabul afterwards—chaired by Neall Ellis and attended by charter company representatives and air crews—a number of suggestions were made about tactics to counter the threat. These included the proposal that when approaching any LZ in the interior, pilots should carefully observe the behaviour of the locals in the area. If any suspicious behaviour was noted, the base operations centre was to be contacted and the helicopter was not to land until cleared to do so by the officer on duty. In other words, added Nellis, 'when in doubt, do not land'.

The dangers of flying in Afghanistan are legion. However, nothing brings the reality home more than the facts. A significant number of aircraft have gone down since the start of the Afghan war in October 2001. Rotary wing losses—both military and civilian—at the time of going to press in the summer of 2011 were approaching the 100-mark. These include an astonishing 25 Chinook CH-46s (eight to enemy fire) and 15 UH-60 Black Hawks (three to enemy fire) and a dozen AH-64 Apaches.

The most recent Chinook crash on 6 August 2011, happened in the Tangi Joy Zarin area of Wardak province, about 100km south-west of Kabul. The helicopter with 30 American troops—many of them from SEAL Team 6—and eight Afghan soldiers on board was shot down by Taliban ground fire. There were no survivors, making it the biggest single aircraft disaster of the war.

On the civilian side, losses have not been as significant. However, there have been some helicopters lost, a few belonging to the same company for which Nellis worked. These include two Mi-8 helicopters operating under contract for NATO forces in Afghanistan One crashed during an emergency landing at FOB Kalagush, Nuristan on 2 May 2010, and the other was destroyed five months earlier when it crashed in eastern Logar Province, killing three Ukrainians.

One of the worst civilian disasters took place on 19 July 2009 when a Russian Hip crashed at Kandahar Airport, killing 16 people: the same number died when a chartered Mi-8 crashed while en route from Khost to Kabul in July, 2006. Only five days before the first disaster, a Mi-26 chopper was shot down with all six crew members on board killed. Seven months prior to that another Mi-26, operating under contract to Dyncorp, crashed killing its eight-man Russian crew.

It is in this hazardous environment that Neall Ellis flies almost daily. He knows the risk yet, as he always has done, he continues to do what he does best with great skill and courage.

ENDNOTES

CHAPTER ONE
1 *Gomos* are bald, granite *kopjes*, or hills that are a feature of much of the country, and which would be of such importance when a youthful Neall Ellis, by then a helicopter pilot, later fought there during the guerrilla war.

CHAPTER TWO
1 Majors Charles M. Lohman and Robert I. MacPherson, *Rhodesia: Tactical Victory, Strategic Defeat*, U.S. Marine Corps Command and Staff College, Marine Corps Development and Education Command, Quantico, Virginia, 1983.

CHAPTER THREE
1 Man-portable air-defence systems (MANPADS or MPADS) are shoulder-launched surface-to-air missiles (SAMs).
2 Paul Els, *Ongulumbashe—Where the Bushwar Began*, Privately published by paul@who-els.co.za, Pretoria, 2008

CHAPTER FIVE
1 Jannie Geldenhuys, *A General's Story: From an Era of War and Peace*, Cape Town, 1995
2 Al J. Venter, *How South Africa Built Six Atom Bombs*, Ashanti Publishing, Johannesburg, 2008
3 Details about arms manufacturing by the South African weapons company Denel can be found at http://www.denel.co.za. For more advanced weapons sys-

tems, see http://www.deneldynamics.co.za/. Denel was formerly Armscor: Armaments Corporation of South Africa

4 At that stage peace negotiations, which never developed into anything concrete, were between Angola and South Africa. Only at the end of the war when Washington, Moscow, Lisbon and the combatant nations sat around the table at the behest of the Americans, was a peace plan finally thrashed out.

CHAPTER SIX

1 Koevoet was also known during the 1970s and 1980s war as 'Operation K', or officially as the 'South West Africa Police Counter-Insurgency Unit' (SWAPOL-COIN). Strictly a police counter-insurgency unit, Koevoet was the single most effective para-military unit deployed against SWAPO fighters and had a higher 'kill rate' than any other military unit deployed during the course of the war.

CHAPTER SEVEN

1 In Afrikaans, *Suidwes Afrika Polisie Teensinsurgensie*.

CHAPTER EIGHT

1 'Natasha' is a synthetic female voice information and reporting system (VIFR) that warns pilots if they are flying too low, if the engine malfunctions or the aircraft is running low on fuel. In American fighter planes it is called 'Bitching Betty'.

CHAPTER NINE

1 Al J. Venter deals with the Executive Outcomes Angolan operation in considerable detail in his previous book on the subject of mercenaries: *War Dog: Fighting Other People's Wars*, Casemate Publishers, Philadelphia U.S. and Newbury U.K., 2006, Chapters 15 to 19 pp349–444.

CHAPTER TEN

1 It's worth mentioning that once Mobutu's regime had been toppled, all three black officers topped Kabila's 'most wanted military and civilian suspects' list, but that was only after they'd ensconced themselves in lavish homes in Johannesburg. When Baramoto fled, he took with him a hundred million dollars in American currency and bags full of raw diamonds, some of them checked through at the airport as luggage. He also took his five wives, an indeterminate number of children and a multitude of freeloaders who seemed to form part of his extraordinarily extended family-in-exile

CHAPTER TWELVE

1 The Economic Community of West African States Monitoring Group, or ECO-MOG, was a West African multilateral armed force established by the Economic

Community of West African States. Essentially, it was a formal arrangement for separate armies to work together, its backbone being the Nigerian armed forces. Its financial resources and sub-battalion strength units were contributed by other regional members including Ghana, Guinea, Sierra Leone, The Gambia, Liberia, Mali, Burkina Faso and Niger.

2 See Al J. Venter, *War Dog: Fighting Other People's Wars*, Casemate Publishers, Philadelphia U.S. and Newbury UK, Chapter 18 'Taking Angola's Diamond Fields from the Rebels', pp425–444

CHAPTER FOURTEEN

1 Hamish Ross and Fred Marafono, *From SAS to Blood Diamond Wars*, Pen and Sword Military, 2011

CHAPTER FIFTEEN

1 Al J. Venter, *War Dog: Fighting Other People's Wars*, Casemate Publishers, U.S. and U.K., 2006: Chapter 6 'The United Nations Debacle in West Africa' pp131–154

CHAPTER SIXTEEN

1 Late 2001, during the UN mandated cease-fire, Nellis' original Hind did come down after its main engine seized while on a sortie in the interior. It crashed in a clearing and a British Army major was killed on impact. Nellis and crew had to revert to using the Sierra Leone Air Wing's 'semi-serviceable' reserve Mi-24 with its 80mm under-wing rocket pods. Without air conditioning in the tropics it was a bit of bind for those who flew in her.

2 Major Phil Ashby, *Unscathed: Escape From Sierra Leone*, Pan Macmillan Publishers, London, 2002.

CHAPTER SEVENTEEN

1 Tim Butcher, *The Daily Mail*, London 29 August 2010

CHAPTER TWENTY-ONE

1 'Taliban Missile Downed Helicopter': *Daily Telegraph*, London, 27 July 2010, p 5

2 U.S. Army Colonel Lester W. Grau deals with these attacks in some detail in his book *The Bear Went over the Mountain: Soviet Combat Tactics in Afghanistan*, Frank Cass Publishers, London, 1998